CONSTRUCTIVIST CO-CURATION

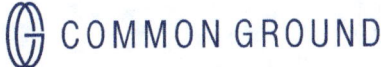

COMMON GROUND

CONSTRUCTIVIST CO-CURATION

A METHOD OF INTERWEAVING MUSEUM AND SCHOOL-BASED ART EDUCATION

VIKI D. THOMPSON WYLDER, MFA, PHD

MARCIA S. MEALE, PHD, NBCT

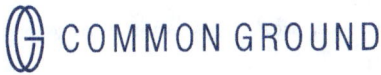

COMMON GROUND

First published in 2025
as part of the **The Inclusive Museum Book Imprint**

University of Illinois Research Park
2001 South First St, Suite 201 L
Champaign, IL 61820 USA

Library of Congress Cataloging-in-Publication Data

Names: Wylder, Viki D. Thompson, 1947-author. | Meale, Marcia S., author.
Title: Constructivist Co-Curation : A Method of Interweaving Museum and School-Based Art Education / by Viki D. Thompson Wylder, MFA, PhD and Marcia S. Meale, PhD, NBCT.

Description: Champaign, IL : Common Ground Research Networks, 2024. |Includes bibliographical references and index. | Summary:"Constructivist Co-Curation: A Method of Interweaving Museum and School-Based Art Education tells a unique story through a retrospective case study of the curatorial convergence of museum educators, utilizing their theory and programs, with art educators, utilizing their theory and pedagogy. The book describes a method that advances museum and school-based practice by asking art teachers to develop projects and curate exhibitions with museum educators. Inherent is the diminishment of unintentional barriers between school and museum systems as school and museum educators strive for mutual conceptualization and purpose. The method nurtures the usage of museums and increased meaning-making within them by the school system audience (teachers, students, and families) . School programs expand and deepen through increased and more easily accessed museum-based resources (original artworks, artist interactions, exhibitions, and museum materials and activities). This book presents Constructivist Co-Curation as a "cutting-edge" model and includes a "how-to-do-it" guide".--Provided by publisher.

Identifiers: LCCN 2024042055 | ISBN 9781963049770 (hardback) | ISBN 9781963049800 (paperback) | ISBN 9781963049817 (ebook)

Subjects: LCSH: Art museums--Educational aspects. | Art--Study and teaching. | Museums and schools. | Constructivism (Education)

Classification: LCC N430 .W495 2024 | DDC 708--dc23/eng/20241016
LC record available at https://lccn.loc.gov/2024042055

Cover Design: Copyright @ Phillip Kalantzis-Cope
Cover Image: Image Copyright @ Viki D Thompson Wylder & Marcia S. Meale. Image of Painting by Jack Dowd. Future of America II. Resin. 36" x 32" x 30". Courtesy of Florida State University Museum of Fine Arts.

TABLE OF CONTENTS

ACKNOWLEDGEMENTS

Our acknowledgments and thanks for this study are many. We wish to acknowledge the Florida State University Museum of Fine Arts (FSU MoFA) as the home for the projects/exhibitions outlined within it. We want to thank the director, Dr. Allys Palladino-Craig, and the assistant director, Jean Young, and all the FSU MoFA staff who supported these projects. Dr. Palladino-Craig gave us the opportunity, the time, the space and materials, and the personnel to work for several years on each project/exhibition. She found grant money to back each one; she designed the accompanying posters for the first two projects. She is listed as the editor of the catalogue for the last project. She even took most of the photographs that are found in this book. Although she retired in 2018, she graciously gave advice for details during the process of preparing to publish. Among the myriad of other helpful details, Jean Young designed the catalogues for *Generations* and *Waging Peace!* and as the current assistant director gave us permission to republish the FSU MoFA photographs and other materials that further the narrative of each chapter. Generations of interns also worked on these projects doing all manner of tasks. They assisted in nearly every step of the process. For example, they assisted at curatorial meetings and with contacting artists, receiving artwork, writing lesson plans, designing activities for K-12 students, hanging the exhibitions, giving tours, and servicing the receptions and events.

The curatorial teams for each of these projects collectively gave hundreds of hours of their time. Their names and affiliations are listed at the beginning of Chapters 4–8, the chapters that directly recount the origin, implementation, and impact of each of the five projects/exhibitions that are part of this study. We want to thank the teachers, primarily art teachers (but not all were art teachers), who served on these committees, but also other art teachers in the Leon County School System (and occasionally outside the county) who participated in various ways in each of these projects.

Three of the five curatorial teams incorporated representatives of community organizations who tended to act as partners of the FSU MoFA in these project ventures. These representatives and their organizations also occur in the lists at the beginnings of the aforementioned chapters. These organizations varied in structure and intent and included the Tallahassee Community College Gallery, The Council on Culture and Arts (COCA) with its connections to exhibition space at the City Hall of Tallahassee, Mission San Luis, the Holocaust Education Resource Council (HERC), the Anderson Brickler Gallery, and The Plant on Gaines Street. Two organizations that offered additional exhibition space were not represented on any of these curatorial committees. We want to thank the Leroy Collins Leon County Public Library for hosting an expansive Student Display for the *Visions of the North Florida Environment* project and the Arts Learning Gallery at the State of Florida R. A. Gray Building for providing space for another expansive Student Display for the project titled *In Print: The Language of Art.*

Amanda Karioth Thompson, who participated in the committees for *Generations* and *Waging Peace!*, represented COCA. As the Education & Exhibitions Manager for the Council on Culture and Arts, and later as Assistant Director, she arranged for an extension of the *Waging Peace!* Student Display at Tallahassee City Hall. She also wrote several articles on these projects for the local newspaper, the *Tallahassee Democrat*. We thank her, COCA, and the *Tallahassee Democrat* for granting permission to utilize the articles in this study.

During the *Waging Peace!* project two graduate students made contributions to the process. The first student, Jennifer Hamrock, a PhD candidate and board member for The Plant on Gaines Street in Tallahassee, joined the curatorial team but developed a parallel program at her institution. The Plant describes itself as a "community D.I.Y. creative space" that welcomes everyone free of charge. With volunteers Hamrock developed a series of "Waging Peace! workshops" for the public and then mounted a parallel exhibition of the artwork emanating from those workshops titled *Waging Peace at the Plant*. We thank Jennifer Hamrock for the extensive verbal and written interview about The Plant on Gaines Street and the program she implemented there.

The second student, Anna Freeman, who was a master's student at FSU in art history, specializing in museum and cultural heritage studies, and an intern at the FSU MoFA, has continued her studies at Ohio State University. She is now a PhD candidate in the Arts Administration, Education and Policy Program there as well as a graduate teaching associate. We want to thank her for researching and writing text for a section of Chapter 2 titled "Identifying Constructivism in Art Museum Education Programs." We indicated her contribution at the end of this section by stating just that: "Based on research and text by Anna Freeman."

For Chapter 2 within the content of the same section, we also interviewed representatives of the Museum Education Programs at the Montgomery Museum of Fine Arts (MMFA) and the High Museum (the High) in Atlanta. We want to thank the education staff of those museums, particularly Kaci Norman, the assistant curator of education for Youth and Family Programs at MMFA, and Kate McLeod, head of School and Teacher Services at the High, who gave of their time and gave much information about the workings of their programs and the concepts behind them. An extended footnote in that section of the book succinctly gives an overview of their programs and names these museum educators.

We want to thank Barbara Davis, photographer, high school art educator from the Florida State University Schools, and committee member for *The Story* and *Waging Peace!*, for photographing the posters from the first two projects, *Visions of the North Florida Environment* and *In Print: The Language of Art*. She stepped in to provide images when most records and images from those early projects had disappeared.

We want to thank Lee McNeil, a former columnist for *Break*, a magazine published by the *Tallahassee Democrat*, who, over the course of several years, read every word of our manuscript as we wrote it, providing feedback and giving editing suggestions.

Finally, we want to thank the target audience, the thousands of students who continually demonstrated meaningful engagement as well as care and respect for the artworks while enjoying the privilege of getting "up close and personal" with each exhibition's components. Their feedback proved valuable for continuing the co-constructivist curatorial process and for providing much documentation of its methods and results.

The process of constructivist co-curation requires the input of many participants. So did the production of this study. We want to express our gratitude to all.

Viki D. Thompson Wylder, MFA, PhD
Marcia S. Meale, PhD, NBCT

INTRODUCTION

"Constructivist Co-Curation"

This book examines a new collaborative or co-curatorial process deemed "constructivist co-curation." Through the presentation of a longitudinal retrospective case study, the procedures, highlights, and findings of five expansive projects using this process, each centered on an art exhibition, are described. Parts of this case study include an autoethnographic approach by including personal narrative to highlight the actuality and authenticity of the constructivist co-curation method. Art educators joined the museum education department at the Florida State University Museum of Fine Arts (FSU MoFA) over a span of 18 years to invent, develop, and refine this comprehensive process. In the five projects examined, art teachers and the museum education director worked together as a co-curatorial team or committee to produce high-quality meaningful projects inclusive of exhibitions and programs that impacted thousands of viewers, from childhood to adulthood, laying a foundation for other institutions to consider. Constructivist co-curation meant that such a committee, influenced by constructivism and other art education theories, determined exhibition content and then also determined and integrated exhibition-based programs via the development and application of related pedagogical materials, interactions, and events. The committee set about to interweave museum and school-based art education. This book stresses the advantages of the constructivist co-curation process for teachers (and community members) in combination with museum education curators/directors. Our hope is that other museums, schools, and organizations will see the benefits of this approach and consider using this method to co-curate projects, which synthesize exhibitions with museum and art educational theory, pedagogy, and programs, to bring more profound meaning-making and understanding to their current constituents and to attract and build new audiences.

Theory

Prior to addressing the book's intrinsic questions—What is
constructivist co-curation, and what is its impact?—the book examines the
constructivist roots that anchor the process. Key constructivist elements
affecting the process are identified and the coalescence of those elements
into a workable method are discussed. In 1998, George Hein published his
influential book/manifesto, *Learning in the Museum,* in which he
described constructivism and the characteristics of a constructivist
museum. Constructivist ideas have affected school-based and museum-based
art education to the present as attested by any brief survey of recent
scholarship but also through the affirmations of museum education
professionals. In interviews conducted in 2019 for this book with personnel
from two major southeastern regional museums, the Montgomery Museum
of Art in Alabama and the High Museum of Art in Atlanta, interaction with
the audience and their meaning-making from the works housed in those
museums proved paramount, indications of the influence of constructivism
on their programs. In his book, Hein outlined the basic points of
constructivist theory, a theory of learning in which learners construct
understanding and make meaning by inserting new information into an
already constructed interior personal configuration of knowledge. The
instructor becomes a facilitator to this process of learning by providing an
environment and activities, mental and physical, which foster connections
between new information and the interior paradigms of learners. That
process is encouraged through various means, for example providing
something familiar in new information that allows connections, providing
interactive pedagogical offerings that allow experiments in thought and action
and the determination of personal conclusions, creating an environment that
gives the learner the ability to select from pedagogical offerings, and
encouraging group learning or constructions. Hein goes on to describe the
role of the constructivist museum as analogous to that of the instructor.

The museum acts as a facilitator of cultural interpretations, not as an authority
of the "truth." The museum is encouraged to become transparent in its method
and process of interpretation, particularly through collaboration, either in its
means of interpretation or in its actual curatorial functions. To be a constructivist museum, connections are augmented and extended to a broad public
inside and outside the institution's walls through interrelated layers of events,

programs, and other offerings. Exhibitions are seen as only one part of this network. Interactive offerings and various types of access—conceptual, social, physical, and developmental—are encouraged. Finally, the museum studies its own audience to better understand the meaning-making of its constituency.

In concert with Hein's idea of transparency, the constructivist co-curation process began with curatorial collaboration. Projects with exhibitions were curated by teams or committees of primarily art educators in partnership with the museum educator. These committees were open and knowable, easily joined upon announcement of their formation. For some exhibitions, community members were also invited to become participants. As stated, committees curated these exhibitions, but the exhibitions acted as nuclei of curatorial committee-developed networks of related programs, events, and interactions. These took place in the museum and outside the museum. These programs offered a range of types of access and combined familiarity, personal connection, and challenge. For example, each project included a parallel student display to accompany the professional exhibition selected by the curatorial committee. All works created by students for display were the result of related pedagogy in the school classroom. These lessons focused on students' responses to various works by the professional artists slated to become part of the museum exhibition. This process of study and creation combined multiple means for personal and group understanding and meaning-making.

Teachers as members of co-curatorial committees also constructed personal and collaborative meanings for individual works and for each project and exhibition as a whole. These meanings guided the development of the network of programs, events, and activities that were developed within each project. Teachers acted as continuous front-end evaluators for each project as it progressed. As the experts on the outlook of the audience of diverse students, other educators, and extended families of students, they became informal qualitative assessors of these projects, their processes, and their potential results or impact on the various members of the intended audience.

In addition to the underlying constructivist theory that informed the museum aspects of the co-curatorial process, art education theories and pedagogy also informed each project and show, and changed over the course of the 18-year period as theoretical pedagogical scholarship evolved and grew. Likewise, art teachers needed to incorporate state standards into their exhibition artwork-based lesson plans which resulted in the application of a variety of different theoretical art education approaches. Just as the standards and art education theory changed over time, so too did teachers' pedagogical strategies and plans for components of these projects within the museum and within their classrooms. Throughout the book, descriptions of the projects and the relevant art education theories are discussed. Art educational theories that impacted these projects and exhibitions reveal an 18-year history of the fluctuation of various theoretical art education influences on participant teachers and include Art as Visual Language (Feldman, 1970), Discipline-Based Art Education also known as DBAE (Clark et al., 1987; Dobbs, 1992) Enduring or Big Ideas (Stewart & Walker, 2005) and Social Justice Art Education (Blatt-Gross, 2017; Buffington, 2014; Darts, 2006; Dewhurst, 2010; Garber, 2004). In the Art as Visual Language approach, emphasis is placed on the elements and principles of art in their use with media as a visual grammar to communicate messages and meanings. Discipline-Based Art Education defines and utilizes four areas for study: art production, art criticism, art history, and aesthetics. Marilyn Stewart and Sydney Walker expanded on the changing adaptations of DBAE to emphasize big ideas and meaning as the focus of art instruction. Social Justice Art Education deals as the title suggests with harder questions and social issues in society through art.

Research Questions

The primary questions to be answered by this book are: What is constructivist co-curation, and what is its impact? Follow-up questions include: What are the benefits of constructivist co-curation to each participant institution beyond benefits normally accrued by museum and school-based art education and beyond usual collaborative processes? To its individual participants? To its audience? How responsive can the process be to current events, social issues, and the community?

Research Process

This book employs qualitative research methods that are retrospective and narrative, with some autoethnographic insights, using a case study approach. A total of five constructivist co-curation projects are the focus of this book that span an 18-year time period. All the projects were developed by local art teachers in conjunction with the director of museum education at the Florida State University Museum of Fine Arts in Tallahassee, Florida.

Since the book is retrospective, primary resources were accessed, all exhibition catalogs and teacher support materials, that is, teaching posters and lesson
plan booklets. In addition, a range of interviews inform the findings. Primarily
teachers who were key to each project and exhibition were interviewed with a
set of questions that was consistent from project/exhibition to project/exhibition.
Another set of questions was developed for interviews of education personnel
from two other regional museum education programs. An informal interview
was conducted with an education director at another state university.

Empirical data were also collected for each project/exhibition. A list of professional artists in exhibitions with numbers of works and numbers of visitors was
recorded. Workshops and numbers of workshop attendees as well as all other
events with numbers of visitors were recorded. Funding sources were noted.

Findings

Chapters 1–3 provide a context and rationale for this case study, including an
explanation of the term "constructivist co-curation." Chapters 4–8 directly describe
the projects within the case study. Empirical data are presented at the beginning
of each of these chapters followed by a description of each of the projects, the
educational theories which influenced them, and qualitative findings. Chapters 9
and 10 provide a summary of the findings. Chapter 9 summarizes the constructivist
co-curation process itself, and Chapter 10 summarizes the impact of the process.

CHAPTER 1

The Contours of Constructivist Co-Curation

Beginnings

On Valentine's Day, 2018, shots rang out. Seventeen were dead at Stoneman Douglas High School in Parkland, Florida, fourteen students, a teacher, an assistant football coach, and an athletic director. But this time thoughts and prayers were not enough. Students demanded and began taking political action immediately, calling for an end to automatic weapons and bump stocks. The Parkland school shooting sent a tsunami of feeling and renewed determination across the state and nation.

The shock of yet another school shooting reached us, a co-curatorial committee of museum and school-based art educators at the Florida State University Museum of Fine Arts (FSU MoFA), just as we were moving toward the final production stages of an exhibition. We had been working together for about two years on a project and exhibition titled *Waging Peace!* Despite the multiyear, step-by-step collaborative effort of selecting imagery, developing programs, making community connections, and planning events, the committee asked, "How could we quickly offer our voices to speak to the Parkland catastrophe and its impact? How could we not address such an event in an exhibition titled *Waging Peace!*?"

Artworks were arriving at the FSU MoFA and included an installation by Patricia Anderson Turner, an Orlando artist whose work embodied a reaction to the June 2016 shooting at the Pulse nightclub. Several art teachers/co-curators of the exhibition acutely felt the imperative of also representing the Parkland incident. For me, as one of two teachers who took the lead, creating and adding a piece focusing on this tragedy presented a conceptual struggle. How could we offer a work that would be thought-provoking but not overwhelming or hopeless in its expression of mourning? After discussion with the entire co-curatorial team, a precursory vision of an installation of piles of backpacks on the floor strewn with black flowers gave way to a *Parkland Memorial Installation* that was poignant but ultimately positive, interactive, and appealing to all ages within the kindergarten through adult audience. A grid of 15 used student backpacks, subtly colored and patterned, as well as a teacher's satchel and a gym bag, were attached to one of the title walls of the exhibition. During the reception on May 17, two interactive stations flanked the installation. Inspired by the making and dissemination of red crêpe paper poppies to memorialize veterans and those who died in war, the audience was invited to design and construct multicolored paper flowers but also to create buttons bearing pertinent personal messages or designs, to be placed on or in the backpacks hanging from the wall. Sadly, on May 18, the morning after the reception, a student at Santa Fe High School in Texas, south of Houston, killed eight students and two teachers and wounded ten others. Prior to a field trip to the *Waging Peace!* exhibition, several students joined me before class to make 10 more paper flowers, white in this case, to add to the base of the *Parkland Memorial Installation* at the FSU MoFA.

> This narrative raises questions. "How could a museum respond to a national event on such short notice? How did teachers become museum co-curators and installation designers? How did these roles affect their teaching and their students? Who were all the members of the co-curatorial team? What was the relationship of the museum to the team? How did the development of this team affect the educational programs of the museum and the reach of the museum into the community?"
>
> —*MM*

The Method of "Constructivist Co-Curation": What Is It?

As a museum educator and an elementary art teacher reflecting on our past collaborative curatorial history at the FSU MoFA, we felt compelled to share our collaborative process with enthusiasm and energy. It is our hope that our process, which developed over time, will not only expand to other museums, schools, and communities but will also expand in scope. We found our process to be a rewarding way of developing and embedding museum exhibitions in extensive projects that merged the skills and aims of the museum and the school system, and often community organizations as well. Our process deepened programs in all three of these sectors and enhanced interaction with the constituencies of each.

Guests entered the Florida State University Museum of Fine Arts to view and interact with the *Generations* exhibition, the culmination of one of the five constructivist co-curation projects detailed in this book.

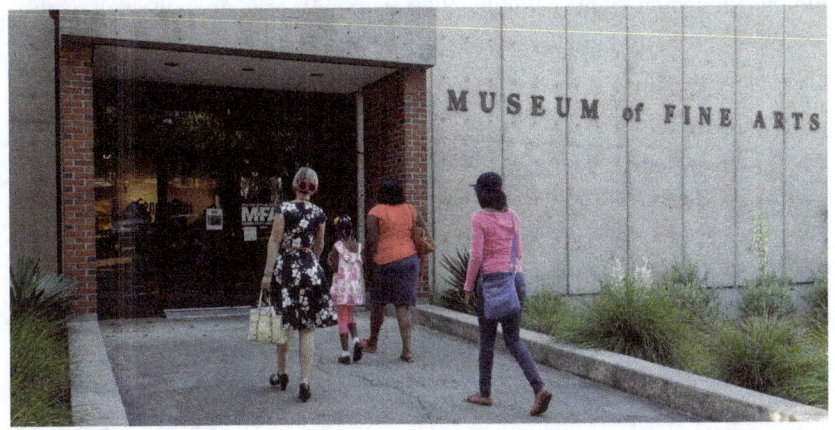

Courtesy: Florida State University Museum of Fine Arts.

These projects and exhibitions found new, young audiences and brought art to people in all walks of life, art to which a diverse public could relate. Through this method, many perceived the exhibitions, the individual artworks, and the museum space as theirs, both figuratively and in many cases literally. Firmly based on constructivist theory, our method offered an inclusive process in which representatives of the museum, the school system, and the community participated in curatorship, one of the core raisons d'être of a museum.

We call our process or method "constructivist co-curation." Constructivist co-curation extended well beyond the limited collaboration typically practiced in a museum setting. Rather it incorporated multiple steps within the comprehensive scope of the curatorial process—exhibition origination, art object selection, organization, presentation, education, and programming. This co-curatorial process supported the constructivist quality of the extended projects for which each of these steps played a crucial part.

Over periods of time, generally over several years per project, representatives of the museum, the school system, and the community met as teams to map and carry out co-curatorial project plans. During the co-curatorial process, each team constructed collaboratively understood meanings that guided the development of the project and the museum exhibition associated with the project. As the process progressed teams set up environments and activities meant to foster constructivist understandings by various sectors of the projected audience. Within schools, artworks, themes, and essential questions from this collaboration became fully integrated into units of study. Students from kindergarten through twelfth grade benefited from the variety of support each project provided from lesson plan suggestions to visual resources to artist interactions to paying for busing students to the museum.

Over the course of nearly two decades the education department of the FSU MoFA established a unique working relationship with the art teachers of the county's public and private school systems. The museum welcomed the participation of local art teachers who, in turn, felt comfortable suggesting and co-curating occasional projects and their featured exhibitions. Undergirded by the tenets of constructivist philosophy, this unique way of working meshed museum education with school-based art education and art educators within the community. By working together, museum and school-based art educators engaged populations and individuals often ignored, introducing community audiences to the vibrancy and relevance of art and the museum.

In this book, we describe the constructivist co-curatorial method while explaining our evolving use of theoretical, philosophical, and pedagogical bases. We then detail the five projects that unfolded over the course of 18 years, and relate the outcomes, impact, or efficacy of this method. Although forms of co-curation have been used by museums, this particular method is innovative and ambitious and points to future directions and connections for educators from both museum and school settings. This book offers a guide for the continuing development of interweaving museum and school-based art education through the constructivist co-curation of exhibitions in which each exhibition formed the nucleus of a larger framework or project.

Who Should Read This Book?

Art educators, museum educators, preservice teachers, community members, and others interested in working together with museums on meaningful exhibitions and programming form the primary audience for this book. This book is meant to join college level textbooks that focus on museum and art education practice and theory. We address theoretical and pedagogical practices interwoven through five projects and their focal exhibitions. These projects offer concise, clear examples of theory in practice. The final project *Waging Peace!* provides an example of integrating Social Justice Art Education theory into practice even at the elementary school level.

How This Book Is Organized

A pertinent, informative reminiscence titled "Beginnings" opens each chapter. Throughout the contents of this book we injected an autobiographical or personal quality to emphasize our enthusiasm for the reality or lived experience of the constructivist co-curatorial method we detail.

Following the basics given in this initial chapter, which includes an explanation of the term, constructivist co-curation, as well as the flexibility of the method, Chapter 2 puts the constructivist co-curation method into the context of other museum programs nationally and regionally and explains the way this method was influenced by Hein's concepts regarding constructivist theoretical application in museums. Chapter 2 also contrasts constructivist co-curation with other collaborative processes to show the ways this interweaving of museum and school-based art education pushes beyond common understandings of museum education practice.

Chapter 3 provides an overview of the five constructivist co-curatorial projects outlined in this book. It identifies the influence of evolving art education theory and practice on each project as well as the curatorial pattern, with some individual differences, that emerged as a defining feature of all five. In Chapters 4–8, we detail the five model constructivist co-curation projects. Discussed, in addition to constructivist theoretical influence, are ways these additional art educational theories and practices—Discipline-Based Art Education (DBAE), the Big Idea, Social Justice Art Education, and the traditional "Art as a Visual Language" approach—guided each of these five projects. Chapter 4 tells the story of the impact of DBAE on the project and exhibition titled *Visions of the North Florida Environment*; Chapter 5 focuses on the project and exhibition *In Print: The Language of Art* with its emphasis on the traditional "Art as a Visual Language" approach; Chapters 6 and 7 recount the use of the Big Idea for two projects and exhibitions, *The Story* and *Generations*; and Chapter 8 describes the application of Social Justice Art Education concepts to *Waging Peace!* the most recent project undertaken.

In Chapter 9 we directly view the constructivist co-curation method or process from each of our vantage points, from the art teacher's point of view and from the museum educator's point of view. This model curatorial process is traced step by step from the origination of a project theme to the completion of a project's many parts.

In Chapter 10, the last chapter, we relate the efficacy of the constructivist co-curation method. This chapter summarizes the success and advantages of this innovative model generally from the perspective of art education and museum education. The chapter ends with a brief look at "Future Outcomes" in which we suggest the use of the constructivist co-curation method for many other museum education programs and school districts.

Implications for the Future

In 2019, when we initiated the writing of this book gun violence in schools appeared to be the most concerning social issue. In March of 2020, we learned to social distance and wear masks as museums, schools, and community sites closed due to the pandemic called COVID-19 (coronavirus disease 2019), caused by SARS-CoV-2 (severe acute respiratory syndrome coronavirus 2). Workers, teachers, students, and many others also learned a new way of working remotely online. In spite of the pandemic, citizens took to the streets across the country and around the world to protest the murder of George Floyd, an African American man who died in 9 minutes and 29 seconds under the restraining knee of an unchecked Minneapolis police officer over a $20 counterfeit bill. Inspired by the protests, the Black Lives Matter movement quickly developed effective visual symbols in the form of community murals. Activists literally painted the words "Black Lives Matter" on streets in communities, most famously in Washington, DC, in front of the White House. Our constructivist co-curatorial method provides important opportunities to continue to curate projects and exhibitions based on a comprehensive examination of current issues deemed urgent by multiple voices and perspectives. During our last constructivist co-curatorial project and exhibition, *Waging Peace!* the co-curatorial committee was able to directly respond to two school shootings through an added exhibition installation with accompanying activities. One of these tragic shootings took place during the final stages of hanging the exhibition, the other happened during the exhibition. Within this process of constructivist co-curation, multiple voices on the committee were heard and multiple perspectives were analyzed. During times of crisis, like the COVID-19 pandemic in which materials and access seem limited, questions arise, "How would this co-curatorial process work for the development of a new project and exhibition?" "Is adaptation possible within the confines of limited access and social distancing?"

Social distancing forced us all to invent new and remote ways of work. Before a vaccine became widely available, in the heart of the pandemic that isolated us, we as human beings needed reassuring connections to one another. We needed a common purpose as a way to make our lives continue to be communally meaningful. We needed something positive to work toward even when we were "alone together." Developing a constructivist project and exhibition addressing COVID-19 and/or the Black Lives Matter movement held potential, and still does, to help heal and fill the gap in many people's lives. We encourage institutions—museums, galleries, schools, community organizations—to step forward to coordinate calls to people interested in developing such projects and exhibitions. Although in-school attendance across the country has resumed, the constructivist co-curation process is workable during crisis situations in which out-of-the-classroom virtual attendance is preferable. Many steps of the process prove viable via Zoom or similar applications. Group or team meetings using virtual video conferencing became commonplace within a few months' time during the height of the pandemic as did virtual exhibitions on institutions' websites. Possible "hybrid" exhibitions that could combine the virtual and the actual, that virtually feature art normally shown in gallery spaces paired with sculpture or other works actually shown on the exterior of buildings, even now would allow in-person viewing in the ventilated safety of the out-of-doors. Teachers using hybrid virtual/in-person pedagogical methods would have the ability to teach from such exhibitions in their virtual or actual classrooms. For example, at elementary schools, instructional support could be found in a "drive-through packet pick-up" of art supplies supported by developmentally appropriate online video or video conferencing lessons incorporating information and discussion including historical background, critical analysis, aesthetics, and artmaking prompts. Students' response works could be digitally submitted for online student displays. Interactions with artists could also take place via virtual media, i.e., streaming, video chat, etc.

This way of work is not completely new. In some past FSU MoFA Education Program projects, artist interactions took place online. In addition, the Education Program previously developed several virtual student displays. Virtual tours of exhibitions are already used by many museums, and virtual video conferencing can provide interaction of tour guides with groups. Teacher workshops in conjunction with such projects and exhibitions can also be conducted in a similar way. The reception for a school-based show could involve a drive-through of an exterior student display along the parent pick-up lane at a school or in the parking lot of a museum. Previously, the internationally recognized painted canvas murals of *Kids Guernica* have sometimes been displayed outside for brief periods of time.

We are in the process of continually inventing new ways to work, display, interact, teach, and learn. Some of these adaptations may be mothballed after the pandemic totally dissipates, but others may remain useful as effective methods going into the future. These methods are suitable for use within a framework of constructivist co-curation regardless of circumstances. Creativity, learning, understanding, and meaning are the stock in trade for constructivist co-curation, a means to help nurture a full and connected life for individuals and the communities in which they live. Constructivist co-curation within the arts can play a role in that fulfillment.

CHAPTER 2

Constructivism—A Broad Theoretical Basis for the Museum and School-Based Art Education "Constructivist Co-Curation" Method

Beginnings

Striving felt continuous for me as the Curator of Education and single staff member of the Education Program at the Florida State University Museum of Fine Arts (FSU MoFA). Effort was made to operate the program within a context of practice, thought, and theory utilized by other museum education programs, particularly in the southeastern United States, while simultaneously adapting to the distinctive qualities of the structure of the FSU MoFA as an institution. As a small university museum, the FSU MoFA encompassed about 16,000 square feet in total for offices, storage, and exhibition space. It maintained a highly eclectic, mostly donated, permanent collection of 5,000–6,000 pieces and hosted primarily rotating exhibitions from outside the collection. As with many universities, town and gown attitudes as well as parking restrictions on campus posed problems for visitation by the community. But the university milieu also offered an array of concepts, theories, and philosophies for meeting challenges posed by the museum's characteristics and situation. At a university, ideas seem to float through the air ready to be plucked. Through partnership activities with the university's Art Education Department, theory and practices were "plucked" from *Learning in the Museum*, George Hein's 1998 book/manifesto for utilization of constructivist practices by museums. Constructivism provided a means to better engage visitors and thus entice the community to overcome barriers to interaction with the FSU MoFA.

—VDTW

Beyond Understandings of Museum Education Practice

In a book edited by Pat Villeneuve and Ann Rowson Love in 2017, titled *Visitor-Centered Exhibitions and Edu-Curation in Art Museums,* Jennifer Wild Czajkowski and Salvador Salort-Pons, an educator–curator pair from the Detroit Institute of the Arts, include a concise, clear summary of the traditional method for curating an exhibition, a method Villeneuve and Rowson Love would like to supplant. Salort-Pons wrote:

> Many times I thought that curating an exhibition was like putting together or organizing the parts of a scholarly article. My audience was my peers, and curating a show was an extraordinary opportunity to clarify a theory or prove a hypothesis. The actual exhibition was better than writing an article because I had the original works of art. My goal was to advance science, to advance the knowledge of art history, and to give new insights about the past. (2017, pp. 240–241)

Primarily, however, Czajkowski and Salort-Pons as well as other curator and museum education authors of the chapters in the Villeneuve/Rowson Love book write about the current pressure for a change from this method within museum culture. These authors who work in institutions which could only be described as diverse—small, large, mobile, commercial, alternative, domestic, and foreign—describe their internal collaborations and their external collaborations with the community to make their exhibitions and exhibition-related programs "visitor-centered." Unlike the assumed traditional audience of professional "peers," as imagined by Salort-Pons for the exhibitions he curated in the past, these professionals think about a broad audience, multifarious in age, gender, ethnic origins, knowledge, career, and work backgrounds, who bring multiple perspectives to their viewing, and who will make individual, independent meanings or socially co-constructed meanings as postulated within constructivist theory, whose set of theoretical principles will be discussed thoroughly in this chapter.

Villeneuve and Rowson Love, in producing their book, hoped to summarize the pressure for change in the museum world as well as apply their own pressure to increase the nascent innovations taking place toward a less hierarchical and less authoritarian institutional system. The professionals invited to share their narratives of collaboration provide models and suggestions for others who wish to also implement programs of institutional transformation. These authors feel their approaches will "lead to deeper relationships" with audiences and bring a more "sustainable future for [their] museums" (Koke & Ryan, 2017 in Villeneuve & Rowson Love, 2017, p. 55). Within their stories of edu-curation and the building of exhibitions and programs tailored to provide, as paramount, personal connections for the active engagement of visitors, these professionals describe a multiplicity of authority-shared cooperative processes or partnerships among various figures: curators, educators, other pertinent staff, artists, university students, and representatives of the community. At times the representatives of the community may be general visitors themselves, but particularly they may be teachers who focus on students in schools, organizations who focus on social justice, and those who focus on underserved communities. The Tucson Museum of Art who partnered with "Owl and Panther, a program of the Hopi Foundation, which is a local expressive arts program serving refugee families affected by traumatic dislocation" (Pegno & Farrar, 2017 in Villeneuve & Rowson Love, 2017, p. 170), and the University of Arizona Museum of Art who partnered with ALLY, a program that "focuses on reducing suicide rates amongst LGBTQ youth (13–23 years old)" (p. 172), provide noteworthy examples.

The list of processes included in the Villeneuve and Rowson Love book extends broadly from audience formative evaluation to the utilization of advisory groups, to an unlikely combining of museum staff to meet their museum's goal of ensuring multiple perspectives through the following emphases—concept, emotion or narrative, aesthetic or pragmatic considerations, and physical experience and sensations. Yet the approach undertaken at the FSU MoFA, interweaving museum and school-based art education through constructivist co-curation of exhibitions and the co-curation of the larger projects within which these exhibitions exist, exemplifies a process that is different, that goes a step or steps further than those detailed by Villeneuve and Rowson Love. None of the processes described in Villeneuve and Rowson Love's book unites the curatorial and education mission thoroughly from the educator's point of view as does the constructivist co-curation method chronicled in the following chapters of this book. Villeneuve and Rowson Love's book does include a combined curatorial/education mission from a curatorial standpoint in which curators acted with a distinct educational intent. But none of the processes in Villeneuve and Rowson Love's book include co-curation of exhibitions by museum and school-based art educators. In the constructivist co-curation method outlined in the following pages of this book, a museum educator or education department assumes the curator and educator role simultaneously with the responsibilities of concept origination, building of an exhibition/curatorial team primarily of art educators from the school system and secondarily of community representatives, selection of artwork for the exhibition, and program development as well as implementation inclusive of textual materials for display and within a catalogue. The five projects, and exhibitions within them, undertaken by the Education Program of the FSU MoFA and the co-curatorial teams working within the auspices of that Education Program depict a process related to but beyond Villeneuve and Rowson Love's description of "edu-curation." The pioneering method described here as constructivist co-curation dramatically extends the usual understanding of museum education practice.

Identifying Constructivism in Art Museum Education Programs

In 2005 and 2008, at the National Art Education Association (NAEA) Conferences, and in 2007 at a Museum Educators of Southern California event, museum educators were invited by Dr. David Ebitz to participate in workshops to identify the common theories that informed art museum educators at the time. Ebitz taught in the Art Education Department at Penn State University, having moved to this position after serving as executive director of the John and Mable Ringling Museum of Art in Sarasota, Florida, from 1992 till 2000. After the workshops, Ebitz wrote about a perceived underlying assumption among museum researchers and professionals that museum educators lacked theoretical foundations to inform their practices. Ebitz hypothesized that this view reflected a perception of the time-pressure under which museum educators must work. He admitted during his tenure as a "museum educator and director [he] had no time for theory," but he also suggested the presumed "lack of theoretical foundation may be equally the result of a lack of the kind of consensus about the aims of museum education that can be easily communicated through a single theoretical rationale" (Ebitz, 2008, p. 14). The job of the museum educator today varies from museum to museum and often depends greatly on the particulars of the museum, as demonstrated by the case of the FSU MoFA, its internal and external structure, and most importantly its audiences and surrounding community.

During all three workshops offered by Ebitz, art museum educators were asked to "write down and add check marks by the names of any theories or theorists that…'informed [their] practice'" (2008, p. 15). Constructivism, listed in seventh place, appeared within the top fourth of the twenty-eight theories and theorists named collectively by those in the workshops. In his essay, Ebitz, himself, referred to his own reliance on constructivism. George Hein, writer about constructivism and author of *Learning in the Museum*, was listed in sixteenth place, but the author, whose doctorate is in chemistry, is better known as a writer within science museum education. The results revealed a contrast to previous thoughts about museum educators and theories, showing that "museum educators readily cite theories and thinkers who have informed their work" (p. 15). Ebitz goes on to say that the theories listed by art museum educators show the "shift of attention in art museums over the last 20 years away from collections to the visitors they serve" (p. 19) and that "constructivist educational practices" seem a "natural consequence" of this shift (p. 20). His closing comments also suggest that a number of educators may view such theories as constructivism as "too general to be directly applied," but they, nevertheless, understand these theories as pertaining to "the nature of meaning making" and "what visitors make of their experiences" (p. 21).

For large-scale collecting museums, there is typically a wide range of educational and outreach programs, including many informed by constructivism. Few museum educational programs state outright the specific theories on which they are built or the theorists that inspired them. Because each museum is unique, most assume museum programs in general are grounded in a variety of frameworks. Furthermore, multiple practice models are used in relation to specific education and outreach activities. At the FSU MoFA though constructivism provided a common framework for the development and implementation of each of the five projects under discussion, each was also influenced over time by the existence, emergence, and evolution of other theories and practices: the mid-20th century "visual language" model, Discipline-Based Art Education (DBAE), the evolution of DBAE into the "Big Idea" approach, and an emphasis on social justice within art education.

A major regional museum in each of the two states bordering Florida, one in Alabama and one in Georgia, provide an extended geographical community context for looking at the FSU MoFA educational practices: the Montgomery Museum of Fine Arts (MMFA) and the High Museum of Art in Atlanta (the High). Each of these museums is different in size and composition of its public and consequently their educational programs reflect these variations. As expected, both utilize various underlying theories and practices within their museum education programs; for example, the High states its use of Visual Thinking Strategies and Harvard's Project Zero. In constructivist fashion, they both use "minds-on" dialogue and "hands-on" artmaking with their tours, "clean artmaking" within gallery spaces and messier artmaking in workshop or studio spaces. The High docents are explicitly instructed to be "interactive" with student tours. Both museums use cross-disciplinary as well as multiple learning modality approaches. Both museums, for example, offer programs that feature movement. The Move with Me Program at the MMFA focuses on dance and the relationship of this movement to an artwork in the Museum. Both museums, under constructivist influence, currently focus on visitor experience and the meaning visitors make as they encounter or confront works of art on display. Though both utilize constructivist concepts, neither has embraced a thoroughly constructivist method like the constructivist co-curation method detailed in this book (M. Meale and V. D. T. Wylder, personal communication, MMFA, August 21, 2019, personal communication, the High, August 23, 2019).[1]

—Based on research and text by Anna Freeman

The Influence of George Hein's Constructivist Museum on the Museum Education Program at the Florida State University Museum of Fine Arts

In the summer of 2005, Fran Kautz, an art teacher from the Buck Lake Elementary School in Tallahassee, approached the museum educator at the Florida State University Museum of Fine Arts to pitch an idea for an exhibition. As unusual

---

[1] Arranged by Kaci Norman, the assistant curator of education for Youth and Family Programs at the Montgomery Museum of Fine Arts (MMFA), a general interview took place with the seven staff members of the Education Program. During the interview, the staff identified the MMFA as a mid-sized regional museum and as a department of the city of Montgomery funded by the city and county. The staff described their extensive educational blueprint for their audience, early childhood through adulthood, which included among their wide-ranging programs some formal art pedagogical activity in the local school system as well as programs within Artworks, an architectural area designed and designated primarily as an interactive space for children. At the High Museum in Atlanta, the head of School and Teacher Services, Kate McLeod, met for an interview. She identified the High Museum as a mid-sized metropolitan museum with 450,000 visitors per year. She described the High Museum as a member of a troika of organizations administered by the Woodruff Arts Center. The other two are the Alliance Theater and the Atlanta Symphony Orchestra. Ms. McLeod outlined the broad educational scope of the museum for its many constituencies while indicating that 5 educational personnel of the staff of 15 educational employees, as well as 9 teaching artists, focus on servicing 55,000–60,000 students and also 5,000–6,000 educators with professional development programs. She stated the museum focuses on the community and uses community partnerships but does not experience the need for much outreach. Like the MMFA, the High operates an architectural space for interactive programs, called The Learning Center, for audience members ages 3–11.

as it seems to propose an exhibition concept to a museum educator rather than a curator, her idea grew into the third project developed by a co-curatorial committee of teachers in partnership with the FSU MoFA Education Program. That day, a three-year plan was set in motion.

The resulting project, named *The Story*, provides an example of the influence of Hein's conception of constructivist emphases at work in a museum with its collaborative, transparent approach to curatorial deliberations, its many interrelated layers of involvement extending connections within and outside the institution, and its interactive "hands-on and minds-on" learning. Not long after the initial meeting with art educator Fran Kautz, a "co-curatorial committee" of teachers gathered to formulate working strategies for the project, strategies that emanated from its overall concept and its many consequent details.

By the time of the exhibition approximately 25 schools, about 50% of public schools in Tallahassee/Leon County, participated in the exhibition in some way. The Council on Culture and Arts for the region provided grant funding and the gallery at Tallahassee Community College partnered to offer additional exhibition space. *The Story* exhibition opened at the FSU MoFA in late spring 2008 with activities for K-12 students and with performances by students as well as an artist in the exhibition. Parents and entire families, inclusive of grandparents, aunts, uncles, and cousins, most of whom, it seemed, had never or rarely visited a museum in the past, attended. This audience expanded visitation numbers to the exhibition and negated social, economic, and population limitations commonly lamented by critics of museum culture.

From the early 1980s to 2018, The FSU MoFA operated more as a facilitator, rather than as an authority, for the university community as well as the broader community in which it resided. Uniqueness grew from necessity since the staff of the Museum at various times numbered between one and five and a half employee positions. The FSU MoFA needed the collaborative efforts of other players. Thus, it operated only with guest curators from across the faculty of the University and sometimes from the broader community. Potential curators presented their ideas about exhibitions, often inclusive of potential programs and speakers, to the director and standing committees that might at various times be required to approve the scheduling of exhibitions. This process tended to ensure interaction by the community with the FSU MoFA and tended to ensure that community players felt they held a stake in the life of the museum. Guest curators offered exhibitions that ranged across subject, media, style, time period, and mode of display. Exhibitions might feature the intertwining of history or science with art, or focus on art historical emphases, or present a cross section of work focused on current societal or aesthetic issues. Displays included varying amounts of didactic material from digital to textual as well as varying amounts of the solicitation of visitor interaction. Guest curators brought themed exhibitions and solo shows for well-known artists like Judy Chicago, or exhibitions featuring artists from the city and region in which the FSU MoFA exists. Although the use of guest curators began as a necessity, the practice deepened the ability of the museum to engage a broader community who demonstrated a complex web of perspectives.

This already facilitative approach toward curation, as well as the development of new theoretical perspectives about museums and their programs, influenced the FSU MoFA K-12 Program. As mentioned, in 1998, George Hein published *Learning in the Museum*, a constructivist theoretical manifesto for museums and their programs. In *Learning in the Museum* Hein succinctly outlined theoretical understandings of knowledge, learning, and pedagogy and neatly compressed the information into one quadratic diagram with brief explanations of didactic/ expository, stimulus-response, discovery learning, and constructivist modes. For each mode placed within a quadrant, he described the characteristics of museums who operated under the sway of that mode. His views greatly influenced the education program of the FSU MoFA thereafter.

Hein viewed constructivism as a group of concepts with several emphases. The most important concept, which affects all other aspects of the approach, is a theory of the mechanics of learning. All learners insert new knowledge into an internal mental organization or configuration of previous experience, knowledge, understandings, and meanings. Thus, the recognition of something familiar within new experience and new information will provide a connection to this new information. Familiarity will allow or ease the incorporation of that information into the already constructed internal mental configuration. Without this connection, the learner will disregard the new either by absence of notice or conceptual denial. During this process of continual insertion with its concomitant internal mental structuring and restructuring, learners "construct" new under-standings and new meanings. This insertion may create small or radical effects, from a detail-sized extension of the configuration, a smaller realization, to its total restructuring, a radical realization.

In essence, the instructor becomes a facilitator, setting up an environment with activities, mental and physical, that will foster connectivity between new experience/information and the multitude of inner configurations of individuals so they can construct new understandings and meanings. The instructor will accommodate a range of learning methods and styles. A constructivist mode of learning is described as interactive, "hands-on" and "minds-on." Learners are encouraged to "experiment" in thought and action to reach a scope of individual conclusions. Mistakes are not measured against a universal "standard of truth" or preordained suppositions, but against "evidence at hand." Group interactions, or social co-constructions of meanings, are encouraged. In addition, learners are encouraged to organize or order their learning experiences through a process of "picking and choosing" activities and aspects grounded in or associated with the new information.

A K-5 visitor experienced work in the Student Display section of *The Story* exhibition.

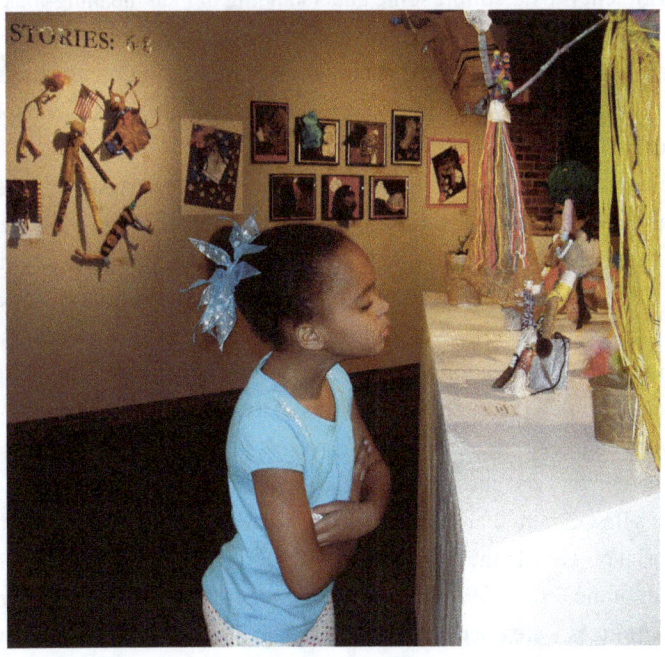

Courtesy: Florida State University Museum of Fine Arts.

Likewise Hein sees the job of the constructivist museum, just as he sees the job for educators, to be that of setting up environments and activities, mental and physical, that foster connectivity between the experience/information provided by the museum and the multitude of inner configurations of visitors so they can construct new understandings and meanings. This constructivist view of the museum is that of facilitator, again similar to the role of the educator. The museum is not seen as the authority, or the place of "truth," but the purveyor of "interpretations" of culture through the display of various exhibitions.

In its role as an interpreter, Hein feels the constructivist museum must do a number of things. To summarize, first, the museum must be transparent in its role as an interpreter, often by including others in its curatorial interpretations, or by including others in the curatorial process, often through some type of collaboration. Second, the museum, to build a broader museum community, must see an exhibition as only one aspect of a larger or expansive program or project that helps to provide additional avenues, or layers of interaction, for constructivist connections of meaning-making. Third, the constructivist museum must study its own constituency to determine some understanding of their meaning-making and shape the environment and activities of the museum to meet their needs. These three main aspects of a constructivist museum require attention to various types of access to the museum's offerings—conceptual, social, physical, developmental, and according to various learning modalities.

These two circumstances—Hein's influential constructivist writings about museums as well as the "guest curator" policy of the FSU MoFA—converged to nurture a unique practice, but a practice that is replicable. From approximately 2000 to 2018, the K-12 Education Program of the Museum acted as a guest curator for five individual exhibitions suggested by local art teachers. From conception to implementation, each exhibition took two to four years to develop. The process ensured the three main aspects of a constructivist museum outlined above were met.

Guest co-curators and guest co-curatorial committees of the FSU MoFA certainly met Hein's first dictum that the constructivist museum needs to be transparent in its curatorial process. In the case of the co-curatorial committees organized under the banner of the FSU MoFA Education Program, the processes and activities of these committees were open and knowable. The formations of these committees were announced, and teachers could join these committees upon announcement. Committee members were charged with "advertising" the exhibition plans to their own scholastic, academic neighborhoods or beyond. Often, some teachers joined after work was under way as did some community committee members. Generally, the process for choosing artworks was suggested by each committee toward the beginning of the multiyear exhibition development. In some cases, committee members presented artwork and artists for consideration with decisions about the artwork checklist determined after all presentations were finished. In others a call for entries was publicized and committee members selected from the artists' applications. Committee members also suggested accompanying programs and accompanying artist interactions with K-12 students and educators. The process for decision-making was flexible and reliant on the consensus of those present at meetings. Those who missed meetings were kept up to date through e-mail, phone calls, and the grapevine. The museum educator also served on these committees and acted as a partner, a facilitator, and the liaison to the museum, implementing the decisions of the committees.

As the previous description indicates, *The Story* exhibition itself was only one part of a larger project, Hein's second dictum that the constructivist museum must see an exhibition as only one aspect of a larger or expansive program that offers additional pathways and interaction to a broader museum community who can make constructivist connections for meaning-making. An extended explanation of the entire *Story* project with its many programs and activities can be found in the project description in Chapter 6.

More difficult for the FSU MoFA, due to its small staff, was Hein's third dictum, that visitors to a constructivist museum need to be studied and their meaning-making understood. The FSU MoFA Education Program opted for informal qualitative measures rather than quantitative. Obviously, the feedback and vocalized opinions of classroom art instructors involved in *The Story* were solicited and followed as a natural part of the process. Their input acted loosely as a front-end study. Those on the co-curatorial committee not only served as curators but also served as informal evaluators of the project and its process. Their feedback about the appropriateness or inappropriateness of artwork selections, texts, activities, learning modalities, and so on for the intended audience provided a continuous evaluation of the process as it moved forward. In 2018, however, the fifth such project for the FSU MoFA Education Program, titled *Waging Peace!* brought a qualitative analysis by a collaborative group anchored in the FSU Art Education Department and will also be discussed in the project description of Chapter 8.

Several quantitative numbers do lend themselves to an evaluation of the effectiveness of *The Story* as well as the other four projects as part of this series. For example, approximately one-third of all public and private schools in the county, which include approximately half of all public schools, participated in *The Story* project. Between outreach and on-site visitations during the last six months of the project, the visitation/participant number of this one project rose to over 7,000, a large number for a small museum whose total visitation/participant figure for all programs for this time frame was approximately 17,000.

Finally, the constructivist museum must pay attention to providing various types of approach or access to its programs—conceptual, developmental, social, and physical. Conceptually, the museum must provide exhibitions/programs that combine familiarity, personal connection, and challenge. The involvement of a sizable group of art instructors helped ensure conceptual access, through their deliberations during curatorial decision-making, their writing of lesson plans for other art instructors, and their teaching from a prepublished catalogue for *The Story* exhibition. This triple requirement—familiarity, personal connection, and challenge—can be exemplified in each of the artworks in a parallel display by the K-12 students from participatory schools. All objects created by students were the result of a preexhibition study in the classroom of an artwork or works by a professional artist or artists in the main *Story* exhibition. This artmaking generated familiarity, personal connection, and challenge on various levels for different categories of people—particularly for participating teachers and students, and the families of students who visited. The simultaneous presentation of a professional exhibition with a K-12 display encouraged ordinary visitors to engage in comparisons and contrasts between the developmental levels of work, an unusual process for meaning-making for most visitors.

Since a small museum like the FSU MoFA cannot erect a permanent children's discovery gallery, these parallel sections of the project, the exhibition by professional artists as well as the display of works by K-12 students, assured attention to developmental access. Social access was implemented by the means of communal curation but also through other features of the project such as tours, which generally utilized physical interaction with art materials, or hands-on art activities, as well as minds-on group discussion for children and adults. During the opening reception, children and adults moving through, or picking and choosing from, a series of make and take tables placed near the artwork on which each was based, also exemplify physical access through interaction with art materials, again demonstrating a hands-on and minds-on quality of the program. Hein feels the constructivist museum cannot overrely on "expert" or didactic information but instead, as in the case of *The Story* and the other four projects and exhibitions carried out in this vein, must emphasize experiences, opinions, memories, and the imaginations of its visitors. In other words, varying types of access and learning modalities must be made available to visitors so each can make his or her own meaning from the museum's offerings (Hein, 1998).

CHAPTER 3

An Overview of the Five Constructivist Co-Curated Projects and Exhibitions—The Influence of Evolving Art Education Theory and Pedagogy

Beginnings

How did the art teachers in the Leon County School District, a medium-sized district in northern Florida, become a group who were comfortable generating, co-curating, and developing five professional art exhibitions and their contextual projects? The answer lies in the national introduction of multiple theories and pedagogies over the past 30-plus years but particularly in the "take the bull by the horns" attitude of teachers in the district with their resultant ever-widening expertise. Theoretical development brought changing teaching standards which brought opportunities for professional development.

Through professional development workshops art teachers in the county started to transform their practice from the traditional strategies of the "art as a visual language" approach in which the elements and principles were the primary focus to pedagogy based on Discipline-Based Art Education (DBAE) theory (discussed in Chapter 4). Other influencing factors emerged. To refine and expand their practice, a cadre of art teachers worked through the certification process together for the National Board for Professional Teaching Standards. In addition, a group participated in a professional reading and analysis of *Rethinking the Curriculum in Art* by Marilyn Stewart and Sydney Walker. Stewart and Walker's book provided an explication of the next-generation DBAE-influenced theory and practice known as the "Big Idea" (discussed in Chapter 6). As art teachers in the district developed their expertise, their relationship to Florida State University Museum of Fine Arts' (FSU MoFA) education department solidified.

Elementary art teachers especially embraced the co-curatorial process and began to confidently instigate the origin of projects and their culminating exhibitions. Elementary teachers pitched *The Story* and *Generations* projects to the FSU MoFA on their own initiative rather than as a result of MoFA invitations to do so. As the FSU MoFA Curator of Education, I did not expect this. The remaining three projects and exhibitions were initiated by the FSU MoFA but themes were suggested by teachers: *Visions of the North Florida Environment* was developed by elementary teachers; *In Print: The Language of Art*, was developed by high school teachers; and the theme for the last project and exhibition (*Waging Peace!*) was suggested by a combined group of elementary and high school teachers who served as members of the FSU MoFA Education Council.

> *Waging Peace!* (the fifth and last project in the series) demonstrated a continuation of theoretical and pedagogical influences. For *Waging Peace!* recent theories and practices underlying social justice in art education held sway (discussed in Chapter 8). Here the emphasis was placed on art as a means to combat social or environmental problems that lead to inequality or a deterioration in the quality of life on this planet.
>
> —*MM & VDTW*

Cover for *The Story* catalogue.

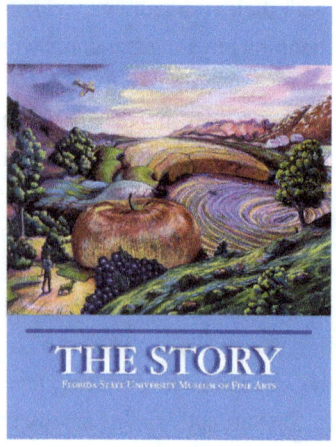

Courtesy: Florida State University Museum of Fine Arts.

Cover for the *Generations* catalogue.

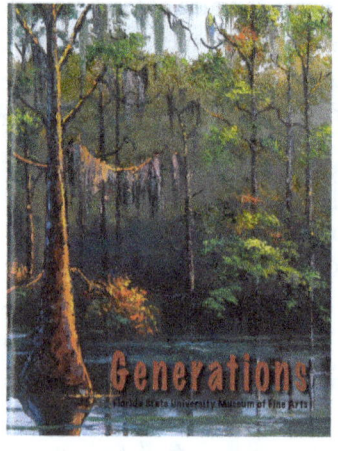

Courtesy: Florida State University Museum of Fine Arts.

Cover for the *Waging Peace!* catalogue.

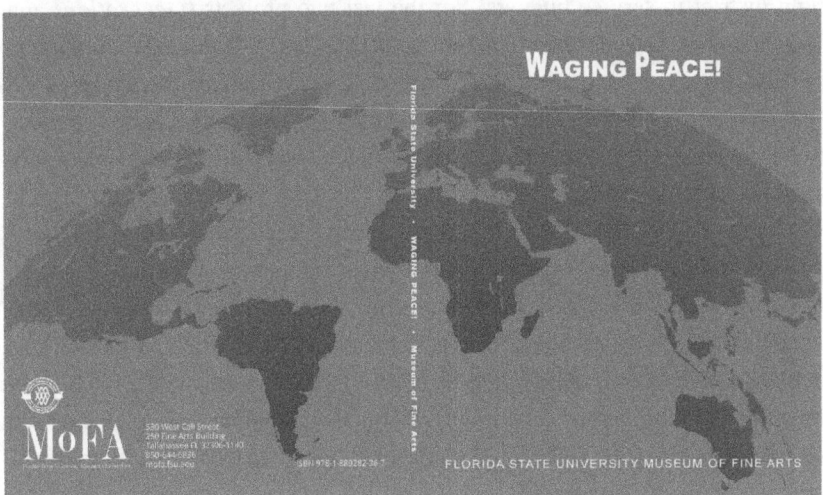

Courtesy: Florida State University Museum of Fine Arts.

Co-Curatorial Patterns

Teachers dominated the composition of all co-curatorial teams, and as such it was natural that art educational theory and praxis influenced each of the projects and exhibitions. This infusion of art educational theory and pedagogy into curatorial implementation was a major characteristic within a pattern, but still only one characteristic of the pattern, which emerged during the formation of the five projects under consideration. Each project and exhibition featured a theme suggested by a teacher or teachers. The FSU MoFA Curator of Education acted as a member of each team and also as a liaison and administrator of the exhibition and larger project within the museum. All teams wrote lesson plans for teachers' packets that were distributed primarily to art instructors and made available to other teachers throughout the county and beyond. All lesson plans followed state standards. All teams developed programs grounded in aspects of the exhibitions. Artist interactions with students and teachers as well as teacher workshops provide two such program examples. Providing in-service opportunities with credit awarded to a broad array of teachers by the county school system was an important aspect of these projects especially in light of tight district in-service budgets. For the last two projects (*Generations* and *Waging Peace!*) besides the usual recertification for the workshop participation process, the county school system awarded co-curatorial members recertification credits via specific documentation simply for their participation in those two projects. Each exhibition featured a professional exhibition catalogue or a poster which acted as a mini-catalogue. For each project a student display of response work, elicited in the classroom by lesson plans from teachers' packets and catalogues, was mounted as an accompaniment to the exhibition of professional work. Plans for each opening night included a series of events generated by the pertinent co-curatorial team. All projects and exhibitions demonstrated community as well as cross-disciplinary elements. University interns were recruited as contributors to the development or implementation of each. Tours of the exhibitions were typically conducted with a "minds-on" and/or "hands-on" approach.

The planning of each exhibition extended from two to four years, and for each of these exhibitions, as stated, the exhibition itself was viewed as the culminating activity of an expanded project which incorporated many activities. In accordance with Hein's dictum for curation in a constructivist museum, the exhibition constituted only one part of a larger project. The extended time for planning fostered the spread of information about the project and exhibition throughout the community of art teachers in the county and to other teachers as well. This nurtured the impulse by many other teachers to join these exhibitions and projects in some capacity, thus increasing their final impact. Following each of the exhibitions, co-curatorial team members reviewed the efficacy of the project for presentation at a state or national conference or as an article for publication.

Within this pattern, differences often emerged based on the influences, concepts, and practices members of the teams brought with them. Some teams emanated from one school; others came from multiple schools. For those exhibitions and projects which represented the involvement of multiple institutions, the FSU MoFA used grant money to assist with busing their students to the exhibition tours. The underlying theories and pedagogies of art education utilized by teachers shifted, changed, and then merged with the distinct qualities characterized by each of the five projects. This made each project and exhibition unique despite the process similarities which carried over from one to the other. Details differed from team to team in the strategies used for the selection of artwork, for the writing of lesson plans, for the mounting of accompanying student displays, and for the creation of programs and events. Generally, these dissimilarities seemed the result of the dominant underlying theory or practice that influenced the selection of a theme for the exhibition.

CHAPTER 4

Project #1: The Influence of Discipline-Based Art Education

Project Title: *Visions of the North Florida Environment*
Planning and Program Implementation: Fall, 1999-Spring, 2002
Exhibition Year: 2002
Co-curatorial Team:
Tallahassee, Florida, Buck Lake Elementary School
- Classroom Educator—Cynthia Braswell
- Classroom Educator—Donna Frinks
- Classroom Educator—Sarah Godwin
- Classroom Educator—Donna Haff
- Classroom Educator—Lynn Janasiewicz
- Art Educator—Fran Kautz
- Art Educator—Sonia McDowell
- Classroom Educator—Nancy Reddick
- Guidance Counselor—Lea Reeves
- Classroom Educator—Betsy Sullivan
Florida State University Museum of Fine Arts
- Curator of Education—Dr. Viki D. Thompson Wylder
Artworks: 38
Artists: Todd Bertolaet, Julie Bowland, Clyde Butcher, Mary Adore Coloney, Molly Mabe, Caroline Madden, and Mark Messersmith

Beginnings

On opening night 2002, as I entered the Florida State University Museum of Fine Arts (FSU MoFA), it was immediately apparent this art show was different, well beyond the usual museum-curated show with an art education component. Little did I know then that two decades later a new way of working would be established, a new approach to curating and collaboration. I did not know *Visions of the North Florida Environment* would be the first of five shows in which the subject was suggested by teachers and co-curated by teachers. What stood out on this opening night were the elementary student docents dressed neatly, well-versed and ready to share their knowledge as mini-experts excited to engage in conversations about artworks.

—*MM*

Poster for *Visions of the North Florida Environment.*

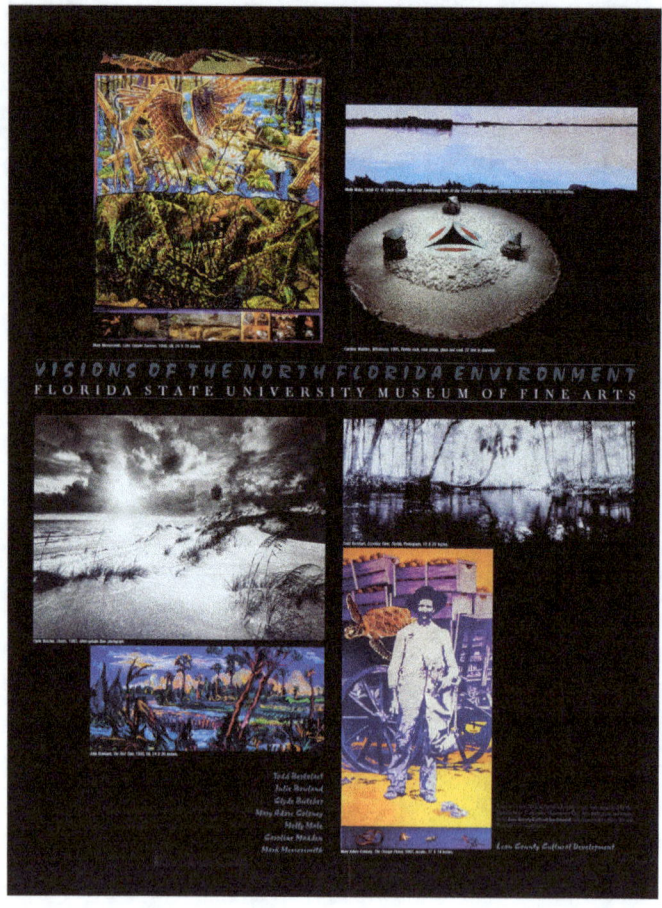

Courtesy: Florida State University Museum of Fine Arts.

The Project Backstory

The *Visions of the North Florida Environment* project resulted from the 1999 invitation by the Education Program of the FSU MoFA to teachers from Tallahassee's Buck Lake Elementary School to co-curate an exhibition. "The Florida State University Museum of Fine Arts and Buck Lake Elementary School [had] enjoyed a partnership for several years" (Florida State University Museum of Fine Arts, 2002, *Visions* poster verso, introduction). At the time, Buck Lake Elementary was steeped in Discipline-Based Art Education (DBAE), also known as comprehensive art education, with an administration, faculty, art and classroom teachers eager and committed to utilizing DBAE theories and practices with their student population. Classroom teachers joined art teachers in using the four disciplines that comprised DBAE—artmaking, art history, art criticism, and aesthetics—as strategies to cross curricular boundaries. Every teacher at Buck Lake Elementary integrated some or all these art disciplines in a natural way within the curriculum of each classroom (M. Meale & V. D. T. Wylder, personal communication with co-curatorial committee members from Buck Lake Elementary F. Kautz & S. McDowell, March 2, 2020). The DBAE emphasis on learning from actual works of art as well as the use of primary sources in teaching, like exhibitions, incentivized a commitment to such a project from Buck Lake Elementary and the FSU MoFA.

DBAE started a shift in art education content and practice in Leon County largely due to summer workshops provided through the *Florida Institute for Art Education*. The Florida Institute was founded and housed in the Art Education Department at Florida State University and funded in 1988 by a grant from the Getty Education Institute for the Arts. It was one of six regional institutes created across the country via grants, which came to be called RIGS (Research Institute Grants) by the Getty Education Institute. RIGS were mandated to conduct training as well as generate resources based on the principles of DBAE. Recognizing that many schools across the state and nation were without or had limited elementary art programs, the goal of the grant was to "develop students' abilities to understand and appreciate art" (Clark et al., 1987, p. 135). DBAE provided both a foundation for art education as well as an essential component for general education as a means to expand art education beyond the art room and into the classroom. To develop students who not only understood theories and contexts of art but who could respond to as well as create art became the comprehensive goal (Clark et al., 1987). DBAE defined and developed strategies for teaching art in the four distinct yet overlapping and organically related art disciplines.

In Florida, in 1996, these four disciplines—artmaking, art history, art criticism, and aesthetics—became the core for teaching art with the approval of the Sunshine State Standards by the State Board of Education (Florida Department of Education, 2020).

In 1997, three schools in Leon County, Florida each received a significant Transforming Education Through the Arts Challenge Grant (TETAC Grant) as part of a five-year initiative funded by the Annenberg Foundation and the J. Paul Getty Trust's Getty Education Institute for the Arts. The Florida Institute for Art Education paved the way for receiving these grants through a previous dissemination of DBAE concepts and prior training of teachers in the school district. After receipt of the grants by these schools, the Florida Institute continued to work closely with them. Buck Lake Elementary School was one of the three grantees and became the first school to participate with the FSU MoFA in the interweaving of museum and school-based art education through the constructivist co-curation of exhibitions and the expanded projects of which they were a part.

In line with the goals of the TETAC Grant, Buck Lake Elementary worked to "infuse…the core curriculum" with the arts via DBAE concepts (Epstein, 2003). "During those same years Buck Lake was awarded a Project Learning Tree Grant which provided money to create an outdoor classroom on school property" (Florida State University Museum of Fine Arts, 2002). Fran Kautz, one of two art teachers at Buck Lake Elementary, worked with the faculty and administration to suggest a theme and title for the exhibition project. Aware of the rapidly changing Florida environment, she wanted Buck Lake students to understand the changes occurring in their own back yards. She felt internally pushed to participate in the project and to influence the framing of it (Meale & Wylder, personal communication, 2020). "Buck Lake art and science initiatives dovetailed into the museum/school curation" and became *Visions of the North Florida Environment.* As their TETAC grant mandate suggested, "the [resultant] curatorial committee decided to build a program for integrating the exhibition into the curriculum of the…school—into language arts, math, social studies, science, as well as the arts" (Florida State University Museum of Fine Arts, 2002). This lead show motivated teachers to participate in further co-curatorial efforts, and it encouraged the idea of art teacher-initiation of future shows and projects at the FSU MoFA.

Description of the Project and Exhibition

At the outset of the co-curatorial process, Buck Lake teachers already knew much of the artwork they preferred for this exhibition. They chose work by local or easily reachable artists with whom they interacted as part of the DBAE emphasis of their school's theoretical and pedagogical focus and they quickly coalesced an exhibition theme from the connected messages of the various artworks selected. Through co-curatorial meetings the committee refined the array of works already considered and chose work by an additional artist. Thirty-eight works by seven artists were picked by the co-curatorial team, which included two art teachers, seven classroom teachers, and one guidance counselor. This first teacher co-curated exhibition opened two and a half years later in May of 2002.

Of the seven artists featured in *Visions of the North Florida Environment*, some had developed a wider audience, yet all were primarily regional: Todd Bertolaet, Julie Bowland, Clyde Butcher, Mary Adore Coloney, Molly Mabe, Caroline Madden, and Mark Messersmith. Photographer Todd Bertolaet's résumé included a book about the rivers of the Big Bend region of North Florida, Molly Mabe's environmental paintings hung in the Museum of Florida History, and Clyde Butcher's black-and-white photographs from across the state earned him the name "the Ansel Adams of Florida." Eventually Mark Messersmith's oil paintings of the encroachment of civilization into North Florida's ecosystems would win him the nationally recognized Joan Mitchell Painters and Sculptors Award in 2006. *Visions of the North Florida Environment* focused primarily on painting and photography, but also featured two installation artists. Caroline Madden concentrated on the use of natural materials like rocks and grass sod and Molly Mabe's single work circled a gallery with a series in oil which created a panoramic strip of landscape only 6½" high but 960" wide.

As an outgrowth of the works selected and in conjunction with the constructivist idea that the exhibition comprised only a part of the project, the co-curatorial committee suggested and developed educational programs. The committee wrote DBAE influenced lesson plans for a teacher's packet that included interwoven activities in areas such as science and language arts as well as the four visual arts disciplines of artmaking, art history, art criticism, and aesthetics. The lesson plan packet "was distributed by the Museum to every teacher at Buck Lake (as well as to art teachers throughout Leon County and in answer to requests from outside the county)" (Florida State University Museum of Fine Arts, 2002). Each lesson plan focused on the work or works of an individual artist chosen for the exhibition.

Coinciding with the writing of lesson plans, Buck Lake faculty received "in-service presentations on each artist" (Florida State University Museum of Fine Arts, 2002). Face to face interaction took place between all seven artists and either the faculty of Buck Lake or the students themselves. Illustrative was the loan of a work by Mark Messersmith to the school as an exhibition preview for its students and teachers. Teachers scheduled their classes for 30-minute sessions with the artwork, much like museum tours, encouraging students to engage in verbal critical analysis or more general dialogue and discussion (Meale & Wylder, personal communication, 2020). Students also conducted an in-person interview of the artist about his work during a visit to the school. Julie Bowland, a plein air painter of the local environment influenced by the fauvist tradition, set up her easel on the grounds of the school and demonstrated her technique. Mary Adore Coloney whose work focused on historical Floridians situated visually in the Florida environment agreed to help students in the painting of an environmental mural in the school's library. The mural can still be seen there today.

Front detail (Julie Bowland: *The Red Tree*) of the poster for *Visions of the North Florida Environment.*

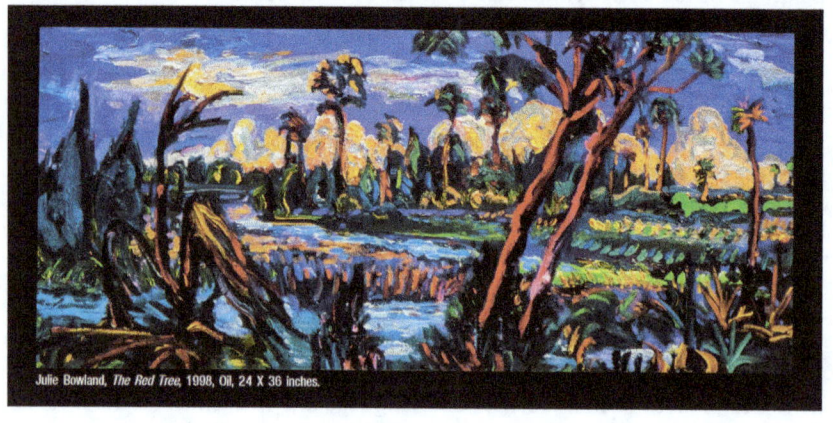

Julie Bowland, *The Red Tree*, 1998, Oil, 24 X 36 inches.

Courtesy: Florida State University Museum of Fine Arts.

The mural became an extended fifth-grade project. Teachers taught lessons merging science and art in which each fifth-grade class researched a North Florida ecosystem and created a collaborative final sketch to act as a template for representation of that ecosystem. The final mural illustrated eight distinct sections of the North Florida environment inclusive of a hardwood hammock, pine flatwoods, sand scrub, a freshwater marsh, a saltwater marsh, a swamp, beach habitat, and sandhill terrain. Six mural sections were painted by the students who were joined by teachers and parents for the completion of the remaining two sections. The mural was finished in three days. The artist, Mary Adore Coloney, contributed to the event by mixing paints during the three-day event and painting the transitions from one section to the next (Meale & Wylder, personal communication, 2020).

The co-curatorial committee mounted a parallel student display at the county public library with an opening reception prior to the exhibition at the FSU MoFA. In this satellite event, each of the 900 students enrolled in the school was represented by his or her own artwork created in response to the study of the professional artists' works in *Visions of the North Florida Environment*. This parallel, simultaneous display of student work set another precedent for future teacher co-curatorial projects in this series.

For the exhibition of professional artwork at the FSU MoFA, the co-curatorial committee organized an active opening reception as well as student field trips. Plans were devised for training students to be docents for the reception. Student docents, whose research of the artists in the exhibition included three in-studio visits, were members of the Buck Lake closed-circuit television class. During their in-studio visits, these students conducted interviews which they then produced and aired at school. At the opening each student docent took responsibility for artists and artworks each personally researched. To broaden the celebration of the arts and coincidentally broaden the audience, the opening also featured a music performance led by the music instructor at Buck Lake. "Reflecting the theme of the exhibition imagery, a group of students will author and [perform] their own song, and other students will recite original poetry based on the imagery of the exhibition" (Florida State University Museum of Fine Arts, 2002). The committee determined every child at the school would visit the exhibition during a field trip and tours in DBAE fashion would be interactive. During a tour with first graders, the painter Mark Messersmith agreed to meet with the students. He spoke a few sentences before hands waved energetically. He was surprised first graders could speak about his "dichotomies," the tension between animals and humans in the eroding North Florida environment (Thompson Wylder et al., 2003). The co-curatorial committee also planned for extended teacher interaction with the exhibition through end-of-the-school-year workshops for which in-service recertification credit was offered. "A two-day teacher workshop [was] held in partnership with…The Mary Brogan Museum of Art and Science" (Florida State University Museum of Fine Arts, 2002).

As part of the project, the museum director approved the production of a poster that would act as a mini-catalogue. An image by each of the artists appeared on the recto-side design. The verso contained multiple sections: an introductory explanation of the exhibition and its process, biographies of each of the artists penned by members of the co-curatorial team, and brief "Suggestions for Activity and Discussion for Teachers K-12." These suggestions abbreviated the lesson plans written by members of the co-curatorial committee for the teacher's packet, which had already been distributed to other art teachers in the county before the exhibition. Like the full lesson plans, the suggestions as a group incorporated the four art disciplines of DBAE as well as interdisciplinary activity. Suggestions for study and use of Caroline Madden's installations comprehensively addressed all four art disciplines and one outside the arts:

- Compare and contrast Caroline Madden's installation with those by artists such as Andy Goldsworthy, Sara Bates, Robert Smithson, Christo, or Nancy Graves (art history and art criticism).
- Artists generally take photographs of their installations and then dismantle them. The memory of the work is retained in the photograph. Decide which is the art—the original installation or the photograph. Can something no longer existing be called art? Can just the memory of it be called art? Can both be called art (aesthetics)?
- Create individual mock-ups of installation works using natural materials arranged on small surfaces. Identify each of the natural materials. Put all the individual installations together to make one large patchwork installation. Create a flyer that lists the natural materials identified (artmaking and science) (Florida State University Museum of Fine Arts, 2002).

Posters were distributed to every student at Buck Lake Elementary before the exhibition and given to viewers at the opening reception. Several of the artists attended the opening and were pleased to find themselves spontaneously inundated with K-5 students, posters in hand, joyfully lining up to ask for the signing of autographs next to images of the artists' works. For these students the artists in the exhibition were viewed as heroes and celebrities. Between the opening reception for the student art exhibition at the public library and the professional artist exhibition of *Visions of the North Florida Environment* at the FSU MoFA, attendees totaled about 1,400 people with students and adults at both venues.

Discipline-Based Art Education and *Visions of the North Florida Environment*

Prior to the adoption of the Sunshine State Standards and the workshops provided through the *Florida Institute for Art Education*, most of the district's art teachers were following the district scope and sequence. As a basis for their programs they planned lessons using some combination of studio artmaking and art history with an emphasis on the elements and principles of art. Often, lesson planning would start with an artist and a work of art or historical exemplar that illustrated an element or principle of art, a technique, or subject matter. Mondrian's work comes to mind with student objectives based on geometric shapes, primary colors, and the process of the artist himself. Formal elements of artmaking were the emphasis. Only occasionally were cultural/historical context, critical analysis, or aesthetic issues engendered by the work considered. Years later, that same lesson based on the influence of "Big Idea" theory and pedagogy shifted focus to questions such as: How did Mondrian capture the rhythm, noise, or structure of a large city?

As art teachers attended *Florida Institute for Art Education* summer workshops, they started to increasingly incorporate DBAE strategies into their lesson planning and teaching. "Aesthetic moments" became an introductory strategy. Students learned a way of talking about art aesthetically and analytically, in other words critically, while they continued to acquire artmaking proficiencies and study art history. Within DBAE, unlike past pedagogies, art history was taught as a cultural context that informed and gave meaning to the art discussion and artmaking following an "aesthetic moment."

What are aesthetic moments? Ron Yrabedra, an art history professor at Florida Agricultural and Mechanical University (FAMU) and an instrumental member of the team that developed the summer Florida Institute workshops, created the teaching structure that came to be called an "aesthetic moment." Yrabedra paired carefully chosen large format images of artworks with music to be shown in quiet darkened settings as a means to create inspirational and meaningful experiences. An inexact illustration of an aesthetic moment is available on YouTube (991bigjohn, 2009). Here, a series of Van Gogh works is paired with the audio of Don McClean singing his ballad, *Starry Starry Night*. With the exception of printed words superimposed on the imagery at the beginning and end of the video and the size of the format, this example follows Ron Yrabedra's prescription for aesthetic moments.

After each aesthetic moment participants were given a quiet moment to reflect. Reflection was generally followed by a question and answer period starting with a question about the viewer's reaction. This led to deeper critical analysis, historical/cultural contextual information, and often to an artmaking session. Created by art teachers and classroom teachers, aesthetic moments became beautiful and moving introductions to art discussions as the beginnings of units. The Buck Lake co-curatorial committee also used aesthetic moments at their meetings or during presentations to inspire and draw their entire faculty into participation.

But aesthetics in the Florida Institute for the Arts workshops went beyond aesthetic moments and the traditional view of aesthetics as philosophical questions about beauty in art to contemporary aesthetic questions about the purpose of art. What makes this an artwork? What makes someone an artist? Who determines what is or is not art?

Art criticism became a key means of talking about art in the art room or classroom. Questions for each of the three core phases of the criticism process were formalized in literature providing a useful set of queries for teachers to use. Feldman and Anderson each added a fourth step; Feldman added analysis (1970, pp. 348–383) and Anderson added reaction. But the three-part approach to art criticism (brief example questions provided here) starts with:

> **Description:** What do you notice first? What material(s) was used? What shapes, colors, textures? What images do you see in the artwork?
>
> **Interpretation:** What does this artwork mean? How does it make you feel? What feelings are expressed in this artwork? Is there a message in this artwork? Provide evidence.
>
> **Evaluation/Judgment:** Is it good in and of itself? Why? Is it clear? Is it well made? Does it have cultural significance? Does it move you? Is the artwork important because of what it means? Why? Would others like to see this artwork? Why?
>
> (Anderson, 1997; Anderson & Milbrandt, 2005)

Over time many local art teachers chose to use the criticism method as outlined by Tom Anderson in his *School Arts* article "A Model for Art Criticism: Talking with Kids about Art". His method started by asking: What is your first response to this artwork? What does it make you feel, think, or remind you of?

Anderson started with reac-tion, then proceeded to description, interpretation, and evaluation/judgment. His method, however, was circular. At the end after evaluation/judgment, he returned to reaction and asked whether the student viewers wanted to revise or add more to their initial thoughts. Teachers found Anderson's method of addressing reaction first more conducive to helping elementary students perceive the purpose of an art criticism session and move through the entire process in a reasonable amount of class time.

Teaching art criticism in the art room and/or classroom empowered students during visits to the museum. When a docent or education director asked questions, students energetically participated: What do you see in this artwork? What do you think it means? How do you know? The process created a meaningful alignment of art education practice with museum education practice.

Art history, using DBAE methods, explores the contexts in which art was or is created to include exemplars from broad categories of time, type, style, culture, and so on. In DBAE as in museum practice, art history includes time periods from ancient to contemporary and across all cultures. It includes all types and styles such as folk art or applied art, as well as that deemed "fine art" (Clark et al., 1987). Art exemplars became central to instructional unit development. Teachers developed and used timelines and maps to help students understand different periods and the location of different cultures.

The expectations for implementation of DBAE included written sequentially organized curricula for all grade levels, inclusive of works of art central to the organization and natural integration of content from all four areas of DBAE. The four areas of DBAE were given comparable attention and respect; they were devised to be developmentally appropriate and organized to increase student learning and understanding. Full implementation included systematic regular art instruction on a district-wide basis, art education expertise, administrative support, and adequate resources. Student achievement and program effectiveness were to be confirmed by appropriate evaluation criteria and procedures (Clark et al., 1987; Dobbs, 1992).

In the summer workshops, classroom teachers were trained side by side with art teachers. These classroom teachers returned to their schools and often paired or consulted with their own school-based art teachers to develop cross- curricular units using art exemplars and DBAE strategies. Titles of thematic units or phrases such as "art and math" or "science and art" were heard around some schools. Buck Lake Elementary School's development of the concepts within *Visions of the North Florida Environment* by art and classroom teachers is certainly an example of this type of thematic merger.

Textbook and multimedia companies responded to the demand for DBAE based instructional information by developing support materials and exemplars with historical background on artists, cultures, and/or time periods, as well as details about technical processes and media used to create the works of art. This information was either provided on the back of prints or in booklets not unlike wall didactics and catalogs found in museums (Clark et al., 1987). This affinity of DBAE-related materials and resources to museum practice is one indicator of the potential for the development of a project like that between Buck Lake Elementary School and the FSU MoFA. DBAE-trained Buck Lake teachers used FSU MoFA printed materials from the *Visions of the North Florida Environment* in their classroom teaching.

The educators of the J. Paul Getty Museum originated DBAE theory and practice. The four disciplines of artmaking, art history, art criticism, and aesthetics are all basic components of the culture of a museum. Museum scholarship and text about artworks often organically combine issues from these four areas. The DBAE attitude toward art teachers' relationships to museums was understandable. Art teachers were prompted to see art museums as the most important art world environment. Exhibitions were touted as major influential factors in the art world. DBAE literature extolled exhibitions, like artworks themselves, as a reflection and shaper of the art world as well as the general culture. Teachers were encouraged to collaborate in some way with museums to work to remove barriers between the museum and the classroom. In DBAE practice teachers were urged to affirm and acquaint students with primary sources by bringing their students to museums for in-person encounters with artworks. Learning in the museum itself was deemed significant.

The main DBAE practice, the development of an instructional unit, bears analogies to the development of an exhibition. Like many exhibitions, units were thematic. Teachers selected artworks, derived a unifying theme of human import from the artwork selection with perhaps additional artworks added to the unit, and then planned instructional processes based authentically on the art disciplines and disciplines outside the arts. Within DBAE practice teachers were advised to look to artwork in a range of exhibitions inclusive of local and community exhibitions as a source for unit issues. Unit teaching methods frequently incorporated face to face exposure and interaction with artwork and artists. Teachers often sought students' production of their own work as a response to the study of thematic unit content.

The co-curatorial process exerted a desirable two-way influence between Buck Lake Elementary and the FSU MoFA. The Education Program of the FSU MoFA used the process to explore the workings of a school in the community in order to better construct the museum education program to meet the needs of public school teachers and students and thus increase the draw and usage of the museum by this population. Collaboration with teachers allowed the one-staff FSU MoFA Education Program to hugely expand and profoundly deepen the meaning of its offerings. Conversely, the co-curatorial process allowed teachers to better fulfill the DBAE method of educating students. The Buck Lake Elementary School community of teachers, administration, and students felt ownership of the museum space and its program. As a result, the *Visions of the North Florida Environment* project, its exhibition and programs, and the museum itself held greater value and relevance for them.

Written by a curatorial member, this biography of artist Clyde Butcher appeared on the back of the poster for *Visions of the North Florida Environment.*

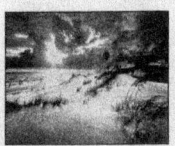

CLYDE BUTCHER's photographs are devoid of the human figure. Butcher's name has become synonymous with the Florida environment. His black and white prints taken with an 8 x 10" or 11 x 14" large format camera capture the detail and texture found in Florida's earth, clouds, and light, not the growth of Florida's cities or the ever-encroaching expansion of Florida's population.

Clyde Butcher was born in Kansas City, Missouri, in 1942. As a child he moved frequently. In 1960 Butcher began to study architecture at California Polytechnic University. Here, Butcher had several defining experiences including an important encounter with photography. In 1963, he was impressed by a visit to an exhibition of Ansel Adams photographs at Yosemite.

During the second half of the 1960s Butcher experienced a number of life changes, both privately and professionally. He continued to work in architecture, beginning a business for photographing scale models in such a way that the pictures looked like they contained real buildings. At one point, Butcher played a part in the process for designing the TransAmerica Tower (San Francisco's signature skyscraper). In 1970, Butcher gave up architecture to pursue landscape photography. Financially, the Butchers lost almost everything and ended up without a home, camping in a tent-trailer in parks. During the 1970s, Butcher found business success and loss again.

In 1980, two years after visiting Florida, Butcher decided to start afresh by moving east. Clyde began to explore the remaining wild environment of Florida, and shot elegant, Adams-influenced scenes of South Florida's last complex and untouched ecosystems.

Butcher, with exacting expectations of himself, estimates that he takes only one truly great picture a year. He states that it takes weeks to find the right setting, days to set up, and hours to prepare before the light and all other features are exactly right.

Butcher was selected for Florida's 1998 Artists' Hall of Fame. He was featured as "Person of the Week" on ABC's Evening News with Peter Jennings. He and his work have been seen on a number of national news programs. He received the Heartland Community Service Award for teaching Floridians about their beautiful state. He has worked "to save nature's places of spiritual sanctuary for future generations" and so was honored by two conservation awards, the Conservation Colleague Award from the Nature Conservancy and the Ansel Adams Conservation Award from the Sierra Club. Clyde Butcher's photography is often found in museum exhibitions throughout Florida, and may be found in his publications.

Written by Betsy Sullivan

Courtesy: Florida State University Museum of Fine Arts.

Written by a curatorial member, this biography of artist Mark Messersmith appeared on the back of the poster for *Visions of the North Florida Environment.*

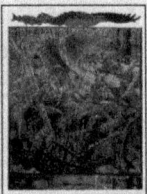

MARK MESSERSMITH's works explore the struggle between humans and the environment. In a time when we see Florida's beaches and forests being replaced by shopping malls, high-rise condominiums, and theme parks, Mark Messersmith's paintings are an important reminder of what we are in danger of losing. Messersmith says that he explores "dichotomies such as good and evil, life and death, humankind versus nature, tastelessness versus taste, chaos versus order; all simultaneously."

Messersmith creates large, colorful oil paintings, often with strong contrast between bright and dark colors. The main characters in his works are bobcats, alligators, snakes, herons, raccoons, owls, and large-mouthed bass. Logging trucks and highways weave through the backgrounds while helicopters and planes traverse the sky. The artist attaches boxed scenes below the bottom edge of his canvases, and carved colorful sculptures above the top edge.

Mark Messersmith holds a Bachelor of Fine Arts from Fontbonne College in St. Louis, and a Master of Fine Arts from Indiana University. He has won both Florida Arts Council Fellowships (1987, 1993, 1999) and NEA grants (1988, 1994), exhibiting his work throughout the Southeastern United States; he is currently an Associate Professor of Painting at Florida State University.

Written by Cynthia Braswell and Lynn Janasciewicz

Courtesy: Florida State University Museum of Fine Arts.

Selected content from the back of the poster for *Visions of the North Florida Environment.*

Florida State University Museum of Fine Arts.

Poster Design: Allys Palladino-Craig
Poster Text: Exhibition Curatorial Team

The *Visions of the North Florida* Environment curatorial team selected works, wrote an explanatory introduction about the project, composed biographies of each artist in the exhibition, and created the following activities for use by both classroom teachers and art teachers within their own school and throughout Leon County. The activities and discussion ideas below demonstrate the concepts behind Discipline Based Art Education including both the interdisciplinary approach of DBAE and the emphasized four art disciplines of art criticism, art making, art history, and aesthetics.

Suggestions for Activity and Discussion for Teachers K-12

1. Todd Bertolaet
   a. Both Todd Bertolaet and Clyde Butcher are photographers who present images of Florida in black and white. However, their photographs show differences in style and message. Compare and contrast the photographs of both artists. What is the message they wish to convey about the North Florida Environment?
   b. Take three photographs of the environment in your neighborhood. Mount the pictures in a triptych sequence. Write two or three sentences about each panel of your triptych; include the relationship that exists among your photos. Todd Bertolaet sometimes adds comments with a gel pen to the borders of his composite photographs. Experiment with the placement and then write your sentences on your triptych using a gel or paint pen.
2. Julie Bowland
   a. Julie Bowland's paintings express her feelings about the North Florida landscape. Make a list of color and emotion words that would help describe her paintings. Write a poem about a single Julie Bowland artwork – rhymng or non-rhyming – that uses the words from your list.
3. Clyde Butcher
   a. Prepare and create an image of a Tallahassee or Leon County area landscape in a black and white medium. In Clyde Butcher fasion, take great care with choosing the location and image you wish to present. Pick a time of day when the light will help to create a dramatic image. Use any black and white medium you choose – photography, collage, pastel, paint or other.

Mary Adore Coloney
   a. In her artwork Mary Adore Coloney includes Floridains interaction
       with their environment. The artist researches her imagery, often
       showing Floridians from the past , for example cutting cane or boiling
       syrup. Look in books about Florida history and find pictures of people
       that show the different ways Floridians before us worked and played.
       Discuss the ways the activities of past Floridians had an impact on the
       animal life found in the borders of Mary Adore Coloney's paintings.
       Discuss ways present day Floridians can preserve their rich wildlife
       heritage.
Molly Mabe
   a. In an ecosystem, living and non-living things are interdependent.
       Looking at Molly Mabe's work, discuss the ecosystem represented.
       What are the relationships between living and non-living things in the
       ecosystem? Or do you consider everything in the painting a living
       thing? Explain.
   b. Imagine that a developer of large condominiums and single-family
       homes purchased the land represented in this painting. What changes
       do you think would occur? How would the balance of nature be
       disturbed if major buildings were erected on this land? Could the
       developer minimize the damage to this environmental area or should
       the building simply not be erected? What could be done to persuade
       the builder to leave this land in a pristine condition? Discuss this with
       an emphasis on finding solutions.
Caroline Madden
   a. Do individual mock-ups of installation works using natural materials
       arranged on small surfaces. Identify each of the natural materials. Put
       all the individual installations together to make one large patchwork
       installation. Create a flyer that lists the natural materials identified.
   b. Compare and contrast Caroline Madden's installations with those by
       artists such as Andy Goldsworthy, Sara Bates, Robert Smithson,
       Christo, or Nancy Graves.
   c. Artists generally take photographs of their installations and then
       dismantle them. The memory of the work is retained in the
       photograph. Decide which is the art – the original installation or the
       photograph. Can something no longer existing be called art? Can just
       the memory of it be called art? Can both be called art?
Mark Messersmith
   a. Mark Messersmith explores the idea of opposites in his work: good
       versus evil, life versus death, human versus nature, and chaos versus
       order. Look for examples of these opposites in Messersmith's work.
       Then discuss this idea of opposing forces at work in our environment
       – are there opposing forces or are there cyclical rhythms? Debate the
       issue. Be sure to support your remarks with clearly stated reasons.

Sample Biographies written by the curatorial team

Julie Bowland has painted the North Florida landscape for over ten years, but she rarely works in a studio. Instead, Bowland prefers weathering the elements to create her vibrant fauve-hued scenes of Florida's pristine rivers, coastal marshes, cypress swamps, and beaches. Bowland feels that, "Color and form may be freely exaggerated, but it is important to me to paint from nature. Standing in a bug-ridden swamp battling the weather and various other changing conditions is a very different experience from the calm control of the studio. I appreciate the dynamic element of dealing with nature during the process of making art."

Julie Bowland was born in Miami, but grew up in northern Indiana and southern Michigan. As a youth, Bowland made frequent trips to the Chicago Art Institute which brought her in contact with the expressive landscapes of Vincent Van Gogh and Claude Monet. She received her Bachelor of Fine Arts from the Florida State University and went on to study painting at Arizona State University where she received her Master of Fine Arts in 1991. Currently, she is the Arts in Public Places Director for the Cultural Resources Commission, the local arts agency for Tallahassee and Leon County.

Bowland's vivid oil paintings evoke feelings of movement and light in the natural world while maintaining close ties to the work of her expressionist mentors. "An expressionist at heart" says Bowland, "I enjoy the experience of playing with color and pushing this oil paint around."

Written by Fran Kautz

Clyde Butcher's photographs are devoid of the human figure. Butcher's name has become synonymous with the Florida environment. His black and white prints taken with an 8 X10" or 11X14" large format camera capture the detail and texture found in Florida's earth, clouds, and light, not the growth of Florida's cities or the ever-encroaching expansion of Florida's population.

Clyde Butcher was born in Kansas City, Missouri, in 1942. As a child he moved frequently. In 1960 Butcher began to study architecture at California Polytechnic University. Here, Butcher had several defining experiences including an important encounter with photography. In 1963, he was impressed by a visit to an exhibition of Ansel Adams photographs of Yosemite.

During the second half of the 1960s Butcher experienced a number of life changes, both privately and professionally. He continued to work in architecture, beginning a business for photographing scale models in such a way that the pictures looked like they contained real buildings. At one point, Butcher played a part in the process of designing the TransAmerica Tower (San Francisco's signature skyscraper). In 1970, butcher gave up architecture to pursue landscape photography. Financially the Butchers lost almost everything and ended up without a home, camping in a tent-trailer in parks. During the 1970s, Butcher found business success and loss again.

In 1980, two years after visiting Florida, Butcher decided to start afresh by moving east. Clyde began to explore the remaining wild environment of Florida, and shot elegant, Adams-influenced scenes of South Florida's last complex and untouched ecosystems.

Butcher, with exacting expectations of himself, estimates that he takes only one truly great picture a year. He states that it take weeks to find the right setting, days to set up, and hours to prepare before the light and all the other features are exactly right.

Butcher was selected for Florida's 1998 Artists Hall of Fame. He was featured as "Person of the Week" on ABC's Evening News with Peter Jennings. He and his work have been seen on a number of national news programs. He received the Heartland Community Service Award for teaching Floridians about their beautiful state. He has worked "to save nature's places of spiritual sanctuary for future generations ." And so was honored by two conservation awards, the Conservation Colleague Award from the Nature Conservancy and the Ansel Adams Conservation Award from the Sierra Club. Clyde Butcher's photography is often found in museum exhibitions throughout Florida, and may be found in his publications.

Written by Betsy Sullivan

Mark Messersmith's works explore the struggle between humans and the environment. In a time when we see Florida's beaches and forest being replaced by shopping malls, high-rise condominiums, and theme parks, Mark Messersmith's paintings are an important reminder of what we are in danger of losing. Messersmith says that he explores "dichotomies such as good and evil, life and death, humankind versus nature, tastelessness versus taste, chaos versus order, all simultaneously."

Messersmith creates large, colorful oil paintings, often with strong contrast between bright and dark colors. The main characters in his works are bobcats, alligators, snakes, herons, raccoons, owls, and large-mouthed bass. Logging trucks and highways weave through the backgrounds while helicopters and planes traverse the sky. The artist attaches boxed scenes below the bottom edge of his canvases, and carved colorful sculptures above the top edge.

Mark Messersmith holds a Bachelor of Fine Arts from Fontbonne College in St. Louis, and a Master of Fine Arts from Indiana University. He has won both Florida Arts Council Fellowships (1987, 1993, 1999) and NEA grants (1988, 1994), exhibiting his work throughout the Southeastern United States: he is currently an Associate Professor of Painting at Florida State University

Written by Cynthia Braswell and Lynn Janasciewicz

CHAPTER 5

Project #2: The Influence of Traditional Formalist Theory and Practice

---

Project Title: *In Print: The Language of Art*
Planning and Program Implementation: Spring, 2001-Spring, 2003
Exhibition Year: 2003
Co-curatorial Team:
Tallahassee, Florida, Lawton Chiles High School
- *Art Educator—Julie Childers*
- *Art Educator—Leslie Cohen*
- *Art Educator—Kelly Little*

Florida State University Museum of Fine Arts
- *Curator of Education—Dr. Viki D. Thompson Wylder*

Artworks: 35
Printmakers: Kabuya Bowens, Chiong-Yiao Chen, Ken Falana, Janice E. Hartwell, Elizabeth A. Heller Mason, Kenneth Kerslake, Joe Sanders, AJ Smith, Barry E. Wilson, Harris R. Wiltsher II

Beginnings

In Print: The Language of Art originated in an unexpected way. I was informally team-teaching a museum studies graduate-level class that met in the museum for the semester. For her final project, Julie Childers, a local high school art instructor who was taking the course, fleshed out the concepts for an exhibition focusing on a process she often liked to highlight in her classroom—printmaking. Her project actualized one of my personal underlying goals for the curriculum of the museum studies class, a long-standing desire for more exploration of direct relationships between K-12 classroom practice and museum practice. Her project provided a practical framework for enacting such a relationship.

The structure of the museum studies final project specified the use of works from the Florida State University Museum of Fine Arts (FSU MoFA) permanent collection. Julie noticed FSU MoFA collected "lots of prints," and she noticed the prints in the collection lent themselves to the study of the elements of design. She commented, "Selecting the prints for the show was like going to an 'elements' candy store." She curated works into her show "with her students in mind." She wanted "to stimulate activity and dialogue," and she wanted her students "to understand elements to the point they could discuss them." To this end she decided to look for prints that allowed comparison and contrast of elements and thus selected prints in pairs or "duets." For Julie, "creating the concept for the exhibition was like creating an artwork" (M. Meale & V. D. T. Wylder, personal communication with co-curatorial committee members from Lawton Chiles High School J. Childers & K. Kawagoye, March 3, 2020).

> I asked Julie if she would consider curating the exhibition for the FSU MoFA. She seemed to hesitate at first, but her plan became a reality. Well before the conclusion of the 2002 project, *Visions of the North Florida Environment*, two other colleagues joined her to begin the co-curatorial process for the second project of the Education Program of the FSU MoFA. The exhibition *In Print: The Language of Art* opened in 2003.
>
> —*VDTW*

Description of the Project and Exhibition

The three teachers who constituted the co-curatorial committee for *In Print: The Language of Art* also constituted the art faculty at Tallahassee's Lawton Chiles High School. Collectively they taught multimedia courses like 2D and 3D Art whose content included an array of traditional art categories—drawing, painting, photography, printmaking, sculpture, ceramics, digital graphic design, and so on. Their overall project with the culminating exhibition was geared primarily, but not exclusively, to high school students.

In Print: The Language of Art featured prints by 10 Southeastern American printmakers who utilized widely varying techniques. Some of these artworks, as indicated, were housed in the FSU MoFA permanent collection while

Poster for *In Print: The Language of Art.*

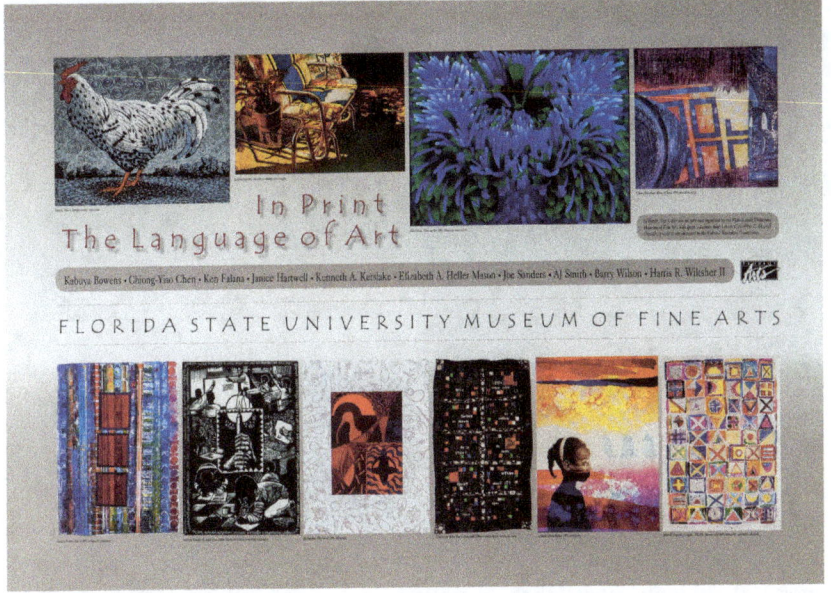

Courtesy: Florida State University Museum of Fine Arts.

others were exhibited as a result of invitation to artists already known by the co-curatorial committee. Print techniques in the exhibition included color intaglio, woodcut, lithograph, linocut, monoprint, as well as more nontraditional processes emphasizing actual three-dimensional elements. For example, printmaker Ken Falana's work, titled *Flowering Tree*, exhibited a unique process he named "silkscreen construction." Small cut sections from large sheets of paper already silkscreened with gradient color by the artist were assembled collage-like into shimmering, hue-saturated, nearly flat bas reliefs. In a piece titled *Crazy Quilt*, the artist Elizabeth Heller Mason sewed together patches from linocuts on canvas with other sections made of surprising materials such as beads and rubber from old inner tubes.

"The purpose of the exhibition [was] threefold: to showcase work and artists in the printmaking medium; to highlight language components of the artmaking process, that is the elements of design; and to teach students interdisciplinary concepts and skills through a project driven process" (Florida State University Museum of Fine Arts, 2003, *In Print: The Language of Art* poster verso, introduction). In the layout of the exhibition, the work was physically paired according to Julie Childers' concept of "duets" so students could more easily analyze, compare,

Front detail (Barry E. Wilson: *Spangled Rooster;* Kenneth Kerslake: *A Corner for Musing*) of the poster for *In Print: The Language of Art.*

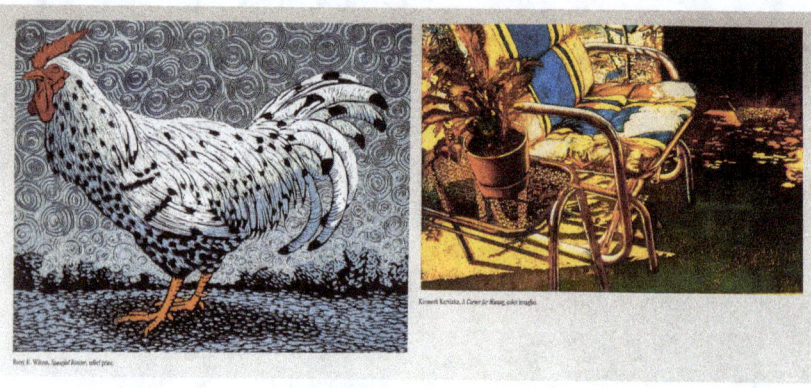

Courtesy: Florida State University Museum of Fine Arts.

and contrast the use of the elements of design. In concert with the third purpose of the exhibition, the project involved Lawton Chiles High School teachers and over 100 students from other disciplines including website design, English, humanities, broadcasting, journalism, culinary arts, chorus, and instrumental music. Chiles students helped write a copy to publicize the exhibition, and they assisted with its advertisement at the school. Culinary arts students prepared and served hors d'oeuvres at the opening reception, while English and humanities students gave readings and music students performed.

Though the exhibition was only one part of the project it acted as guide and determiner of its many parts. Half of the artists interacted with Chiles students primarily through artist/student dialogue and demonstration of printmaking techniques. Chiles faculty "wanted students to see real art and artists and wanted the students to understand the communication of the artists' voices through printmaking, to deeply understand that process and communication, then to find their own personal artistic voices using the printmaking medium, which they did" (Meale & Wylder, personal communication, 2020). Janice Hartwell visited classrooms to present her low-technology monoprinting technique using cardboard. Chiles students also took field trips to the Florida State University Print Lab where A. J. Smith, an artist from Arkansas, invited a small group of students to contribute to the production of a lithograph and where Kabuya Bowens demonstrated her collograph techniques with their emphasis on the visibility of her own hand in the process as well as her African American heritage.

During this artist interaction for *In Print: The Language of Art*, AJ Smith demonstrated lithographic processes to Lawton Chiles High School students.

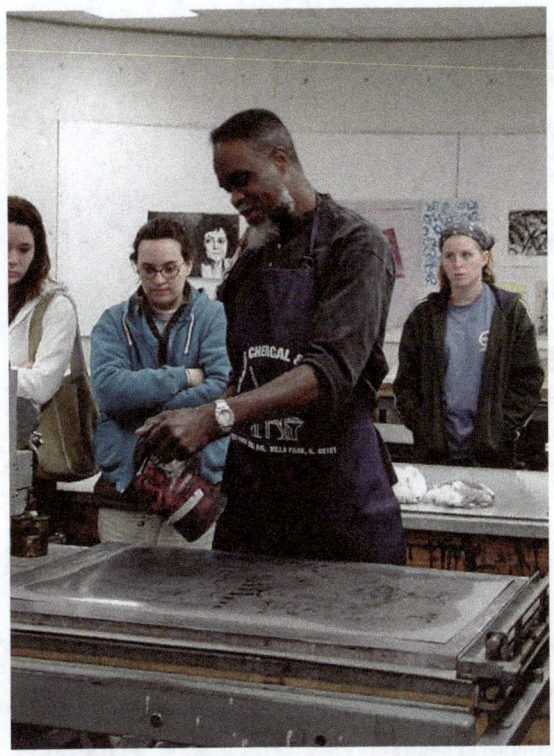

Courtesy: Kelly Little Kawagoye

Harris Wiltsher visited Lawton Chiles High School to give a lecture as part of the school's Arts Day, an across-the-board recognition of the arts at the school. About 350 students from all classes and disciplines involved in the project at Chiles attended the lecture. The Chiles art faculty prepped the audience beforehand by giving each student attendee a one-page handout about the speaker with specified areas on the handout to note artwork ideas inspired by the lecture. They also described the speaker as a successful and accomplished artist, a "real artist." The Chiles faculty "saw Wiltsher as opening the art world" for these students.

Wiltsher's talk connected the students to the perspective and career of a professional. Wiltsher brought actual artworks, original fine arts prints and prints on

Front detail (Kabuya Bowens: *Blue II*) of the poster for *In Print: The Language of Art.*

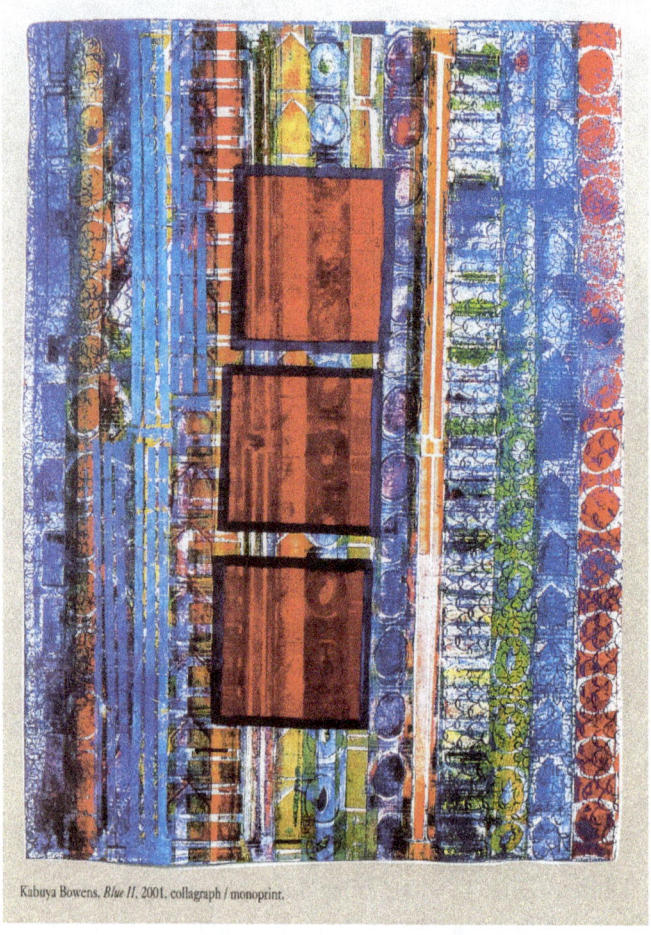

Kabuya Bowens, *Blue II*, 2001, collagraph / monoprint.

Courtesy: Florida State University Museum of Fine Arts.

t-shirts. He talked about his trip to South Africa and the way this changed his production, that he began to put more of himself into the work, that he began to incorporate within his compositions imagery centered on social dynamics and living conditions. He captured the attention of the students and related to them partially by inviting audience participation. After the presentation students wanted to also speak with him personally. (Meale & Wylder, personal communication, 2020)

The curatorial committee of three teachers authored a teacher's packet of lesson plans based on the work in the exhibition that was distributed to art teachers throughout the county school system. In this case the co-curatorial committee also solicited informal comments and written input from a sampling of their own art students during the writing of lesson plans. The resultant teacher's packet featured a pair of sections titled "From the Teachers: Creative Classroom Activities" and "From Their Students: Creative Classroom Activities" (Childers et al., 2003). Toward the end of the packet the co-curatorial committee defined 34 printmaking terms in a glossary. In addition a group of students under the direction of the art instructor from Deerlake Middle School in Tallahassee researched and composed exhibition wall text for nine main print processes—digital transfer, etching, intaglio, linocut, lithography, monoprint, relief printing, serigraph, and woodblock. Middle school students, working with partners, defined each of the nine print processes and added general historical information about each to the text.

For teachers to earn in-service credit toward recertification, several printmakers from the exhibition presented at a day-long workshop that was offered at the end of the 2002–2003 school year (Florida State University Museum of Fine Arts, 2003). Ken Kerslake presented his photolithography process. Chiong-Yiao Chen, a native of Taiwan and a professor at the University of North Alabama, presented her woodblock techniques for merging her Eastern and Western aesthetic sensibilities, clarifying the process through a visual organization and layout of the tools for each step in her method (Meale & Wylder, personal communication, 2020).

The parallel and simultaneous display of student artwork done in response to the work of the exhibition was mounted in an official gallery setting in another state building. For this parallel display, student works from grades K-12 were solicited through official calls to art teachers in the county. "This student display [was] designed to profile the wide variety of printmaking techniques employed by classrooms in the county at various grade levels. In addition, it [paid] tribute to the creative teaching of the elements of art by teachers throughout the school system" (Florida State University Museum of Fine Arts, 2003).

The FSU MoFA produced a poster to accompany *In Print: The Language of Art*. Images of artwork from the exhibition were illustrated on the front side with several components written by the co-curatorial committee printed on the back. These components included an overview of the project, biographies of the artists in the exhibition, and "Idea Starters for Your Classroom." These ideas were categorized under the four components of Discipline-Based Art Education (DBAE). Since the work in the exhibition was hung as pairs or duets to call attention to the elements of design used within each work, an art criticism starter asked students to compare and contrast works in the exhibition using a Venn diagram. An aesthetics starter asked students to consider the criteria used by the co-curatorial committee to select the prints in the exhibition. An art history starter asked students to create a timeline of important events, artwork, and artists in the history of printmaking. And an artmaking starter asked students to explore a variety of print techniques from woodblock to glueline to stencil processes (Childers, Cohen, & Little, 2003, poster verso).

Traditional Formalist Theory and Practice and *In Print: The Language of Art*

Despite this nod to DBAE philosophy and practices within the content of the exhibition poster and in contrast to the full immersion in DBAE practice in *Visions of the North Florida Environment*, this second project and exhibition represented an adherence to a more formalist philosophy that influenced and still influences pedagogical practice, one that presents visual art as a visual language composed of elements, principles, and media. Only elementary teachers sat on the *Visions of the North Florida Environment* co-curatorial team. Teachers at the elementary level often instruct using fluid disciplinary boundaries in their daily pedagogy and therefore more readily welcome the interdisciplinarity of DBAE practice. Secondary art instructors teach within a highly categorized framework that makes a DBAE practice seem more awkward. Art classes at the high school level are typically studio art classes, which often make a point of teaching formalist elements and principles. Art history is taught as its own subject separate from a studio art class. Classes that shed light on other contextual concerns within DBAE like a broad view of aesthetics or societal context might be learned in humanities classes or courses that deal with philosophy or societal relationships.

Even the title *In Print: The Language of Art* reflected the 20th century ideas of art educators such as Edmund Burke Feldman who talked about the necessity of a study of the "language" of the visual arts in order to understand the messages and meanings that its specific language conveyed. Feldman compared this visual art analysis to the study of the vocabulary, structure, and semantics of grammar in order to understand words, sentences, and literature. Feldman advocated an education that would teach the ability to " 'read' a work of art" (1970, p. 219).

Feldman portrayed style as the characteristics of formal organization, and he portrayed aesthetics as viewers' understandings of formal organization within individual works of art, "the viewer's act of reconstituting these forms in his own consciousness" (p. 183). He viewed media as the elements of form "embodied in specific materials" (p. 171), but he saw the characteristics of a medium affecting the use of those elements and thus the meaning of an artwork. Feldman is well known for developing a method of art criticism (adapted for use by DBAE practitioners), which he divided into a sequence of steps—description, formal analysis, interpretation, and judgment—as a means of evaluating an artist's use of the visual language. And he advocated for a study of the visual arts language as a part of art history, that is a study of the elements and principles as seen in "real works of art" (Feldman, 1992, p. 125) made over time by various cultural groups. He did not advocate for a study of the elements and principles as mere definitions or diagrams (Feldman, 1970, p. 183). He saw reading of form as a means to at least partially unlock the meaning of works from history. In his Preface to his book *Becoming Human Through Art*, Feldman mentions that he "built as well as I could on all the art disciplines: philosophy of art, art history, art criticism, art education, and studio performance" (pp. vi & vii). As seen in the discussion above, he viewed all these disciplines via a formalist lens. He saw visual art as a means of communication in which a work of art was created because the artist wanted to converse "through the language of visual form rather than some other language" (p. 171).

Becoming Human Through Art was published in 1970, but in 1992 as the emphases in art education were evolving away from Feldman's emphases, he wrote an essay titled *Formalism and Its Discontents* in which he urged art educators "against throwing out the baby with the bath water" (p. 125). Certainly this project demonstrated a continuing valuation of Feldman's concepts as relevant. The work in this exhibition, which opened at the FSU MoFA in 2003, was presented as forms embodied in the specific materials of printmaking, and the study of these forms was presented through looking at real works of art. With *In Print: The Language of Art*, all parts emanated from the context of this formalist premise, even the occasional flirts with other theories or practices like DBAE.

The printed exhibition pedagogical accompaniments for this project were hybridized. The "Idea Starters for Your Classroom" published on the poster for the exhibition and the lesson plans in the teachers' packet on which they were based dallied with DBAE categories. Yet a traditional formalist and genre-based approach to teaching from *In Print: The Language of Art* was built on the following:

- exhibition exemplars
- exemplar printmaking processes or techniques to produce aesthetic and communicative effectiveness of the imagery produced in the classroom
- exemplar elements and principles to analyze for their contribution to aesthetics or meaning and to highlight in student production
- the developmental level of the students.

For instance, one of the lesson plans used in the classroom at Lawton Chiles High School followed this formalist format to a significant degree. Ken Falana's prints were selected as exemplars, and his "silkscreen construction" was selected as a printmaking process. The elements, color and shape, were highlighted. "The emphasis was on the aesthetic experience/meaning, looking at color and shapes used by Falana, and then asking students to print their own color, feel the printed paper, use scissors to produce the cut shapes, and collage the shapes together" (Meale & Wylder, personal communication, 2020).

Though high school students formed a primary target audience for this exhibition, elementary art teachers were invited to include their students' response work in the parallel student display. For example, a fifth grade teacher might choose the screen prints of Janice Hartwell as exemplars from the poster or teacher's packet, while focusing on paper stencils and paint as an elementary adaptation of the professional silkscreen process used by Hartwell. While artmaking would comprise the bulk of the lesson, such a lesson could be accompanied by a discussion of the reasons for and messages from Hartwell's media choice. Hartwell's work would easily accommodate a focus on the formal concepts of positive and negative space with a discussion of their contribution to the works' aesthetics or meaning.

A focus on genre and formalist elements does bring students a deeper appreciation of process as well as insight into the use of media and elements as part of a visual language. The depth of appreciation depends on the developmental level of the students. An understanding of the relationship and effectiveness between an artist's message and/or aesthetics with the choice of media and manipulation of elements of design often results from such pedagogy for older students. Near the beginning of the curatorial process, the Chiles faculty expressed their desire for this outcome for their students. They felt their students "began to see printmaking as very personalized, as voice through the medium of printmaking, as a validation of the artist's voice" (Meale & Wylder, personal communication, 2020).

As with the bidirectional effect of the co-curatorial process with an elementary school during the first project sponsored by the Education Program at the FSU MoFA, *In Print: The Language of Art* exerted a two-way influence between Lawton Chiles High School and the FSU MoFA. This co-curatorial process facilitated an exploration of the workings of a high school in the community in order to better construct, expand, and deepen the FSU MoFA Education Program to meet the needs of secondary art programs in the public school system, their teachers and students. Five artists interacted in classroom settings with 415 students. The co-curatorial process allowed teachers to better fulfill their need to give students the ability to learn the visual language of art through a more intimate and profound face to face experience with artists and their works of art in the classroom and in a museum setting.

The exhibition opening at the FSU MoFA brought over 900 visitors. The parallel student display of response artwork in the print medium was held in an additional gallery space at a state building and featured 400 students from the classrooms of 12 teachers in the community. The opening for the student display numbered approximately 300 people. The teacher workshop offered at the end of the school year attracted 45 teachers. In the years following the project, teachers at Lawton Chiles continued to bring students annually for a series of classes with the same pedagogical intent demonstrated during the project. As a result of this co-curatorial experience, Lawton Chiles teachers and their students remained engaged with the FSU MoFA as a teaching space.

Selected content from the Teachers Packet for *In Print: The Language of Art.*

Courtesy: Florida State University Museum of Fine Arts.

Disseminated to teachers in hard copy and CD format: inclusive of all images for exhibition by exhibition artists.

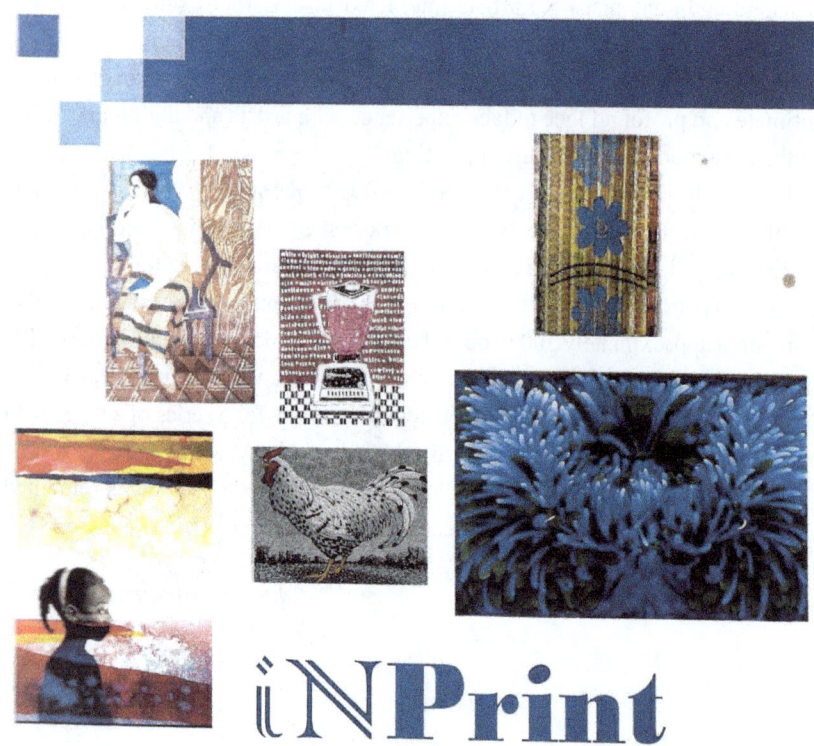

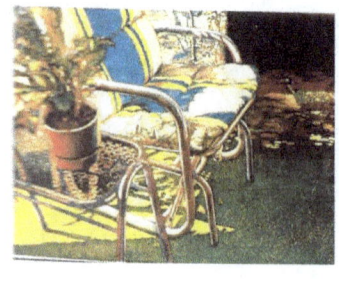

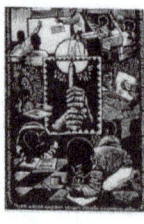

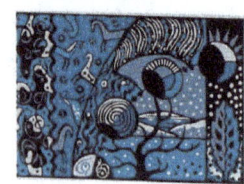

In Print: The Language of Art
Florida State University Museum of Fine Arts
May 12, 2002 – June 6, 2002
With reception: Friday, May 16, 2002 7-9 p.m.

An Educational Supplement to the Museum's Exhibition

Table of Contents

Edited by Viki D. Thompson Wylder, Curator of Education
& Matthew Fenner, Volunteer Coordinator

Graphic design by Julie Childers and Daniel Hoge (student: Lawton Chiles High School)

Thank you to the FSU Museum of Fine Arts volunteers and interns for the reproduction
of this packet.

Courtesy: Florida State University Museum of Fine Arts.

In Print Insight

The exhibition – *In Print: The Language of Art* – and the packet of the same name are the result of a partnership between the Florida State University Museum of Fine Arts and Lawton Chiles High School. The exhibition itself will consist of two components of artwork: pieces by artists working in the Southeast and work that already resides in the permanent collection of the FSU Museum. The purpose of the exhibition is threefold: to showcase work (and artists) in the printmaking medium; to highlight language components of the artmaking process, that is the elements of design; and to teach students interdisciplinary concepts and skills through a project driven process. In part, the work will be exhibited in duets, pairs of works that will emphasize the use of various elements or principles through visual comparison and contrast.

Likewise, the two very visible aspects of the partnership – the exhibition and the packet – are only part of the story. The partnership involves planning and implementation over a two year duration to include: teacher and student involvement in the curation of the exhibition; specific involvement by exhibition artists with the students; a teacher's packet written by teachers and students to be distributed throughout Leon County and some teachers in the surrounding counties; tours of the exhibition using student docents; student writing of press release material; student design of publicity materials such as an exhibition card and poster; interviews of teachers and students by local television personalities; the development by students of a closed circuit tv program on the exhibition; performance by students at the opening reception to include other arts such as drama, dance, and music. Students from the following subject areas will participate: studio art, graphic design, English, humanities, broadcasting, journalism, drama, dance, and music.

The project features an opportunity for participation in a unique K-12 student exhibition based on the concepts of the FSU MoFA exhibition. Titled *In Print: Learning the Language of Art* (see overview on next page), the student display will be held in tandem at the Learning Arts Gallery at the RA Gray Building. The student display is designed to profile the wide variety of printmaking techniques employed by classrooms across the county at various grade levels. In addition, it will pay tribute to the creative teaching of the elements of art by teachers throughout the school system.

Julie Childers, Leslie Cohen, and Kelly Little comprise the Chiles curatorial team. They solicited and selected the artwork, planned the packet, and developed the activities as a group. The contents of the packet have been slated to both elementary and secondary grade levels. All materials can be xeroxed or duplicated. A CD Rom is included with a series of images from the exhibition as well as student activity materials. The packet will become a website (address forthcoming). The FSU Museum of Fine Arts will offer an Outreach Program (Museum representatives will come to your school) in March and April. Tours will be offered at the Museum in May. A day long workshop on this exhibition and packet (as part of a two day workshop also in partnership with the Brogan Museum and Buck Lake Elementary) will be offered for all area teachers at the end of the 2002-03 school year.

Viki D. Thompson Wylder, Curator of Education, FSU MoFA

In Print: The Language of Art
May 12 - June 6 with reception: Friday, May 16, 7-9pm

Selection from Overview in Teachers Packet

InPrint:
The Language of Art

Introduction
The audience is a major focus for this exhibition. *In Print: The Language of Art* is meant for the general public, but it is first and foremost a teaching exhibition that keeps primary and secondary teachers and students in mind. *In Print*, as the exhibition title suggests, is a collection of prints, in this case by artists from the Southeast.

Prints are introduced to the viewer as pairs, or duets. Each pair or duet has many similarities, but each is different in terms of subject, composition, and content. Unrelated prints are placed together to create tension – a tension meant to produce the beginnings of critical analysis as well as a dialogue between the viewer and the artwork. The viewer is encouraged to compare and contrast the pieces to better understand the basic visual grammar from which the language of art is composed.

The Language of Art
In every field there is a language that helps outline and define the tenets and structure of that field. Be it soccer, computers, or engineering, each's language helps people understand and participate.

The visual arts has its own structural system – and language – composed of basic elements and principles. This exhibition will deal specifically with the ELEMENTS of art: line, shape, form, space, color, value, and texture. By analyzing the *elements of art* the viewer will gain some insight into the structure and language of the system as well as each individual image.

An individual work of art can be divided into three components: the subject, the composition, and the content or message of the image. By looking at a work of art using these three components, a better grasp of the piece is achieved.

1. • The **subject** of a work of art, usually referred to as the main character or idea, can be recognizable or realistic. It can be based on reality and look like a photo, or be based on reality and be abstracted from nature. It can also have no subject at all and be nonobjective. No matter which is chosen – realism, abstraction, or non-objectivity – the subject is arranged in a composition using the elements and principles of art.
2. • When the artist uses the elements and principles of art concurrently in his/her work, the artist creates a **composition**. The composition is the sum of all parts.
3. • The subject arranged in a composition (according to the elements and principles) is created to communicate a message or an idea. The **content** of the image can center on any issue or aspect of life the artist wishes to address.

The works in this exhibition all vary in terms of subject, composition, and content.

The Duets
Each duet will focus on one element at a time. However, the following information should be considered as the first step in an ongoing exploration of the elements. Each image uses all of the elements in some form or another. Following are brief descriptions of the ways each *element of art* can be illuminated within one pair of images.

Sample of a Duet: Line

Line is the path of a moving point through space. The first duet is comprised of works by Janice Hartwell and Barry Wilson. While each image handles its subject in a different manner, line is a major element in both images.

Both Wilson and Hartwell use line to create pattern. Hartwell uses repeated bold and solid lines in a variety of directions - horizontal, straight, and diagonal. Some curved lines are used to form shapes. Wilson's lines, in contrast, tend to be more delicate and more curvilinear. All of Wilson's lines tend to be repeated and rhythmic, a means for creating a sense of energy, in this case to animate an otherwise straightforward image of a rooster.

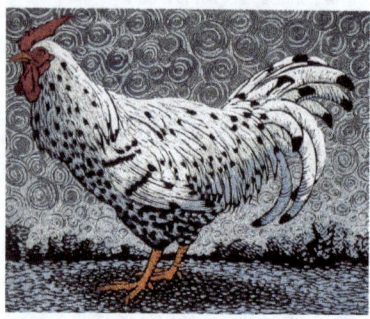

Barry Wilson, *Spangled Rooster*, relief print, 21" x 25".

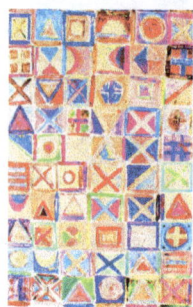

Janice Hartwell, *97 degrees / 4PM / Tallahassee, Summer 1998*, 21" x 28", monoprint, water-based relief ink.

Sample Biographies

Biographies

At first glance a number of **Kabuya Bowens**' prints look like pieces of African-inspired cloth. Streaked and striped, they also incorporate patterns of primary shapes – squares, rectangles, triangles, circles – in primary colors. Bowens has given them titles like Yellow III or Blue I. But they may also include schematically drawn house shapes and flowers. Bowens seems to be offering us a fundamental visual translation of the fabric of life. "Art can communicate a common ground we all share," states Bowens. "The language of art is the recognition of all life and the relationship of our daily experiences." Bowens wants her art to function like a growing connective tissue between herself and the viewer.

Bowens sums her mental processes as her own "3Rs" – reflection, relationship, and response. Through reflection Bowens pulls together her memories of experiences and relationships. These reflections may be affected by a variety of personal issues and everyday interactions with others. She observes the way in which people define themselves, the way in which they stake out their separate cultural and political places. She can be inspired by music, performance, literature, and other visual art. Bowens' own art – her means of connection or relationship – is her response.

Bowens production shows her emphasis on the physical act of art-making. Her prints demonstrate a non-slick, authentic love of the evidence of her hand in the process of constructing the print. She is interested in using various tools and materials. For her, even the gathering of these tools and materials is as important as the use of them or the existence of the final work. She views the work of creating as a learning continuum, one that often speaks to her and directs her actions.

Bowens is currently an associate professor at Florida State University teaching printmaking. Bowens studied in Washington, DC, New York City, and Rome and received her MFA from the Tyler School of Art in Philadelphia. She has received various awards including a fellowship from the New York Foundation for the Arts and a fellowship from the Southern Arts Federation/ National Endowment for the Arts and Humanities. Her resumé includes various group and solo exhibitions. Her work can be found in a number of collections including the Metro-Dade Artbank in Miami, the Brandywine Workshop in Philadelphia, the Virginia Miller Gallery in Coral Gables, and the Polk Museum in Lakeland, Florida.

Written by Julie Childers

Although printmaking is considered a way to create multiple originals, ironically **AJ Smith** is interested in using the print medium to create images that are one-of-a-kind. In works like *Calm, Bodygear* (1995) he experiments with the overlay of graphite on a print that is part lithograph and part monoprint. The black and white portions of the work are a combination of lithography and drawing. The color is a combination lithograph and monoprint.

In *Calm, Bodygear*, Smith prints a confetti of frenzied lines. His energized registrations coalesce like molecules forming unstable matter. Here emerge ephemeral looking letters that fade as they descend on a little African-American boy who looks up at us through the window of the image. Smith's letters spell out the word "calm." The word is not reassuring. This monoprint seems a clear demonstration of Smith's belief that "creative expression provides an effective means to communicate feelings and emotions where words are often inadequate."

In the last several years, Smith's production has focused on portraiture. In this body of work, Smith combines his influences – the principles of African art, the imagery of historical European art, and the realism of American artists of the 1920s and 1930s. Thomas Hart Benton is of particular interest to Smith. Benton was the teacher of his teachers.

AJ Smith, now a Professor of Art and Coordinator of Printmaking at the University of Arkansas at Little Rock, received his Master of Fine Arts at Queens College, City University of New York in Flushing in 1977. For two years following, he apprenticed with Robert Blackburn at the Printmaking Workshop in New York City. Numerous exhibitions, awards, and fellowships extend throughout his career. He has had 20 solo exhibitions. His fellowships include those from the Brandywine Center in Philadelphia in 1991 and the Tamarind Workshop in Albuquerque the year before. His work can be found in a number of public and corporate collections including the Columbia Museum in South Carolina, the Philadelphia Museum in Pennsylvania, the Studio Museum in Harlem, the Arkansas Arts Center, the Kansas City Art Institute, Library of Congress Prints & Photographs, the Schomburg Center for Research in Black Culture, the Central Institute of Fine Arts in Beijing, China, the Bank of America in Charlotte and Philadelphia, and USA Today, Gannett News Service in New York City.

Written by Viki D. Thompson Wylder

From the teachers:
Creative Classroom Activities

Use the following as idea starters for your classroom activities.

ART CRITICISM
1. Duet Comparison/Contrast Activity (by Julie Childers)
Have xeroxes or prints of the images available. Use the Image Index Sheet in the CD to print the images. Hand out pairs or "duets" of images. Ask the students to compare and contrast the images using the Venn Diagram provided. Then ask the students to share information with the rest of the class.

2. Create Your Own Duet (by Julie Childers)
Using the *Create Your Own Duet* worksheet, have the students place one image in each of the boxes. They can do this on the computer using the file and the Image Index provided. Or, have worksheet and samples of the images from the Image Index file available for cutting and pasting. Have the students share their duets with the rest of the class or their table.

3. Categorizing by Style (by Leslie Cohen)
Picture this scenario.... The harried teacher is about to show slides of the artwork from the show, *In Print: The Language of Art*, when she drops all the slides on the floor. Have your students help this teacher get organized. Refer them to the Image Index on your CD. Your students should group the images by individual style.
> Options:
> 1. The classroom teacher will print the images on individual sheets of paper – one image per page. The students will place the images in ten piles according to style.
> 2. The students will access the Image Index on their computers. Via powerpoint, the students will sort the images into ten stylistic categories.
> Note: The options above call for ten stylistic categories because the exhibition contains artwork by ten artists. Stylistic similarities between and among the varying artists' works may emerge during this exercise. Stylistic categories can be changed or adjusted. Students must justify their choices. There is not necessarily a right or wrong answer. Instead, the visual justification for placing works into categories is important.

4. Creative Interpretation (by Leslie Cohen)
Project a single image from the Image Index on your classroom screen. Arrange the students in a circle in front of the visual. Starting with one student, have the student begin a story reflecting on the subject matter of the print. She/he should use only one sentence. Continue around the circle, in order, following the story line. Have the last student end the story with two sentences. Have one student record the story to share with others.
> Options:
> 1. The classroom teacher can use a document camera to display the print on the classroom's screen.
> 2. The classroom teacher can produce a transparent image and use an overhead projector to show the print on the classroom's screen.

5. The Significance of the Parts (by Leslie Cohen)
> 1) **Secondary teachers** should show the following three prints:
> *Margaret* by Chiong-Yiao Chen
> *Digital Mirror* by Kenneth Kerslake
> *South Africa: A Better Life for All* (the image of the series that contains the fist in the center section) by Harris Wiltsher.

Allow each student to pick the image that best communicates to him/her. Group the students into three sections according to prints chosen. Each group will discuss and share the meanings of the chosen print with each other in the group.

Next introduce the idea that part of the selected print has faded due to improper storage or display. Individually each student will write the way the meaning of the chosen print would change.

a) In the Margaret *print, the image of the woman disappears. How would the print's message change?*

b) In Digital Mirror, *the digital writing disappears. How would the print's message change?*

c) In the image from the South Africa Series, *the center box with the fist vanishes. How does the print's meaning change?*

2) **Elementary teachers** can do the same exercise with their students. Tell the students that an art thief stole into the Museum to cut out the sections described above. Ask the students if the meaning of the work is changed with the section removed. Ask the importance of the section to the art work. Ask the students to interpret the meaning of the work without the section.

Individually each student will write two paragraphs comparing and contrasting the meanings of the original to the altered work of art.

AESTHETICS
1. Using Criteria (by Leslie Cohen)
Pretend the teachers in charge of curating the show, In Print: The Language of Art, are having trouble selecting the prints they want to be displayed at the FSU Museum of Fine Arts. What criteria should they use to select the images? Choose the criteria and have the students choose the works they deem worthy for the show.

Options:
1. *Students can use criteria that assesses monetary value to each work.*
2. *Students can use criteria that reflects contemporary issues or images.*
3. *Students can use criteria that best demonstrates the elements of art.*

2. Theories of Art (by Kelly Little)
Each student will choose an artwork from the exhibition Image Index. Using the worksheets provided, each student will decide which of three theories of art would best allow an evaluation of the work chosen: realism; formalism; or emotionalism.

ART HISTORY
1. Timeline (by Kelly Little)
Using the worksheets provided, each student will place historical printmaking events onto a timeline. A list of famous printmaking artists is provided. These names can be researched and also placed onto the timeline.

PRODUCTION
1. Elementary: Finger Paint Prints – Line and Color (by Leslie Cohen)
Elementary classroom teachers should prepare their classrooms for a production lesson focusing on two art elements, line and color.

Cover the students' desks with newspapers. Place on each student's desk a slick paper with finger paints in the primary colors – red, blue, and yellow. The teacher should pick and play a contemporary music recording. First, ask the students to draw in the air with their eyes closed to the beat of the music. Perhaps slow dance music would invoke curvy lines. Rap songs might dictate short, jagged movements or stokes.

Next tell the students to open their eyes and paint the rhythm or beat of the selected music on their papers. The paintings should be non-objective. Encourage the students to switch colors and cross lines.

Now have the students clean their hands. Next distribute clean white paper to each student to press on top of the finger painted slick paper. Each child should rub the entire top sheet with the palm of the hand in a circular manner. Then the students should gently pull the papers off and view their prints. The teacher should discuss with them their new colors and lines.

2. **Secondary Projects (by Kelly Little)**

Following are a number of suggestions for middle and high school teachers, but even more ideas for class artwork production can be found in the "Resources on the Web" section at the end of the packet.

1. Artist: Harris Wiltsher
   Technique: woodblock or linoleum
   Choose a social issue to address and create a print with imagery that suggests a
     social message.
2. Artist: Elizabeth Heller Mason
   Technique: fibers with image transfer to paper or fabric.
   Use imagery and text from everyday life, study other artists like Jim Dine, Faith
     Ringgold, and Claus Oldenberg.
     Select images from magazines. Xerox copies or do actual drawings.
          a) Cover with at least 5 coats of gloss medium and let dry. Soak image in water
          and remove paper backing. Let dry. Image can be applied to any surface with
          adhesive.
          b) Use Design colorless blender marker to rub on reverse side of toner style
          copies, paper or fabric. Embellish surface with beads, threads, or other
          materials.
3. Other relief ideas:
          * Gyoko Fish prints – art catalogs now carry the "less fragrant variety of fish that can be
          used for several days"
          * Rubber stamps – explore texture and layering of images by repetition
          * Woodblock prints – Japanese
          * Block printing on fabric
          * Make plates by drawing glue lines for raised edges
          * Monoprints – print from a negative image drawn with a foam brush on a plexi plate
          * Stencils – a form of basic screenprinting

From their students:
Creative Classroom Activities

Use the following as more idea starters for your classroom activities.

ART CRITICISM
1. Music Matching
Have students discuss an art print from the exhibition and its relationship to a particular kind of music they feel would be most compatible with the print image.

2. Relate to an Experience
Have students discuss an art print from the exhibition. Have them talk about the way the mood of the work reminds them of particular personal experiences.
(Art Criticism suggestions by Will Graper from Kelly Little's class)

PRODUCTION
1. Drawing the Elements: Line
Have the students select a print from the exhibition that demonstrates interesting line quality. Create and pass out worksheets that depict a square within a larger square. In the small box have each student draw lines as seen in the print from the exhibition. In the surrounding larger square/box have each student free-draw in the same line quality for UNITY or different line quality for CONTRAST.

2. Drawing the Elements: Shape
Have each student look at a print, select a shape, and draw it anywhere on his/her paper. Have the student draw more of the same kind of shape in different sizes for REPETITION.

3. Drawing the Elements: Texture
Have each student create a nine or six square grid. The student will then draw a sample texture from various prints in the exhibition – one print texture per each of the grid spaces.
(Production suggestions 1 – 3 by Will Graper from Kelly Little's class)

4. Printmaking
1. Have students think of a product that could be sold. Have each student use a needle tool to draw/gouge an image of the product by pressing the tool into a foam plate. Roll ink on the foam plate until it is totally covered. Press the foam plate onto paper until the ink has transferred from the plate to the paper. Make the print of the product into an advertisement by adding a title and other words.
        Materials needed for this project: foam plate, roller, ink, needle tool/other pointy tool, and paper.
(Printmaking #1 by Katherine Salesses from Leslie Cohen's class)

2. The object of this project is to make a print of leaves in kaleidoscope form or a form that could be seen through a kaleidoscope. Paper, various kinds of leaves, as well as different colors of paint are needed.
        Have the students first paint a selection of leaves. Have each plan a composition (where the individual leaves would be placed on the print to be produced). Dip each leaf into paint (colors of choice) and print.
(Printmaking #2 by Beth Duncan from Leslie Cohen's class)

3. The end product of this project is a "United States Quilt." The quilt is to be made of printed squares of fabric. Follow this process:

        a) Have students pick states and trace their outlines onto sheets of paper.

b) Cut out the state shapes.
c) Find landscapes or pictures that illustrate characteristics of the state.
d) Find textures that resemble the pictures in some way.
e) Glue the textures to the state cut-outs.
f) Use a roller to ink the cut-outs.
g) Place inked cut-outs onto fabric squares, so that the result is a print of each state.
h) Arrange fabric squares together to form a quilt of the states. Glue quilt together on matboard
       or sew squares together and hang.
Materials needed for this project: fabric, glue, glue gun, ink, brayer, textures, paper, map of USA.
(Pintmaking #3 by Andrea Arce-Trigatti from Leslie Cohen's class)

Selected Activity Worksheets From Teachers Packet

Line

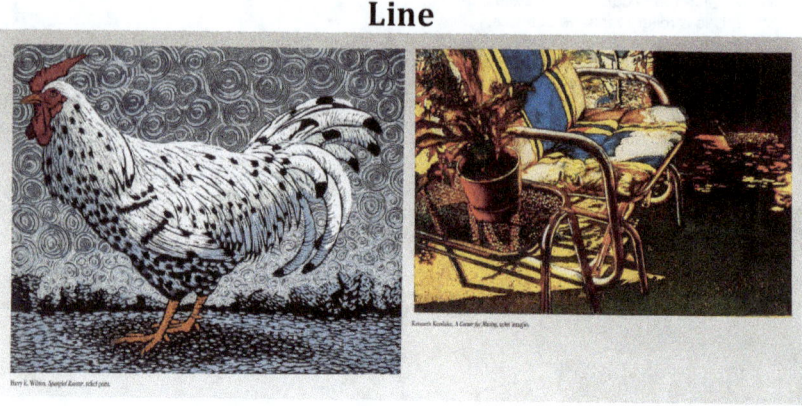

Line is an element of art that is the path of a moving point through space. (Arttalk)

Compare these two prints. How is line used?

Create your own Duo!

PICK TWO IMAGES THAT HAVE A SIMILAR

USE OF AN ELEMENT OF ART

COPY AND PASTE THE IMAGE IN THE SQUARE USING THE COMPUTER

OR CUT AND GLUE THE IMAGES IN THE BOXES PROVIDED

A

B

Circle the Element of Art that is similar in both images:

Line	Shape	Color	Value	Space	Form	Texture

Artist: _____

Title of Work _____

Artist: _____

Title of Work _____

Aesthetics

Aesthetics (ess thet ix) is a branch of philosophy concerned with the nature and value of art. All art can have different qualities-literal, design, or expressive.

LITERAL QUALITIES-Realistic qualities that appear in the subject.

DESIGN QUALITIES-How a work is organized or composed and how the artist uses the elements and principles of art to create the work.

EXPRESSIVE QUALITIES–How a work conveys ideas or mood.

3 Theories of Art

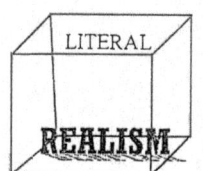

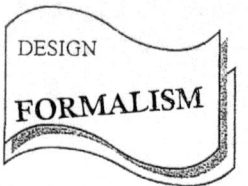

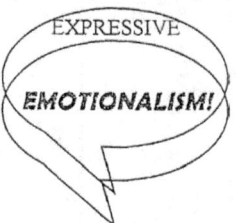

_ *If* you are a critic that thinks that the most important thing about the artwork is the realistic presentation of subject matter....

_ *If* you believe that a work is successful if it looks like and reminds the viewer of what he or she sees in the real world...

_ *If* you think that art should imitate life...

_ *If* you think that the art is successful if it has a good composition...

_ *If* you are satisfied by an arrangement of shapes, colors or textures...

_ *If* you agree that not all works of art must look like something...

_ *If* it is o.k. to have art just be abstract....

_ *If* you do not need to "see" what the artist sees or feels...

_ *If* you are most concerned about the expressive content of the work itself...

_ *If* you want to understand the artist's message...

_ *If* you expect the artwork to cause an emotional response...

_ *If* you think art's purpose is to get a reaction out of the viewer..

In Art Criticism*, there are four steps in gathering information about a work of art...

Describe
When, where, and what ....?

Analyze
Elements & principles: style or art movement....................?

Interpret
Influences on the artist: time period, environment, personal life, and other artists ....?

Judge
The artwork's value is assessed.......................... by first asking which philosophy is most important ....?

Realism ....or ....*Formalism*............ or ....*Emotionalism?*

You be the judge!

Sometimes the best way to judge an artwork is to use all three theories of art criticism-
Realism, Formalism, and Emotionalism. However, for this activity you will choose
the one philosophy that most proves that the art is

successful!

1. Sketch a work of art you have personally chosen in <u>one</u> of the boxes.

Title:_____

Artist:_____

2. Use the checklist to see which philosophy seems to be the best one to represent
the artwork as successful. *Mark a check by each one that applies, then tally which theory wins!*

_ R   The most important thing about this artwork is the <u>realistic</u> presentation of subject matter.
_ e   The artist has a clear message in the work.
_ e   When I look at this artwork it causes an emotional response.
_ R   This work is successful because it reminds the viewer of what he or she sees in the real world.
_ R   This artwork imitates real life objects.
_ e   This artwork has a distinct mood or emotional quality.
_ F   This artwork is simply abstract-no message here.
_ F   This art has a good composition and does not need to have recognizable objects to look good.
_ e   I think this artwork was created to cause change-either socially, politically or emotionally.
_ F   This artist was most concerned with an arrangement of shapes, colors or textures.
_ R   This artist was concerned with using techniques that allow the art itself to look like something real.
_ F   This art is simply about colors, shapes or elements of art and how they are combined.

Which theory had more tallies?   *Circle one*
R= Realism   e= emotionalism   F=Formalism

*Art Criticism defined from ART TALK text

Printmaking Timeline

Cut and paste the dates in history onto the timeline page correctly by date.

Where do these artists belong on the time line?

868 AD Buddhist Scroll created (17 ft long)

1100 Transmission of paper to Europe

1397 Birth of Johannes Genfleisch Gutenberg

1450 Gutenberg uses his jeweler skills to improve movable typography

1460s The 36 Line Bible, a first book printed typographically

1481 William Caxton prints *The Mirror of the World*, an illustrated book

1600s Posthumous impressions – entrepreneurs purchasing plates from estates of deceased artists to republish prints (ex: Rembrandt's work was printed from many versions of plates)

1640s *Mustard Seed Garden*, a painting encyclopedia, was printed in China

1790s Lithography invented by Senefelder

1850s Artists begin to produce limited editions

1860 Hand signing prints by artists a new trend

1890 Gravure printing invented – metal plate

1910 Offset printing begins

1907 Silk fabric used for screen printing by Samuel Simon – England

1900s Numbering system begins (1/100)

1920 Almost all prints signed by artist. They became more valuable.

1960 3D Flexography invented

20th Century Mixed Media, monoprints

Hiroshige

Hokusai

Albrecht Dürer

James Whistler

Thomas Hart Benton

Grant Wood

Larry Rivers

Honoré Daumier

M. C. Escher

Robert Motherwell

Helen Frankenthaler

Andy Warhol

Roy Lichtenstein

Robert Indiana

Mary Cassatt

Printmaking Timeline

| 800AD | 900 | 1000 | 1100 | 1200 |

| 1300 | 1400 | 1500 | 1600 | 1700 |

| 1800 | 1900 | 2000 | present day |

Glossary Sample Page

Printmaking Glossary

Aquatint Aquatint, an intaglio process similar to etching, produces a print of an entirely different appearance. Large segments of the plate are exposed to the acid bath, creating tonal areas rather than lines. Aquatint prints date from the 18th century, when artists endeavored to recreate the effect of watercolor and wash drawings in prints. To create an aquatint, certain areas of the plate are immersed in a mild acid, which bites the areas of the plate not covered with resin. If the artist wishes some areas to be darker than others, those areas are exposed to the acid longer to become pitted and thus retain the ink more readily. The aquatint method is often difficult to control and is usually used in combination with etching and drypoint techniques.

Artist's Proofs Artist's proofs are those impressions from an edition that are specifically intended for the artist's use. These impressions are in addition to the numbered edition and are so noted in pencil as artist proof or A/P.

Baren A baren is a tool for burnishing or rubbing the back side of the print as it is pressed to the plate to transfer ink from the plate to the paper.

Drypoint Drypoint technique is similar to line engraving. A pencil-like tool, usually with a diamond point, is used to draw an image on an untreated copper or zinc plate. Each movement of the tool makes a furrow with a soft metal ridge on either side (called a burr). The burr is pushed up from the plate by the tool. The artist endeavors to retain the fragile burr throughout printing because the burr holds the ink and results in a print with rich, velvety lines. The delicacies of the burr and the continuous pressure of the press seldom allow more than 20 to 30 impressions to be printed before the burr is lost. As in the aquatint process, the drypoint print is produced by inking the plate, wiping it clean, placing dampened paper over the plate, and putting the plate through the press.

Edition The number of images printed from the plate, stone, block, or the like is called an edition. These identical images are pulled or printed either by the artist or, under the artist's supervision, by the printer. The body of the edition is numbered (for example, 1/100 through 100/100) directly on the print, usually in pencil. Additional proofs, such as the artist's proof, are also part of the edition.

Elements of Art Line, Shape, Space, Texture, Form, Color, Value.

Engraving In an engraving, the artist, by the placement and thickness of the line, determines either a dense and detailed image, or an image with a sketchy or feathery quality. After the image is cut into the plate, soft ink is applied with a roller across the entire plate, making certain that all the incised lines are filled with ink. Next, the surface of the plate is carefully wiped clean, leaving behind only the ink held in the drawn lines or crevices. The plate is then placed on the bed of the press. Dampened paper is placed over the plate and felt blankets or padding are laid on top of the paper. Under the pressure of the rollers from the press, the paper and padding draw the ink up from the incised lines onto the paper.

State of Florida Visual Arts Standards

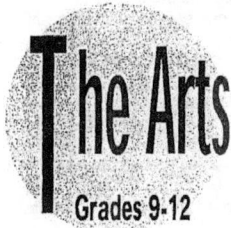

Grades 9-12

Visual Arts

Skills and Techniques

Standard 1:

The student understands and applies media, techniques, and processes. (VA.A.1.4)

1. uses two-dimensional and three-dimensional media, techniques, tools, and processes to communicate an idea or concept based on research, environment, personal experience, observation, or imagination.
2. uses tools, media, processes, and techniques proficiently, knowledgeably, and in a safe and responsible manner.
3. knows how the elements of art and the principles of design can be used to solve specific art problems.
4. uses effective control of media, techniques, and tools when communicating an idea in both two-dimensional and three-dimensional works of art.

Creation and Communication

Standard 1:

The student creates and communicates a range of subject matter, symbols, and ideas using knowledge of structures and functions of visual arts. (VA.B.1.4)

1. applies various subjects, symbols, and ideas in works of art.
2. understands that works of art can communicate an idea and elicit a variety of responses through the use of selected media, techniques, and processes.
3. understands some of the implications of intentions and purposes in particular works of art.
4. knows how the elements of art and the principles of design can be used and solves specific visual-art problems at a proficient level.

Cultural and Historical Connections

Standard 1:

The student understands the visual arts in relation to history and culture. (VA.C.1.4)

1. understands how social, cultural, ecological, economic, religious, and political conditions influence the function, meaning, and execution of works of art.
2. understands how recognized artists recorded, affected, or influenced change in a historical, cultural, or religious context.

Aesthetic and Critical Analysis

Standard 1:

The student assesses, evaluates, and responds to the characteristics of works of art. (VA.D.1.4)

1. understands and determines the differences between the artist's intent and public interpretation through valuative criteria and judgment.
2. understands critical and aesthetic statements in terms of historical reference while researching works of art.
3. knows the difference between the intentions of artists in the creation of original works and the intentions of those who appropriate and parody those works.

Applications to Life

Standard 1:

The student makes connections between the visual arts, other disciplines, and the real world. (VA.E.1.4)

1. knows and participates in community-based art experiences as an artist or observer.
2. understands and identifies the skills that artists use in various careers to promote creativity, fluency, flexibility, and elaboration within the arts and across life.
3. knows how to communicate with the public, the consumer, and the artistic community about aesthetic questions, entertainment, resources, and choices in education.

NATIONAL VISUAL ARTS STANDARDS

Understanding and applying media, techniques, and processes
* Students know the difference between materials, techniques and processes.
* Students describe how different materials, techniques and processes cause different responses.
* Students use different media, techniques and processes to communicate ideas, experiences and stories.
* Students use art materials and tools in safe and responsible manner.

Using knowledge of structures and functions
* Students know the differences among visual characteristics and purposes of art in order to convey ideas.
* Students describe how different expressive features and organizational principles cause different responses.
* Students use visual structures and functions of art to communicate ideas.

Choosing and evaluating a range of subject matter, symbols and ideas
* Students explore and understand prospective content for works of art.
* Students select and use subject matter, symbols and ideas to communicate meaning.

Understanding the visual arts in relation to history and cultures
* Students know that the visual arts have both a history and specific relationships to various cultures.
* Students identify specific works of art as belonging to particular cultures, times and places.
* Students demonstrate how history, culture and the visual arts can influence each other in making and studying works of art.

Reflecting upon and assessing the characteristics and merits of their [a student's own] work and the work of others
* Students understand that there are various purposes for creating works of visual art.
* Students describe how people's experiences influence the development of specific artworks.
* Students understand there are different responses to specific artworks.

Making connections between visual arts and other disciplines
* Students understand and use similarities and differences between characteristics of the visual arts and other arts disciplines.
* Students identify connections between the visual arts and other disciplines in the curriculum.

For more information, visit the **National Art Education Association** website.

Artist interaction handout to accompany a talk by the artist Harris Wiltsher given to Lawton Chiles High School students.

Harris Wiltsher, Printmaker

Lawton Chiles High School & Deerlake Middle School

Printmaking Partnership

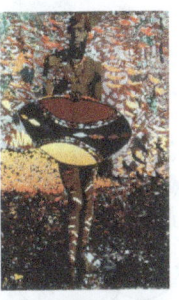

Although he is an ocean and a hemisphere away from South Africa, **Harris R. Wiltsher II** is working to preserve the uprooted culture or "setso" of that country. Wiltsher, an artist and an Assistant Professor at Florida A&M University, believes it is culture that makes us powerful and that art can be a narrative tool to educate, stimulate change, and build appreciation of the history of a culture. Putting his beliefs to work, Wiltsher has brought a direct South African perspective to his campus in Tallahassee, Florida. For example, he curated a traveling exhibition of South African works and has facilitated workshops inviting several visiting artists from Cape Town. This South African link allows him to broaden others' awareness of social, political, and educational issues, the same issues that influence his personal works.

In his series *South Africa, A Better Life For All*, Wiltsher combines imagery and text. The text, printed in the various languages of the people of South Africa, speaks about voting privileges, education, housing, business, race relations, culture, the arts, politics, the future, and life in general. Wiltsher, a graduate of FAMU in 1990, received his MFA from Cranbrook Academy in Michigan in 1993. He returned to FAMU in 1996. He has received numerous scholarships and fellowships including the William and Camille Cosby Fine Arts Scholarship, Cranbrook Scholarship Award, Phillip Morris Fellowship Award, J. William Fulbright Scholarship Award, and the Bronx Recognizes its Own Fellowship (BRIO). His work has been exhibited in New York, Michigan, Chicago, Mississippi, and Florida where he spreads "die booskap" or *the message* of his work, a valuation of past while looking to the future.

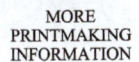

MORE PRINTMAKING INFORMATION

Museum of Printing
www.museumofprinting.org

Imprint on the World Contest
Www.speedball.com

Vocabulary
Www.zimmerworks.com/vprintmaking.htm

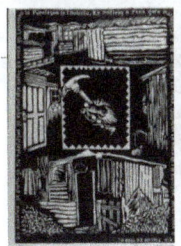
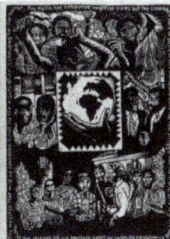
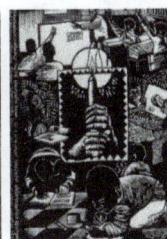

Lecture Notes

Printmaking Facts

Think about a social issue you would like to bring attention to by creating your own artwork.

LIST IDEAS in box

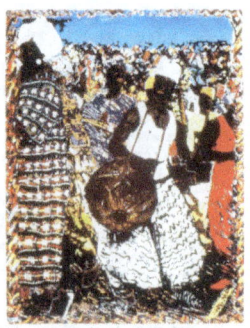

Want to know more about Harris R. Wiltsher's artwork?

Write to him at semelo@hotmail.com.

Courtesy: Art teachers, Julie Childers, Leslie Cohen, and Kelly Little Kawagoye; artist, Harris Wiltsher.

CHAPTER 6

Project #3: The Influence of the "Big Idea"[1] Approach

Project Title: *The Story*
Planning and Program Implementation: Spring 2008
Exhibition Year: 2008
Co-curatorial Team:
Tallahassee, Florida K-12 inter-school art educators
- Apalachee Elementary School—Pam Brewster
- Belle Vue Middle School—Althea Valle (English for Speakers of Other Languages or ESOL)
- Buck Lake Elementary School—Fran Kautz
- Chiles High school—Julie Childers, Leslie Cohen, Kelly Little
- Deerlake Middle School—Linda Johnson
- Florida State University Schools—Barbara Davis, Pam Wallheiser
- Gilchrist Elementary School—Julie McBride
- Lincoln High School—Dr. Marilyn Proctor-Givens, Shannon Smale
- Pineview Elementary School—Sara Chang (ESOL), Sunny Spillane
- Raa Middle School—Teresa Coates
- Riley Elementary School—Megan Garriga
- Ruediger Elementary School—Dr. Marcia Meale
- Trinity Catholic School—Maria Augustyniak'

---

[1] The term "Big Idea," derived from the book *Rethinking Curriculum in Art* (2005) by Marilyn Stewart and Sydney Walker, seems to carry dual meanings within their thinking. In a section of their "Introduction," called "What's the Big Idea" (pp. 2–3), Stewart and Walker appear to simultaneously use the term to refer to their proposal of the use of the "enduring idea" in curriculum planning but also to use the term to refer to their own "Big Idea" for the book in its entirety, a holistic guide for curriculum planning. Later in the book they identify enduring ideas as "themes, topics, or issues that reflect big questions" or "broad, umbrella-like ideas" (p. 25). In this book on the constructivist co-curation method, the term "Big Idea" generally refers to use of the "enduring idea" as a foundation and guide for the co-curation of extended projects with embedded exhibitions.

Florida State University Museum of Fine Arts
- Intern—Ashley Hickman
- Curator of Education—Dr. Viki D. Thompson Wylder

Tallahassee Community College Gallery
- Coordinator—Laura Thompson

Artworks: 60

Artists: Mary Lee Bendolph, Richard Bickel, Romero Britto, Kevin Cole, Melinda Copper, Lenore DePree, Nancy Baur Dillen, Jack Dowd, Mark Fletcher, Minuette Floyd, Adrian Fogelin, Jonathan Green, Wennie Huang, DeLoss McGraw, Dean Mitchell, Mark Priest, Sandy Proctor, Eluster Richardson, Faith Ringgold, Sydney Scherr, Franz Spohn, Peggy Banks Sword, Carol Walker, Kathleen Wilcox

Beginnings

In late summer of 2005, Fran Kautz, the art instructor from Buck Lake Elementary School who drove much of the organization of her school for the *Visions of the North Florida Environment* project of 2002, called me to say she wanted to come by the Museum of Fine Arts (MoFA) to talk. I was intrigued as she sat down in my office area and began to describe a new project and exhibition, one that was bigger than the two previous teacher co-curated projects and exhibitions in number of works, scope of artists, and involvement of schools and teachers. "I think this exhibition should be about art and stories...We should look at any work that suggests a story—like Faith Ringgold's quilts or work that focuses on heroes or myth or the everyday person" (Thompson Wylder, 2007, p. 4). And Fran wanted to offer this co-curatorial opportunity to teachers at schools from across the school district, not just one school.

By the fall of 2005, a co-curatorial team was meeting monthly, and the Museum issued a statement which outlined a potential schema for the entire project, formally titled *The Story*, for a variety of purposes inclusive of grant support. After this statement was published, a gallery coordinator at Tallahassee Community College and a Florida State University student joined the co-curatorial committee for this exhibition.

The Florida State University Museum of Fine Arts is currently planning to host an exhibition in May/June of 2008 titled *The Story*. The title is indicative of the theme selected for this show—all works in the exhibition will show a merger of formal aspects, style, and technique with a narrative quality. This narrative tone may be suggestive or palpable.

The exhibition, and program to accompany it, is unique in its conception, planning, and process. A committee of Tallahassee/Leon County K-12 visual arts and language arts teachers from 13 schools are joining the Museum to curate the exhibition and plan the educational program and activities surrounding the exhibition. This includes an educational packet with lesson plans written by teachers on this committee to be sent to all visual arts and language arts teachers (and others) in this school district. A goal of this committee is to insert the images from this exhibition into the academic curriculum of schools within Leon County. The works in this exhibition will be used as a stimulus for student writing and art production (K-12). A parallel exhibition of K-12 work will be developed. Other activities include teacher workshops and a program of interaction between students and artists. A number of administrators from the Leon County School Board Office will lend their advocacy and assistance for this exhibition and program. A catalogue of the exhibition will be produced.

(Thompson Wylder, 2005)

During the spring of 2007, a little more than half-way through the co-curatorial planning process, Fran Kautz and a handful of teachers from the committee enjoyed an unexpected, exciting curatorial experience which emphasized the bigger scope of this project. These teachers attended a National Art Education Association Conference in New York City. They knew the ACA Galleries (American Contemporary Artists) located in New York City's Chelsea district agreed to loan several artworks under consideration for the exhibition. Fran described the teachers' visit to the ACA Galleries where they were stunned "due to the caliber of the work viewed, the status of the artists represented, many mega-artists, the money value placed on the work, and the welcoming attitude of the director." From the "abundance of work on hand, the gallery director presented pieces for them to review and even touch." During this conversation, they "viewed new work by Faith Ringgold and they selected work by DeLoss McGraw, an additional artist suggested by the gallery owner/director not previously known or discussed by the co-curatorial team." Fran summarized their visit to the ACA Galleries as, "amazing, a once-in-a-lifetime experience, an experience beyond anything I could imagine" (M. Meale & V. D. T. Wylder, personal communication with co-curatorial committee members from Buck Lake Elementary F. Kautz & S. McDowell, March 2, 2020).

—VDTW

Description of the Project and Exhibition

For *The Story*, the third project out of the five undertaken, the committee selected 60 artworks by 24 artists from across the country. Among the wide-ranging artists was a mix of internationally, nationally, regionally, and locally known artists. The work of each artist showed distinct media and style. The exhibition checklist incorporated the painted story quilts of the internationally celebrated Faith Ringgold; the quilts of Mary Lee Bendolph of Alabama's Gee's Bend African American tradition; the pop art serigraphs of Miami-based Romero Britto; the illustrative drawings of awarded author Adrian Fogelin; the watercolors of Dean Mitchell who was described by one New York critic as the modern-day Vermeer; the Apalachicola, Florida photographs of Richard Bickel; the ceramic sculpture, drawings and verse of North Florida naturalist Mark Fletcher; and the installations of emerging New York artist Wennie Huang. Interactions with Ms. Huang provided an example of the additional curation of programs and activities essential to these extensive projects. The co-curatorial committee invited her to travel from New York to Tallahassee to meet and make art with several classrooms at a Title I school. She also staged a one-woman performance at the exhibition opening using her installation. Her installation and her performance, jointly titled *Between Heaven and Earth*, focused on her Taiwanese heritage.

In accordance with Hein's constructivist museum dictum that the exhibition is only one aspect of a larger project that provides additional avenues or layers of interaction for constructivist connections of meaning-making, the committee decided to sponsor several significant events well before the opening of *The Story* exhibition. The first was a "Preface" event held a year prior in which a teacher workshop was offered against the backdrop of a small display of narrative works from the museum's permanent collection mingled with K-12 student work stimulated by the permanent collection pieces. The three-hour for-credit workshop,

This artist interaction and performance titled *Between Heaven and Earth* was given by Wennie Huang at the opening reception for *The Story* exhibition.

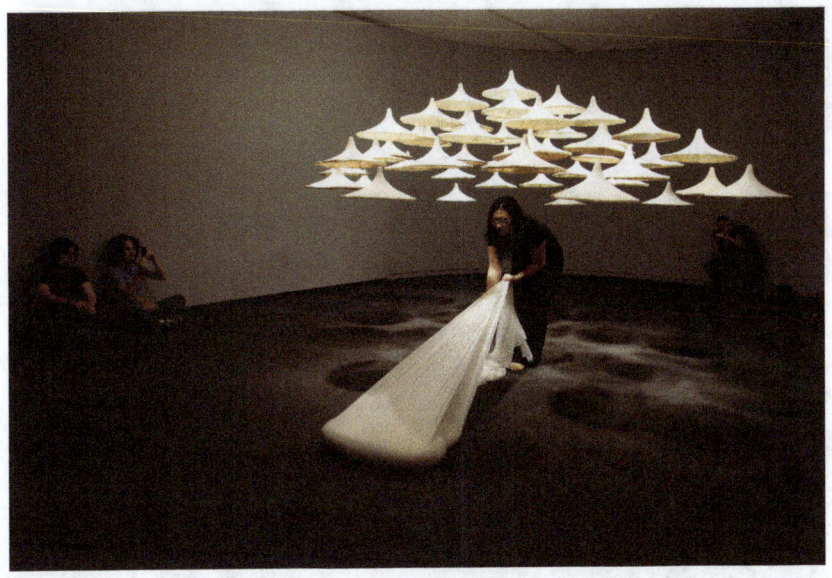

Courtesy: Florida State University Museum of Fine Arts.

billed as "Dinner and A Story" using the name of a past television show, was held on a Friday evening and included several parts. K-12 students and families were welcomed to an hour reception for the display. The reception was followed by a "for teachers only" buffet dinner with wine during a presentation by the award-winning author Julianna Baggott, who publishes under the pen name N. E. Bode among other monikers. In a cross-discipline fashion that describes a number of *Story* programs and activities, her talk focused on helping students integrate the visual arts with writing.

The second early event was promoted and funded by the Council on Culture and Arts in Leon County eight months before the exhibition. For this occasion the artist Faith Ringgold addressed teachers and K-12 students at a state-operated auditorium. During her presentation which consisted of a lecture, a reading of her Caldecott Award-winning children's book, *Tar Beach*, and audience interaction, the artist invited K-12 students to ask questions and join her at the podium to read from an offshoot of *Tar Beach* titled *Cassie's Word Quilt*.

During this artist interaction, Faith Ringgold invited students to read her book aloud during a presentation sponsored by the Council on Culture and Arts in Tallahassee.

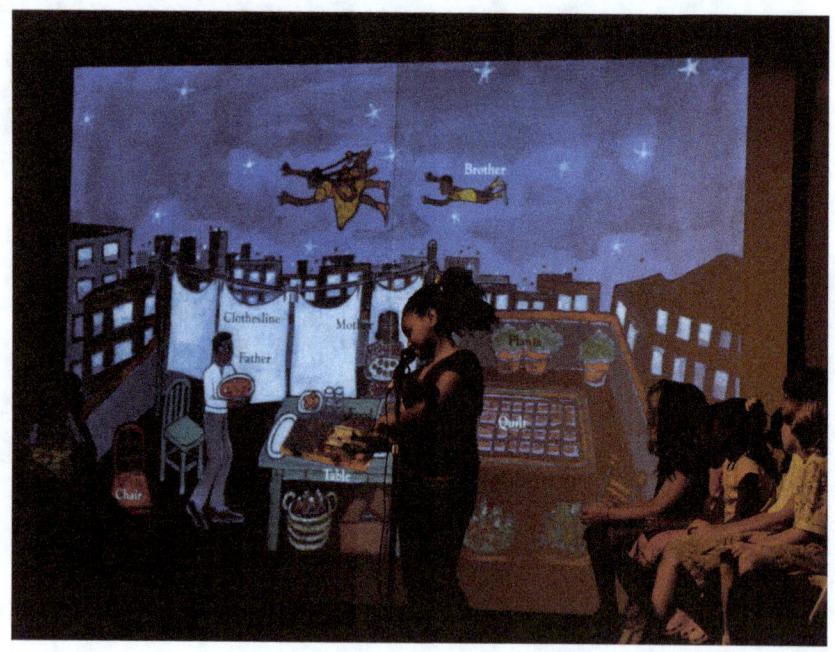

Courtesy: Curatorial Team Member for *The Story*.

In addition to these early facets of the project already mentioned, 15 other artists interacted with K-12 students, often through a personal visitation to classrooms but sometimes through other methods such as communication with classes via email. Dramatically crossing curricular boundaries, several *Story* artworks included turtle/tortoise imagery leading to the visitation of some classrooms by Tallahassee area herpetologist Bob Walker, also known as Turtle Bob, who traveled with live gopher tortoises which are considered a "threatened" keystone species in the Southeast.

The museum printed a catalogue and teachers' packet of lesson plans several months in advance to distribute to all art instructors (and others) in the school system so that *Story* artwork could be used in the classroom as a stimulus to inspire student inquiry and artworks. Rather than offering a student display outside the premises of the Florida State University (FSU) MoFA galleries, a section of the viewing space within the MoFA was set aside for K-12 student artwork. Student artwork

In response to Romero Britto's works, high school students created characters, costumes, and setting for a student performance at the entrance to the Florida State University Museum of Fine Arts during the opening reception for *The Story* exhibition.

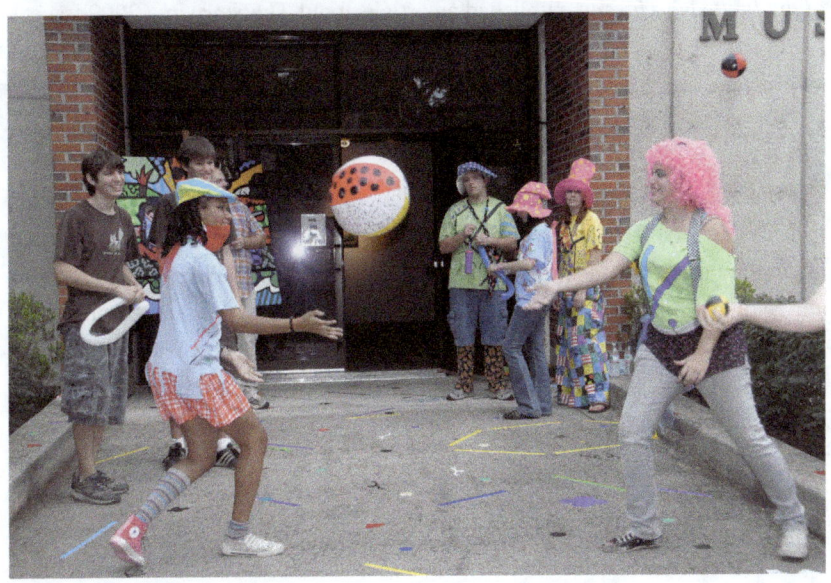

Courtesy: Florida State University Museum of Fine Arts.

overflow, created by students from schools who began participation toward the end of the project and not long before the exhibition date, was shown in a partner exhibition at the Tallahassee Community College Gallery (TCC Gallery). At the opening of *The Story* exhibition, K-12 student groups performed music and readings. With kinesthetic liveliness, a high school group greeted visitors in Romero Britto-inspired costumes demonstrating the pop art spirit of the two pieces of the artist's imagery included in the exhibition. Tables were placed throughout the exhibition with "make and take" activities designed by museum interns and volunteers. Each activity was based on an artwork in the show. At one "make and take" table, visitors could "Make Your Own Edible Romero Britto Inspired Artwork." Interactive tours were also given over the course of the exhibition with busing financed for many groups by grant money awarded to the FSU MoFA.

The after-exhibition activity for *The Story* project exceeded that for any of the other four projects. A two-day teacher institute of workshops based on the content of the exhibition, for which teachers could earn in-service credit, was hosted at the FSU MoFA at the end of the school year. Presentations about *The Story* project were made at the Florida Association of Museums Conference and the National Art Education Association Conference. *The International Journal of the Inclusive Museum* published an article about *The Story* in a 2009 issue.

The "Big Idea" Approach and *The Story*

The planning for *The Story* project and implementation of its many components spread out over a three-year period. The co-curatorial team for *The Story* operated under the influence of the principles and strategies outlined by Marilyn Stewart and Sydney Walker in their book titled *Rethinking Curriculum in Art* published the same year that project planning began in 2005. Stewart and Walker promoted a framework for teaching centered on the "Big Idea," a framework also loosely adaptable to the curatorial process. Interestingly, Stewart and Walker expressed their hope that museum educators as well as art instructors would heed their philosophical and organizational concepts.

The "Big Idea" framework consists of two major components:

- broad unit plans, each inclusive of an "enduring" or "big" idea with a rationale, key concepts, essential questions, objectives, standards, and assessment criteria, and
- series of lesson plans, each series addressing the idea, concepts, questions, and objectives of a unit.

This framework is interdisciplinary across subject matters and utilizes inquiry methods within the four disciplines of art—artmaking, art history, art criticism, and aesthetics. It is multicultural, requires connections to the self and the real world, and focuses on the communication and meanings inherent in artworks or artifacts. Finally, it charges the teacher with moving in and out of two roles, that of expert as well as facilitator/guide/coach to engage students in the learning process. The "Big Idea" framework is constructivist in nature with an emphasis on connections and construction of knowledge by the learner through hands-on and minds-on activities, discussion, and often collaborative work.

The educator planning within the "Big Idea" framework can start anywhere within that framework. The intent may be the teaching of a cultural practice or teaching from an art historical piece, but the unit of study must ultimately be based on and unified by an "enduring" or "big" idea. This idea must be a concept that is adaptable across developmental levels, holds import to humans in general through the ages, and in so doing exceeds one subject area. Ideas may be encapsulated in a single word such as conflict, power, nature, change, communication, and so on, or if desired, expanded slightly into a phrase. From the enduring or big idea, a small number of meaningful key concepts are developed that explain the enduring idea from several perspectives. Stewart and Walker provide samples of key concepts using the enduring idea of communication—"communication requires interpretation" and "communication can be both public and private" (Stewart & Walker, 2005, p. 33).

Formulating one to three essential questions to guide the study of the unit comprises the third step in the process. "What counts as communication? Why is communication often difficult? Why is communication important?" (Stewart & Walker, 2005, p. 35). These three steps—1) the selection of the enduring or big idea, 2) the development of key concepts, and 3) the formulation of essential questions—create the foundation for a unit of study and its objectives, as well as a number of coherently related lesson plans and lesson objectives. These plans allow the educator to primarily guide learners by incorporating activities, discussion, and collaboration using art disciplines and other subject matter disciplines. They encourage connections among details, concepts, messages, cultures, the self, and the world to help the learner find and make meaning and bring the learner to important art understandings, that is, to construct knowledge.

Stewart and Walker want to give students the ability to question, analyze, and participate in the processes within, about, and around art (all of equal importance). For them this constitutes the broad goal of the study of the discipline. The authors promote this comprehensive framework so that learners can gain insight into the "range of purposes" (2005, p. 9) for art within cultures and the way those purposes affect individuals within those cultures, including the lives of the learners themselves. They want learners to become savvy enough to ask their own conceived questions about any aspect of art which can then result in personal or collaborative analyses and actions.

From the museum's curatorial perspective, the enduring or big idea is analogous to the theme of an exhibition and the project of which it is a part. The project itself is analogous to the unit. In this case the enduring or big idea/theme of the unit/project/exhibition was expressed in the title—*The Story*. This curatorial theme or enduring idea proposed by teachers met the criteria stated by Stewart and Walker for selecting such an idea. Adaptable across many levels (pre-K through university level, and general adult audience), the concept and construction of the story reaches across all humanity categorized by age, gender, race, ethnicity, culture, economics, and history. It has "lasting human importance and appear[s] to be a continual concern to humans at different times and in different cultures" (Stewart & Walker, 2005, p. 144).

The brain generally organizes information via stories and in this way provides an effective transfer of information and a mode for understanding. Stories, particularly myth-like stories, act as the foundational building blocks of the values and beliefs of all cultures by conveying messages from past generations, spreading messages within the contemporary generation, and passing on messages to future generations. Stories offer personal and cultural perspectives of civilization and environment that assist individuals with a comprehension of geographical and societal values that affect them. Stories allow vicarious experience and the development of empathy. Analysis of stories stimulates interpretation, sometimes leading to change of beliefs and values which promotes the evolution of stories over time or the development of new stories (multiple websites offer a summary of the cultural role of stories). In addition, the enduring or big idea of *The Story* exceeds the single discipline of art. At the outset the co-curatorial team integrated literature and writing into plans for this unit/project/exhibition. Eventually other disciplines like history, the environment, and even dance were addressed.

The rationale for developing *The Story* unit/project/exhibition is nearly self-explanatory. Teaching about and from the story and its form is basic to educational practice. Of course, narrative art is based on story and much of art history includes a focus on the narrative. The importance of narrative in art is contemporaneously underscored by the building of a new museum in Los Angeles—the Lucas Museum of Narrative Art. This unit/project/exhibition provided opportunities for looking at multiple visual stories in multiple media from multiple perspectives in a concentrated space. It offered teachers and students simultaneous opportunities for questioning, analyzing, and identifying the information and perspectives communicated by these narratives. It offered abundant inspirational opportunities for the development of new narrative art by students. That new narrative art was shown at the FSU MoFA (and at the TCC Gallery) in conjunction with the professional artwork chosen by the co-curatorial committee.

With the developmental level of K-12 students in mind, the following key concepts guided the proposal and selection of unit/project/exhibition programs and artworks by teachers on the co-curatorial committee.

- Much visual art is structured as a story or narrative.
- A story, or narrative, takes multiple forms of organization.
- A story, or narrative, transmits information and point of view.
- A story, or narrative, can be questioned and analyzed to identify the information and point of view it holds.

The essential questions posed by the unit/project/exhibition and derived from the key concepts were basic.

- What is a visual story or narrative?
- How do artists—in several disciplines—tell stories or narratives within their artwork?
- How does the viewer analyze a visual story or narrative and receive a message?

The objectives for viewers, especially students, for this unit/project/exhibition were:

- To experience the organization inherent in a visual story or narrative by looking at or studying the exhibition artwork.
- To analyze examples of visual stories (either in the exhibition or suggested by the exhibition) to determine the narrative information and messages within them.
- To understand the way artists use narrative to create an artwork, particularly by students through creation of artworks inspired by the stories or narratives curated into the exhibition.

In addition, the programs within the unit/project/exhibition held before and during the exhibition ensured the unit/project/exhibition objectives were met.

- Two major events that targeted teachers, students, and families were scheduled long before the exhibition: the "Preface" event titled "Dinner and a Story," which meshed narrative work from the MoFA permanent collection and student artwork based on the permanent collection with dinner and a talk by the award-winning author Julianna Baggott; and a talk and discussion by Faith Ringgold, the artist historically famous for her development of painted "story quilts."

For this artist interaction, Jack Dowd invited students to the installation of his work titled *Future of America II* for *The Story* exhibition.

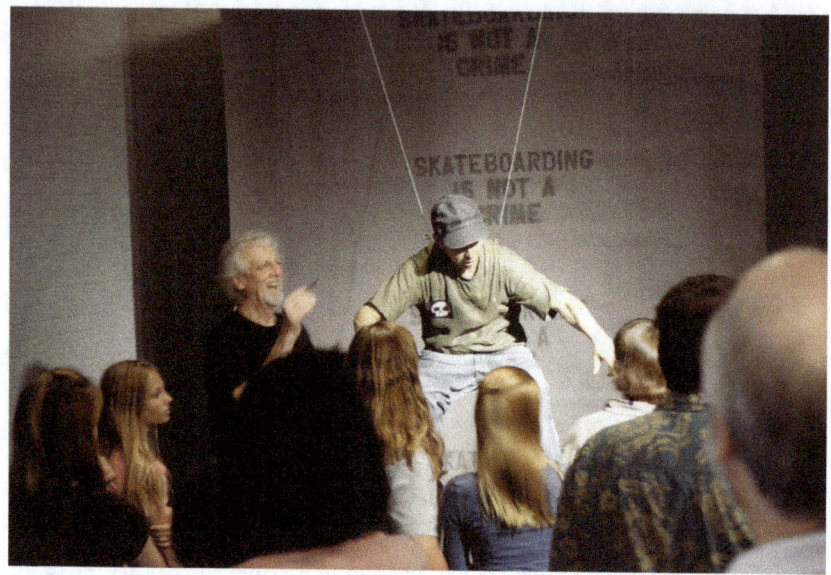

Courtesy: Florida State University Museum of Fine Arts.

- A catalogue of the exhibition was printed early and distributed to all schools in the district in which the FSU MoFA resides.
- A teachers' packet or lesson plan book written by teachers and interns based on works in the exhibition was similarly distributed to schools in the district.
- Various artists visited or interacted with classrooms in some way to work with students to present aspects of their lives and artwork but also to help students begin to create their own narrative art.
- Student displays of narrative art produced in the classroom were mounted.
- A full program was offered on opening night with hands-on make and take opportunities based on works in the exhibition, and performances such as that by artist, Wennie Huang, in which she presented a symbolic narrative of her experience as a person of Taiwanese heritage in the United States.
- Hands-on or minds-on tours for various audience constituencies were given throughout the course of the show.
- From grant money, the FSU MoFA subsidized the cost of busing students to the exhibition for tours.

- A two-day institute for teachers was held with sessions run by an educator from the John and Mable Ringling Museum of Art, teachers from the co-curatorial committee, a biographer of one of the artists in the show, and several artists from the exhibition.
- All teacher workshops (the institute, Dinner and a Story, and the Faith Ringgold event) offered teachers the possibility of earning recertification credits awarded by the county school system.

The catalogue for the exhibition was devised with story or narrative organizational structure in mind. A page represented each artist in the exhibition and showed a work by the artist at approximately half-page size, a smaller photo of the artist, and a very brief biography told in story format despite the brevity. Written by co-curatorial team members, each biography utilized bare-bones organizational parts of a story—setting, character, rising action, plot, and resolution. The early printing and distribution of the lesson plan packet and the catalogue allowed teachers in the classroom to teach from the foundational aspects of the unit/project/exhibition while accessing or utilizing *Story* artwork content. Especially in the classroom, objectives came to fruition. Students in classrooms produced their own narrative creations inspired by the artwork in the exhibition to show in the student display sections of *The Story* at the FSU MoFA or at the TCC Gallery, which housed student display overflow.

Even a brief scan of state and national standards for art and language show alignment by a range of those standards with this comprehensive unit/project/exhibition. Many Florida visual arts standards at various grade levels deal with the acquisition of analytical skills as a means to develop critical thinking. They also address the transferability of skills among disciplines. Florida's reading standards for literature on multiple grade levels cover the craft and structure of various types of texts such as "story." In addition, national standards like Common Core Standards for "Reading: Literature" do the same. The National Board for Professional Teaching Standards does not refer to the specifics of student outcomes and therefore does not directly address potential objectives of this unit/project/exhibition. Instead the National Board presents standards for teacher professionalism and advocates for primary and secondary level collaborative projects with entities like museums to "extend...classrooms beyond school... to promote student learning and involvement with art" (*Early Childhood and Middle Childhood/Art Standards*, 2000, p. 48) and to "connect students and their artwork with the larger community through exhibitions, programs, and field

The opening reception of the Student Display of high school response work, titled *Stories 9-12* .

The opening reception of the Student Display of elementary and middle school response work, titled *Stories K-8*.

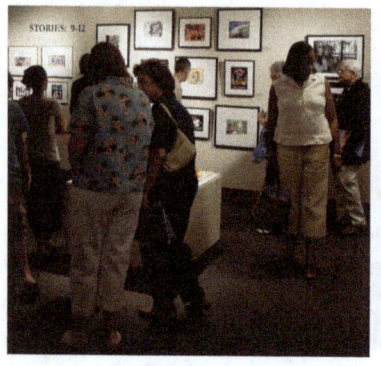

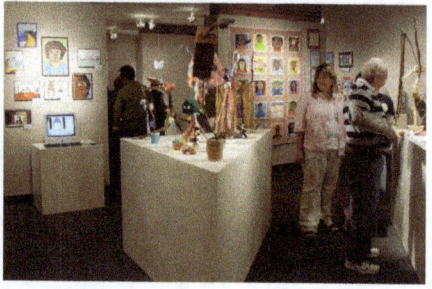

Courtesy: Florida State University Museum of Fine Arts.

Courtesy: Florida State University Museum of Fine Arts.

trips." A "long-range experience" (*Early Adolescence through Young Adulthood/ Art Standards*, 2001, p. 81) with museum educators is suggested.

Assessment strategies to measure the final success of the fulfillment of the objectives of this unit/project/exhibition could not be as defined or as formal as assessment strategies used in the classroom. In fact, art teachers (and several outside the visual arts discipline) at 25 schools in the region whose students produced *Story* response artwork for the student display at the FSU MoFA or the overflow site at the TCC Gallery hosted lessons in the classroom based on at least one or more of the objectives of this unit/project/exhibition. Success could be informally evaluated by the artwork produced in the classroom and then shown in student displays or by comments and feedback from teachers who taught or hosted those lessons. For example, Adrian Fogelin, an artist in the exhibition and writer/illustrator of novels for a young audience, visited Kelly Little's Chiles High School classroom to talk about her work and help students develop their own stories and illustrations as part of a lesson. Little's plan involved the writing and illustration of a chapter book by each of the students. Although brief, a written statement by Kelly Little subtly suggested Fogelin's session with the students featured the three unit/project/exhibition objectives—analysis of story organization, analysis of visual information, and development of understanding of the process for creating visual narratives. Little's words also indicated the depth of that analysis and understanding by her students. "Students commented that the process of creating characters became easier as they built more and more layers of details about the character and settings and started sketching their illustrations" (Little, 2008, p. 16).

Riley Elementary School students took a field trip with *The Story* artist Mark Fletcher during this artist interaction to explore nature as inspiration.

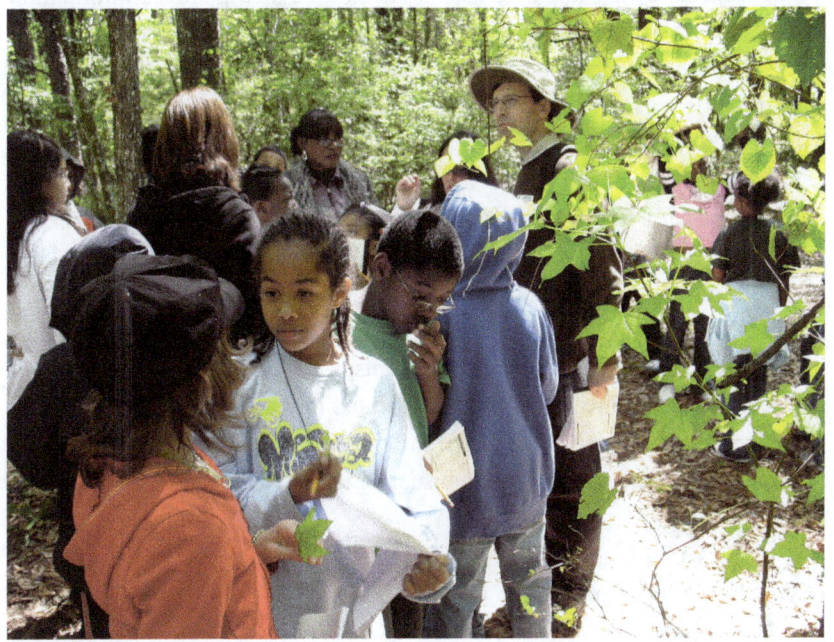

Courtesy: Megan Garriga.

Lesson plans featuring much of the work in the exhibition were written and distributed in a teachers' packet or lesson plan book prior to the exhibition. Over 700 students produced K-12 artworks based on visual and textual narrative and inspired by works in the exhibition. Several classes utilized plans centered on the work of Mark Fletcher, a ceramicist, graphic artist, and narrative poet. Fletcher, who enjoyed art residencies at state parks in several states, concentrated on facets of the environment captured in storybook style in many of his works no matter the medium. Like Adrian Fogelin, Mark Fletcher worked directly with students.

Megan Garriga, an elementary art instructor at Riley Elementary, a Title I school, collaborated with Fletcher to inspire and guide the production and illustration of narrative poetry by her students through a series of activities aligned with language, visual arts, and science standards. Garriga and Fletcher planned presentations by Fletcher in the classroom in which he outlined his methods for observing and retaining detail, creating imagery, and writing poetry. Students, with notebooks and worksheets in hand, visited a state park during a school field trip with the artist to observe, make notes on their observations, and sketch. In the classroom during days following this field trip, students used their gathered information and sketches to author and illustrate their own narrative poems. Several finished works were shown individually framed at the FSU MoFA as part of *The Story* student section. The rest were combined into a book titled *Poetry Inspired by Nature* (2008) that was also displayed. Fourth grader Keith Singleton's poem *On the Hike* appeared in the book accompanied by pencil drawings of the trunk and branches of a tree, a gray woodpecker with a red head and yellow beak, a gray and yellow bee, as well as red ants. His imagery of the woodpecker and bee seemed to also reflect a consultation of scientifically accurate photos or drawings. The poem narratively recounted the field trip to the state park and made reference to all these images except that of the red ants. Certainly, this student's artwork attested to the fulfillment of the unit/project/exhibition objectives—analysis of story organization, analysis of visual information, and development of understanding of the process for creating visual narratives.

> *On the Hike*
> Everywhere I looked I saw a tree
> They smelled so sweet, just like honey.
> Shh, Listen—
> I heard the breeze
> Gusting through the dark green trees.
> I saw a sink hole,
> In it was a duck.
> I thought I heard a woodpecker
> As he began to peck.
> This is what I experienced
> On our nature hike
> Everything felt perfect and just right!
> (Mrs. Greenberg's 4th Grade, 2008, Keith Singleton section)

Tours were also used to provide informal assessments of the achievement of objectives. One tour was devised for various grade levels in which students reviewed the basic parts of stories—setting, character, plot, conflict, and resolution or ending. Then students selected works or were asked to discuss a specific work using these terms. Worksheets were provided to assist recall of thoughts. Students' responses revealed their understanding of the way artwork sometimes creates a narrative, the organization within the visual narrative, and the information or message given. During the visual process, students often had to verbalize a narrative through a personal reading of the work.

Museum assessments of programs usually include a recounting of numbers of visitors and participants. Numbers tallied for *The Story* could not gauge the success of internal pedagogical objectives met, but they did give some idea of the drawing power of this expansive project and exhibition to targeted audiences. By the end of the project, 25 schools had participated with *The Story* student display. Artworks by 600 students were represented in the parallel K-12 exhibition at the FSU MoFA and 124 students were represented at the overflow gallery site at Tallahassee Community College. The opening reception audience for the exhibition at the FSU MoFA numbered approximately 800.

Page from *The Story* catalogue.

The Story ⬤━━⬤ 17

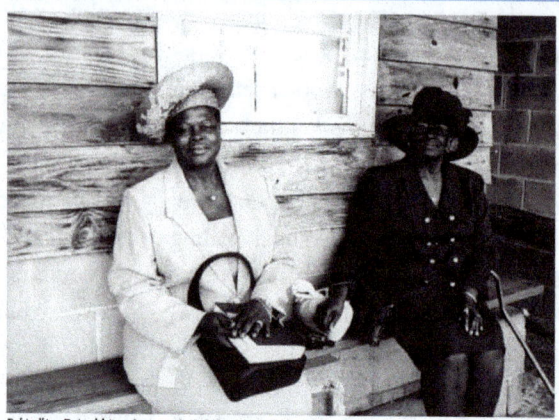

Rekindling Friendships, photograph, 8.25" x 12.5".

Minuette Floyd

Minuette Byers Floyd is the Coordinator of Art Education at the University of South Carolina, a position that incorporates her background as an artist and as a former elementary art teacher. Born in Mooresville, North Carolina, she grew up experiencing "that old-time religion" at camp meetings—dusty roads, tents, rocking chairs, reunions, renewals, hand clapping, foot stamping, preaching, singing, fellowshipping, fish frying, pound cake baking, children playing, and families praying. As an artist in a changing world, she looked for a way to capture the richness of her youth. She returned to the camp meeting tradition with her camera to document the history, events, and spirit of such African-American assemblies in North and South Carolina. She talked with people at the campgrounds and recorded their earliest memories. In the spirit of education, she placed her camera in the hands of children so they too could document the camp meeting experience through their own lenses.

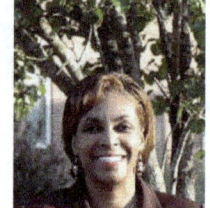

Marilyn Proctor-Givens: Lincoln High School

Minuette Floyd is an Associate Professor of Art Education at the University of South Carolina. She maintains a studio in Columbia, SC. Contact Information: 803-777-3137, mbfloyd0@gwm.sc.edu.

Selected Awards and Exhibitions: 2007–Artistic Excellence Grant, National Endowment for the Arts; 2005–Outstanding Art Educator/Higher Education, National Art Education Association; 2004–*Generations: African American Campmeeting Traditions in South Carolina*, Monsanto Gallery, Lander University, Greenwood, SC and Arthur Rose Museum, Claflin University, Grangeburg, SC; 2002–Outstanding Art Educator/Higher Education, South Carolina Art Education Association.

Courtesy: Florida State University Museum of Fine Arts.

Page from *The Story* catalogue.

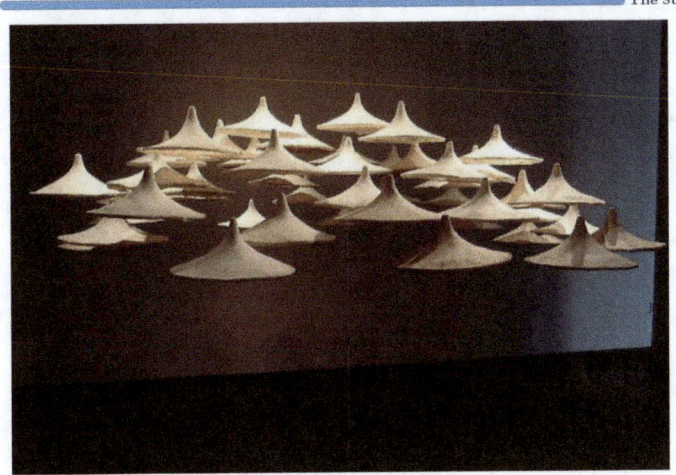

20 ━━━━━━━━━━━━━━━━━━━━━━━━━━━━━━━━━━━━━━━ The Story

Between Heaven and Earth, installation, 16' x 10'. Courtesy: Dieu Donné Papermill.

Wennie Huang

As a high school student, Wennie Huang stood out. She was a talented musician, a gifted artist, and class valedictorian. She was also the only Asian-American in her high school class. Wishing to be recognized more for her talents than her ethnicity, Wennie impressed her classmates with her drawing skills, and decided to become an illustrator.

At Pratt Institute in New York City, Wennie discovered that she was neither the only talented artist, nor the only visibly ethnic person. Both her art and her sense of identity began to change. After college, Wennie's closest uncle died, and her parents gathered the family for a series of ancient Taiwanese mourning rituals. Fascinated, Wennie dug deeper into her family's history. With newfound inspiration Wennie began using her artwork to explore her own Taiwanese-American experience, an exploration that she continues today.

Sunny Spillane: Pineview Elementary

Wennie Huang is an art instructor at the 92nd Street YMCA and a visiting instructor at Pratt Institute. She maintains a studio at 100 Ocean Parkway #1T, Brooklyn, NY 11218. Contact Information: 347-398-3875, wennie_huang@hotmail.com.

Selected Awards and Exhibitions: 2007–Public Art Commission PS 263, Percent for Art, New York City, NY; Sculpture Space Artist Residency, Utica, NY; *Evidence*, Kleinart-James Gallery, Woodstock, NY; 2006–*Celebrating Winter through Nature*, Wave Hill, Bronx, NY; *Ragdale's 30th Anniversary Exhibition*, Ragdale Foundation, Chicago, IL.

Courtesy: Florida State University Museum of Fine Arts.

Page from *The Story* catalogue.

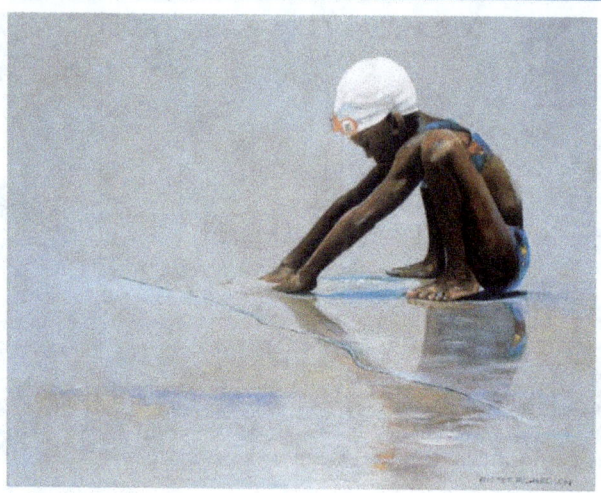

Seashore, oil, 16" x 30".

Eluster Richardson

The children in the front of the line whispered as they were re-entering the classroom at John C. Riley Elementary after recess. The whispering grew louder. "Eluster, Eluster, you did that?" The thin boy with a shy smile stopped in the doorway. "Yeah!" he said.

That memory of his classmates is hazy but Eluster, born at Ayavalla Plantation in Tallahassee, knows he discovered himself in the third grade when his teacher pinned his drawing of simple machines on blue-lined paper to the bulletin board. His confidence swelled.

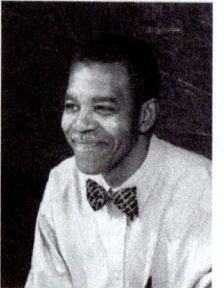

In a way Richardson's art career began that day. Self-taught, he loved to draw and later honed his skill in oils. Richardson prefers painting people and their expressions, stating that "people are such a challenge." In 1992, right before the birth of his daughter, Jasmine, the artist established his now favorite medium of watercolor. Jasmine continues to be a source of inspiration.

Julie McBride: Gilchrist Elementary School

Eluster Richardson maintains a studio at 7056 Bradfordville Road, Tallahassee, FL 32308. Contact Information:850-893-0059, eluster7@earthlink.net.

Selected Awards and Exhibitions: On-going–Permanent Artist-in-Residence, Riley House Museum and Resource Center of African-American History and Culture, Tallahassee, FL; 2006–*International Directions*, LeMoyne Art Foundation, Tallahassee, FL; 2005–*Contemporary Art*, Three Person Exhibition, Museum of Florida History, Tallahassee, FL; *Reclaiming Midwives*, Smithsonian Institution, Washington DC; *Florida Watercolor Society*, Leepa-Rattner Museum of Art, St. Petersburg, FL.

Courtesy: Florida State University Museum of Fine Arts.

Selected content from the Teachers Packet for *The Story*.

Florida State University Museum of Fine Arts.

Table of Contents

Edited by: Maxie Balthrop (Viki D. Thompson Wylder)
Graphic and Cover Design by: Maxie Balthrop

For exhibition tours please contact Curator of Education, Viki D. Thompson Wylder, at (850)644-1299.

*images for education use only

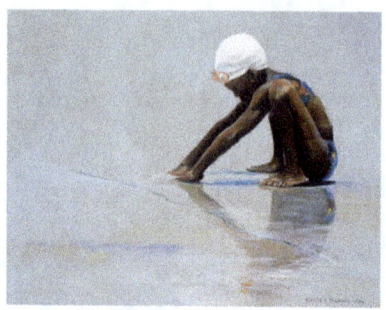

Eluster Richardson: Contemplative Places and Spaces
By Julie McBride

Description:
Students will be introduced to Eluster Richardson's life, paintings, and inspirations. The students will produce artworks stimulated by the watercolor work of Richardson.

Sunshine State Standards:
Visual Arts:
VA.A.1.2, VA.B.1.2, VA.C.1.2, VA.D.1.2, VA.E.1.2

Social Studies:
SS.A.1.2, SS.B.1.2, SS.C.1.2, SS.D.1.2, SS.E.1.2

SRA Units: Language Arts
3rd grade: Friendship, Imagination, Storytelling
4th grade: Communication
5th grade: Heritage, Journeys and Quests

Grade Level(s): 3-5

Time Needed: 3 to 4 class periods, each a 45 minute session

Objectives:
1.   To utilize artwork as a springboard for the exploration of one's own life and feelings
2.   To utilize artwork as a stimulus for analysis of artist's purpose and technique
3.   To utilize artwork as an inspiration for creativity and the self-evaluation of personal accomplishments

Materials:
Magazines
Pencils
Glue
Scissors
Watercolors
Water
Paper towels
Assorted brushes (some wide for the wash and some thinner for details)
Painting cloths
Tagboard, heavy drawing paper, or watercolor paper
Salt (optional – a small amount of salt lightly sprinkled on parts of the wet watercolor will create a white crystal effect. Eluster Richardson sometimes uses this technique in his watercolors.)

Vocabulary:
Wash
Collage
Depth: foreground, middle ground, background
Contemplative

Procedure:
1. The Artist
Tell the class about Eluster Richardson.
- Eluster Richardson (1951 – present)
- Eluster Richardson's oil paintings and watercolors may be familiar to many in the north Florida area. He was born and raised in Tallahassee. He worked for the telephone company for 30 years, always painting in his spare time. "Most people come home and watch TV. I paint." His daughter, Jasmine, is frequently featured in his paintings. Eluster uses photographs he has taken to serve as a plan for his artworks. His paintings often depict family, a place of worship, or someone in quiet reflection.

2. The Artworks
Discuss the works with the class as in the following.
1. Look at Eluster Richardson's artworks, slowly and carefully. Do the artworks have anything in common? What words would you use to describe these paintings? Loud or quiet? Hard or soft? Lively or still? Colorful or dull? Outside or inside? Joyful or sad?
2. What kind of a space or place has Eluster Richardson created in his paintings? What is the background like? Where is it? Where in the painting did Eluster place his people? What are people doing? Within the painting where are they looking? Would you like to know these people? If you were in one of these paintings where would you be? Who would you be?

3. Artworks inspired by Eluster Richardson's watercolors
Discuss with students the following. After the discussion students will follow the directions given.
1. Contemplative means thoughtful. To contemplate means to think, or to be in thought. Can you think of another word for contemplate? (reflect, ponder, consider)
2. Describe a place to which you go to be thoughtful, or to contemplate something? (tree house, church, room, library, etc.) This place could exist in your mind and not be an actual physical place that anyone else can actually see or use or visit. Use your watercolors to create a quiet place or space where you would like to be. You may put yourself in your painting or not. What colors would you choose? Which ones would you avoid? What are you thinking about, or contemplating, in your artwork?

A wash in watercolor uses a large amount of water and a small amount of color to spread across your paper. Artists frequently blend several colors in a wash. Spread water across your paper with a wide brush and then quickly add a touch of color to see what happens.

Your painting can serve as a background for drawing, painting in details, or for collaging (gluing cutout pictures) later when it is dry.

Evaluation:
Students will be led through a self-reflective discussion. Questions will be asked as follows.

1. Is your place real or imaginary?
2. What colors did you choose for your wash? Why?
3. Are you in the painting? If so what are you doing?
4. What is the most interesting part of your artwork (usually it is the part you spent the most time on)?
5. What else is in your artwork that is important to you?

Extensions:
Introduce Jonathan Green's paintings while making connections between the two artists and their works.

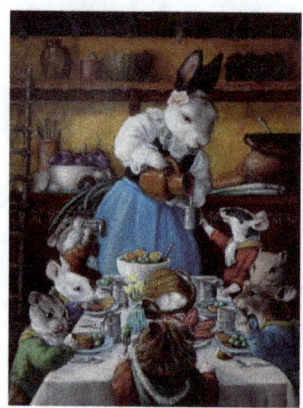

A Personified Parody: A Lesson Plan Inspired by Melinda Copper
By Julie Childers

Description:
In this lesson, students will use the art of Melinda Copper as inspiration. Students will use famous paintings to stimulate ideas for the personification of animals that exemplify the students' personalities.

Sunshine State Standards:
Language Arts:
LA.910.3.1.1, LA.910.3.2.1, LA.910.3.5.3

Visual Arts
VA.A.1.4, VA.B.1.4, VA.D.1.4

Grade Level(s): 9-12

Time Needed: Two weeks

Objectives:
1. Students will define and understand the meaning of the vocabulary below.
2. Students will view famous works of art to use as interpretation and appropriation for their parodies.
3. Students will choose famous works that seem to describe or mesh with some parts of their personalities.
4. Students will research the historical and stylistic backgrounds behind the paintings and produce short, one-page papers on the works.
5. Students will take digital images of family pets or favorite animals as a means to personify the main subjects of the paintings.
6. Students will each create a narrative diptych of two computer-generated images or paintings.
7. Students will write brief stories that describe the settings, the primary events of the paintings, as well as incidents occurring after the primary events. They will share with the class.

Materials:
Access to art historical images to use for appropriation
Acrylic or tempera painting materials
Photoshop software

Vocabulary:
Personification
Parody
Appropriation (http://en.wikipedia.org/wiki/Appropriation_art)
Diptych (optional)
Narrative

Procedure:
1. Students will be shown a PowerPoint of the works by Melinda Copper and the famous works she appropriated. Discussion will be held on the aesthetics of appropriating images. During the PowerPoint, students will compare and contrast the images and also define the vocabulary and discuss meanings and examples.
2. Students will search through art history books, art cyclopedia and other internet links to find images that best describe parts of their personalities. Each of the images must include a person or two "doing something" and must be realistic.
3. Students will research the famous paintings and the artists. They will produce written descriptions of the historical backgrounds of the works, the styles used, the original purposes, and facts about the artists. Students will include the images in their one-page papers.
4. *Homework:* Looking at the works, the students will take digital photos of family pets to match the positions of the subjects in the famous works.
5. (Option: Painting) Using the digital photos, students will draw and then paint images stylistically matching the famous works of art. . Students will substitute the animals for the people in the images. They also may add additional items to personalize their paintings.
6. (Option: Photoshop)If the students are using Photoshop, they will combine the digital images with the famous works of art. Images must be seamlessly combined so that no parts look as if they were merely added into the original works. Students will use the tools in Photoshop to do this.
7. (Option: Photoshop)To add to this lesson, students in the computer class will create second narrative images to produce diptychs. In these second images, students will tell what happened next to the subjects of the first works. The styles of the second paintings must match the first, but the subjects can be doing something different.
8. (Option: Photoshop)After the original images or diptychs are complete, short narrative stories will be written that describe the events of the images and what happened before and after them. Prewriting, drafting, and final writing will be emphasized.

Evaluation:
Students will be evaluated on the following:
1. Successful completion of the vocabulary definitions.
2. Successful completion of one-page historical background papers on the images and the artists.
3. Successful recreation of the famous works of art in the exact style of the original images with animals substituted for the main subjects.
4. Successful completion of short stories in relation to the works created.
5. Successful presentation of the narratives and images to the class.

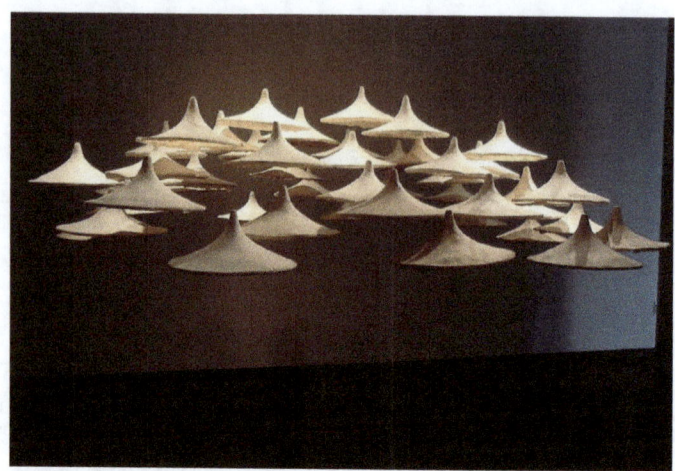

Papier Mache Installation: Inspired by Wennie Huang's *Between Heaven and Earth*
By Sunny Spillane

Description:
Students will look at Wennie Huang's installation piece, *Between Heaven and Earth*, which consists of a group of papier mache hats hung at varying head heights, suspended from the ceiling. Students will discuss her use of symbolism and connections to her ethnic identity and cultural history. Each student will then make his/her own papier mache cast of a baseball cap, using layers of colored tissue paper. When the papier mache caps are finished, students will arrange them as a group into their own class installation, with each hat hung at the child's actual head height.

Grade Level(s): 4-5

Time Needed: Five to six 30-45 minute art class periods

Sunshine State Standards:
Visual Arts:
VA.A.1.2.1-4, VA.B.1.2.1-4, VA.C.1.2.2, VA.D.1.2.3

Language Arts:
LA.C.1.2.4-5, LA.C.2.2.1-2, LA.C.3.2.1, 2, 5

Objectives:
As a result of this lesson, students will:
1. understand the unique qualities of installation art (as opposed to two dimensional art, or a single three-dimensional sculpture) by comparing and contrasting installation art with other art forms
2. understand artists' use of symbolism by discussing several different artworks that employ symbols
3. create their own artworks using papier mache
4. arrange their artworks into a group installation through teacher-mediated group discussion and experimental placement of each individual artwork into a group installation.

Materials:
20-30 second-hand or cheap baseball caps (enough for each child to use his/her own)
colored tissue paper
white drawing paper
white glue
water
bowls (for glue-water mixture)
paintbrushes
plastic food wrap
acrylic clear (or translucent) gloss medium
tape measure
scissors
monofilament (fishing line)
paper clips
KWL chart (see attached page)

Vocabulary:
Installation
Papier Mache
Cast
Culture
Ethnicity
Symbolism

Procedure:
1. Class will view Wennie Huang's installation piece, *Between Heaven and Earth*, and discuss her background and artwork, the installation medium, and her use of symbolism. The class will begin KWL charts dealing with three subjects: installation art, symbolism in art and Wennie Huang herself.
2. The teacher will demonstrate the papier mache technique (teacher pre-mix one part glue to two parts water, and divide into bowls for students to share) using layers of colored tissue paper. The students will experiment with layering different colors of tissue paper onto white drawing paper. Since tissue paper is so delicate, students will probably need to lay tissue paper onto white paper, and then "paint" glue mixture on with brushes.
3. The teacher will pass out one baseball cap to each student, cover each with plastic food wrap, and then let each student papier mache his/her cap, using the color scheme worked out in #2 above.
4. While the papier mache caps are drying, brainstorm as a class the different possibilities for arranging the caps into a class installation. Then, have students physically move into different group arrangements to visually assess the potential configuration and to discuss differences in meanings that each group configuration might convey.
5. When caps are dry, lift papier mache artworks off baseball caps and trim edges with scissors. Students may then paint over their artworks with acrylic gloss medium.

Before installation: The teacher will attach monofilament to each cap to hang each cap at that child's head height. During the project, the teacher will measure each student and note his/her height.

Evaluation:
Students will be evaluated with a 5 point rubric, as follows:
1. Student participated thoughtfully and respectfully in all class discussions and group activities; papier mache cap was well-crafted with no rough edges or loose paper pieces; student layered 2-3 different colors of tissue paper to create a harmonious, unified color scheme in the artwork.
2. Student participated respectfully in all class discussions and group activities; papier mache cap was fairly well-crafted without many rough edges or loose paper pieces; student layered 2-3 different colors of tissue paper to create a simple color scheme in the artwork.
3. Student participated in most class discussions and group activities, possibly with minor behavior issues; papier mache cap had rough edges and loose paper pieces; student either used one color of tissue paper to create or created a dissonant or haphazard color scheme.
4. Student had major behavior issues, no participation or inappropriate participation in class discussions and group activities; papier mache cap was very poorly crafted or incomplete; student was extremely thoughtless and/or careless in choosing colors for the cap.
5. Student did not participate at all due to extreme behavior issues, artwork was substantially incomplete, or student did not follow directions at all in any stage of the project.

KWL Chart

What I Know	What I Want to Know	What I Learned

kwl

CHAPTER 7

Project #4: Revisiting the "Big Idea" Approach

Project Title: *Generations*

Planning and Program Implementation: Fall 2009-Spring 2013

Exhibition Year: 2013

Co-curatorial Team:

Tallahassee, Florida K-12 inter-school art educators

- Bond Elementary School—Dr. Michelle Davidson
- Buck Lake Elementary School—Fran Kautz
- Conley Elementary School—Dr. Marcia Meale
- Deerlake Middle School—Linda Johnson
- Florida State University Schools—Eileen Baumfield Lerner (Gifted Program)
- Gilchrist Elementary School—Julie McBride
- Lincoln High School—Shannon Takacs
- Montford Middle School—Donald Sheppard
- Pineview Elementary School—Sara Chang (ESOL [English for Speakers of Other Languages]), Katharyn Jones, Kati Yates
- Raa Middle School—Teresa Coates
- Rickards High School—Jeff Distefano
- Riley Elementary School—Walter Thorner
- Sullivan Elementary School—Evelyn Pender
- Trinity Catholic School—Maria Augustyniak

Council on Culture and Arts

- Education and Exhibitions Manager—Amanda Karioth Thompson

Florida State University Museum of Fine Arts

- Curator of Education—Dr. Viki D. Thompson Wylder

Holocaust Education Resource Council
- Board Member—Eileen Baumfield Lerner

Mission San Luis
- Programming and Audience Engagement—Lindsay Douglas
- Programming and Audience Engagement—Erick Lopez

Tallahassee Community College Gallery
- Coordinator—Laura Thompson

Artworks: 70

Artists: Lauren Austin, Carrie Ann Baade, Maria Balingit, Ananda Balingit-Lefils, Trevor Bell, Aletha Butler, Judy Chicago, John Edward Cogswell, Bradley Sr. and Bradley Jr. Cooley, Lisa Kearsley Cowling, Jean Charles Duffaut (Dufo), Préfète Duffaut, Mark J. Fletcher, Linda Freeman, Hans Fuchs and Margarete Lalak, James Gibson, Hodges and Rogers Glenn, Valerie S. Goodwin, Jim Graham, William Harper, John Hathorn, Mariann B. Kearsley, Brent Kington, Samella Lewis, Robin Lewis-Wild, Henry Lin, Maya Lin, Lucy Martinez, Grace Matthews, Tom McCarthy, Arie Waldrop Meaders, Whelchel Meaders, Eluster Richardson, Faith Ringgold, Aminah Brenda Lynn Robinson, Peggy Simmons, James Wallace, Kathy E. Wilcox, Nancy Youdelman

Beginnings

Shortly after school let out for the summer in 2009, I met with Fran Kautz and Evelyn Pender, two other elementary art teachers, to do some plein air painting at a nearby lake. When the temperatures rose to the melting point we called it quits for the day, walked up the street to Fran's house to cool off, and began chatting. My 60th birthday was approaching, and I said I would like to do an exhibition with my daughter and maybe granddaughter. As Fran, Evelyn, and I talked, this idea altered and grew. Eventually the conversation coalesced around an exhibition/project proposal, and it was decided that Fran would ask the Curator of Education at the Florida State University Museum of Fine Arts (FSU MoFA) about doing another collaborative effort, this time with the theme of generational legacy. Although the idea of an exhibition with my daughter and granddaughter fell by the wayside, it inspired *Generations*, the fourth museum/school co-curation project at the FSU MoFA.

—MM

Description of the Project and Exhibition

An interesting factor in the development of these projects was the way the co-curation process helped modify and ultimately define the concepts that drove the exhibitions as well as the larger projects of which each exhibition was a part. The multitude of voices brought a depth to each exhibition and project beyond the original conception. In this case, defining the "big idea" or "enduring idea" of "legacy" was a necessary step. Through discussion the original key concept that "art legacy is passed generationally through families" changed to "art legacy is passed generationally through multiple paths." The co-curatorial team defined four paths for passing art legacy from one generation to the next by posing the essential question, "What are the paths of passage for artistic legacy?" (Thompson Wylder, 2013, p. 3). In the consideration of artists and works for this exhibition, the following four paths were determined which were accepted into the show.

Guests enter the *Generations* exhibition at the Florida State University Museum of Fine Arts.

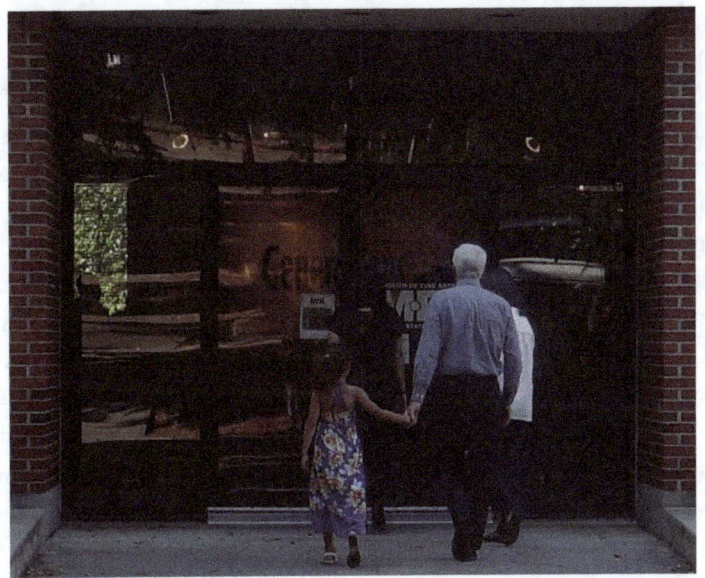

Courtesy: Florida State University Museum of Fine Arts.

- Legacy is passed from family to family.
- Legacy is passed from teacher to student.
- Legacy is passed from the first generation of an art movement to the second generation of an art movement.
- Legacy is passed from a specific culture or tradition to the society or culture-at-large.

This expanded concept for the *Generations* project provided co-curators with the advantage of a broad slate of prospective artists and media from which to make suggestions for incorporation into the show. As in the previous three projects team members curated into the exhibition the work of local and regional artists and also work by internationally recognized artists such as Faith Ringgold, Judy Chicago, and Maya Lin. Art teachers on the team often made and assessed curatorial suggestions according to the pedagogical possibilities of effective lesson planning and potential interactions with the artists selected. Middle school art teacher Linda Johnson suggested the work of blacksmiths Brent Kington and Jim Wallace for the exhibition and then partnered with elementary art teacher Fran Kautz to author a lesson plan which focused on the history of ironwork objects. Elementary school art teacher Walter Thorner suggested ceramic pieces by North Georgia potters Arie Waldrop Meaders and Whelchel Meaders and then wrote a lesson plan on the North Georgia decorated pottery tradition which includes face pots. Middle school art teacher Donald Sheppard suggested the work of three generations of African American teachers and students beginning with the local painter Eluster Richardson. Richardson admired twin artists Hodges and Rodgers Glenn with whom he studied, and the favorite professor of the Glenns, the noted printmaker Samella Lewis. Sheppard's lesson plan combined an exploration of the personality attributes of figures that inspire admiration with the artist's ability to convey such traits in print imagery. Maria Augustyniak, a K-8 art teacher, proposed a dramatic bobbin lace piece, 10′ in diameter, by artist Robin Lewis-Wild and developed a lesson plan based on furthering the legacy of lace art through the use by students of little-known lace techniques. The final *Generations* exhibition included a fascinating eclectic mix of story quilts, pottery, sculptures, metal works, prints, paintings, drawings, collages, enamels, and bobbin laces all united under the "big idea" of legacy. The exhibition featured 70 works by 42 artists.

Among the multiple components of this project, the FSU MoFA published a *Generations* catalogue. The co-curatorial team wanted to acknowledge the

During this *Generations* tour, students and chaperones enjoy the giant bobbin lace by Robin Lewis-Wild titled *Meandering*.

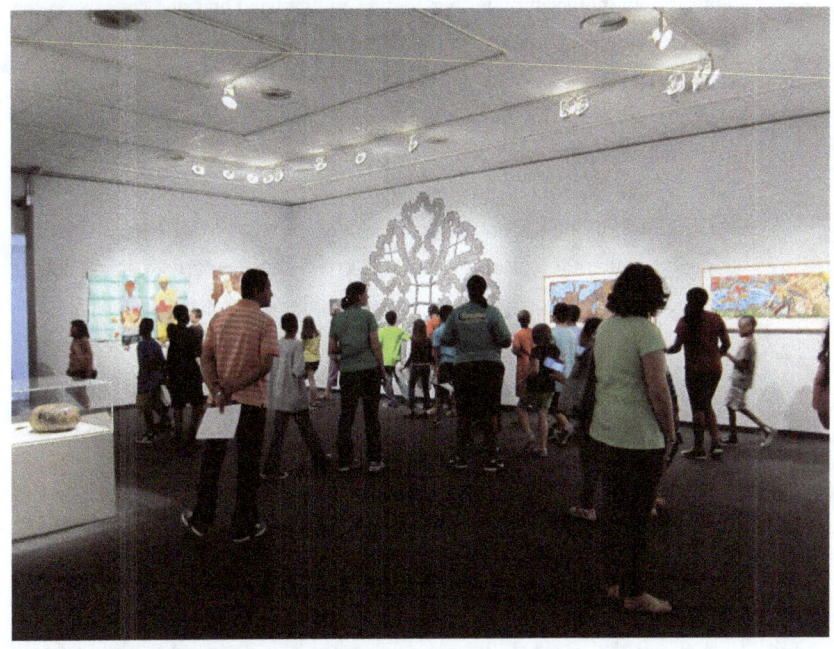

Courtesy: Florida State University Museum of Fine Arts.

paths of legacy within the exhibition and suggested...icons that run throughout the catalogue to designate inheritance—family member to family member, teacher to student, specific culture or tradition to wider culture, and first generation to the second generation of an art movement.

(Thompson Wylder, 2013, p. 3)

The catalogue design dedicated a full page to each artist. Each artist's page included photographs of the artist's work or works in the exhibition, a photograph of the artist, a legacy icon placed at the top corner of the page, and an artist's statement. The paperwork sent to artists asked them to write about the relationships of their works to the concept of legacy in the artist statements. Mark Fletcher, whose composite art incorporates natural observation, illustrative style, and poetry, wrote about the influence of his grandparents' works.

Being raised by a Holocaust-survivor parent certainly influenced my view of life and affected my art...Imagine you lost your parents, your home, and your country...My mother brought her brother in one hand and one suitcase in the other. That suitcase contained not food or clothing but her parents' artwork, poems, and letters. My grandparents' original illustrated books, recently translated letters and journals, my grandfather's poems, and my grandmother's sketches are my only communications with family who died before I was born...Much of the artwork was optimistic, whether for their children's protection or their own spiritual survival is not clear. What is clear now is that I have inherited their appreciation for their short lives. I also received their artistic lines, love of wordplay and reverence for nature as a restorative inspiration for art.

(Fletcher, 2013, p. 17)

Nancy Youdelman, who travelled from California to Tallahassee to give a more formal lecture on her work, combined incarnations of female clothing like dresses and shoes with forms of household objects in her sculpture. She wrote about the influence of her feminist college professor.

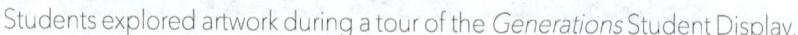

Students explored artwork during a tour of the *Generations* Student Display.

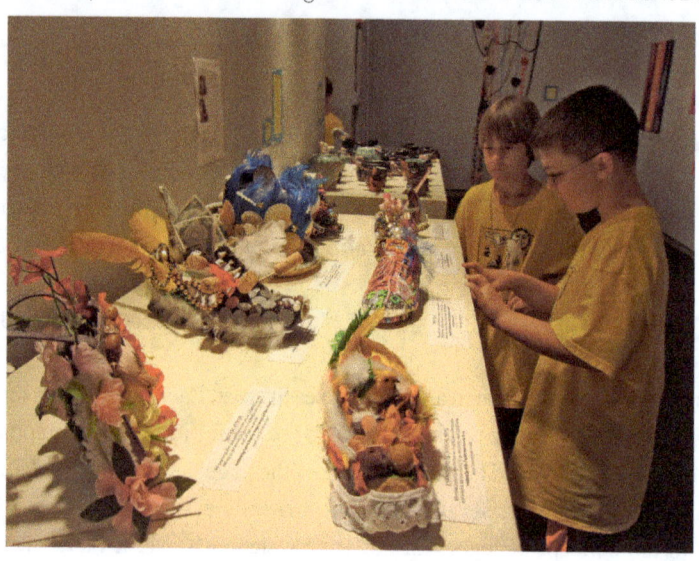

Courtesy: Marcia S. Meale.

Music students from the local school system performed at the opening reception for the *Generations* exhibition.

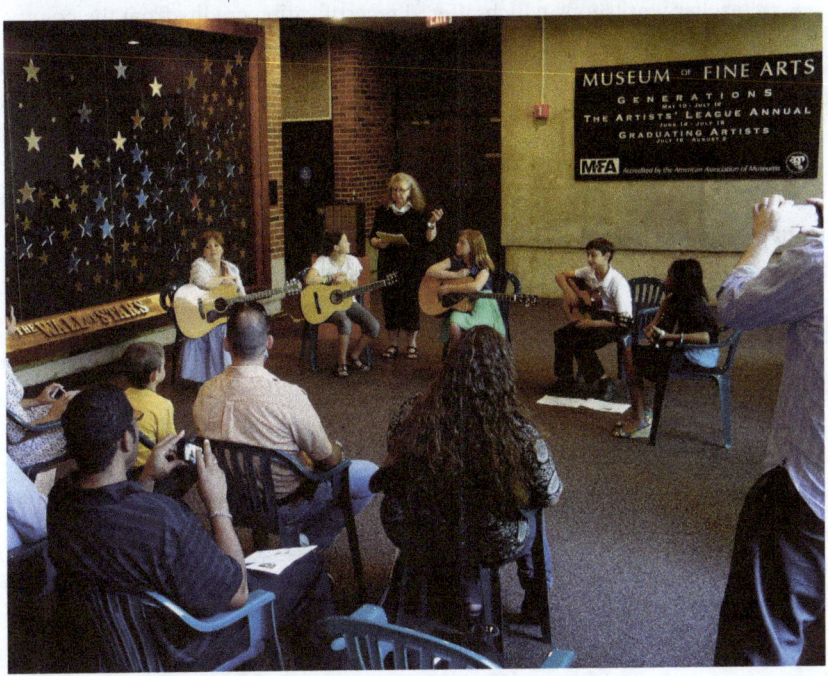

Courtesy: Florida State University Museum of Fine Arts.

Having a role model is essential to becoming an artist, and for me, having Judy Chicago for a teacher when I was at the impressionable age of 22 was phenomenal…From Judy, I got a real taste of what it was like to have artistic vision, plan what to do with it, refine it, and take it through to completion. In the process, I learned to do things that I had never done before. That is the greatest gift a teacher can give a student.

(Youdelman, 2013, p. 43)

The catalogue also furnished a brief overview of the project and named its components. Besides the exhibition, teachers' packet, and catalogue itself, other aspects, now traditional for these projects, were listed:

- a parallel K-12 student display, once again with the Tallahassee Community College Gallery hosting the overflow,

- opening reception activities, again with musical performances by students and "make and take" opportunities,
- teacher workshops which offered recertification credits from the county school system, and
- interaction between artists in the exhibition and schools.

Included in the overview was a particular-to-this-project event. Two educa-tion curators from Mission San Luis in Tallahassee joined the co-curatorial team and then sponsored a *Generations* Family Day at their site. Mission San Luis is a living history museum showcasing a reconstructed settlement. Research shows approximately 1,400 people, Spanish and Apalachee Native American, lived at this mission established between the 1560s and 1690s. Mission San Luis today makes available to the public a gallery of Apalachee and Spanish artifacts as well as Spanish Colonial art, reconstructed buildings, and expansive grounds. During the Family Day, held prior to the exhibition, "artists and artisans [including a number of *Generations* artists] demonstrated their traditions" at stations spread across the Mission San Luis setting "while offering hands-on opportunities to students and their parents" (Thompson Wylder, 2013, p. 3).

Also described in the catalogue was a *Generations* day-long teacher workshop in large part monetarily sponsored by the Tallahassee Holocaust Education Resource Council and supported in alternate ways by six other local organizations. Offered a month before the exhibition, the workshop

> featured Ela Weissberger[,]...a Terezin survivor and performer in *Brundibar*, the children's opera staged at the concentration camp [Weissberger] honored the legacy of her own art teacher at Terezin, Friedl Dicker-Brandeis. Dicker-Brandeis saved the work[s] of many of her students by hiding them in several suitcases before she was sent to Auschwitz and her death.
>
> (Thompson Wylder, 2013, p. 3)

Weissberger likewise became the special guest and speaker at a Holocaust Remembrance program at the Florida State University Schools, a K-12 school represented on the *Generations* co-curatorial team.

Teachers attended two other *Generations* teacher workshop events. The first took place eight months before the exhibition and the second occurred several weeks after the show opened. For the first workshop the co-curatorial committee organized an

Artist Mariann Kearsley worked with students during a *Generations* event, a Family Day held onsite at Mission San Luis, a partner institution.

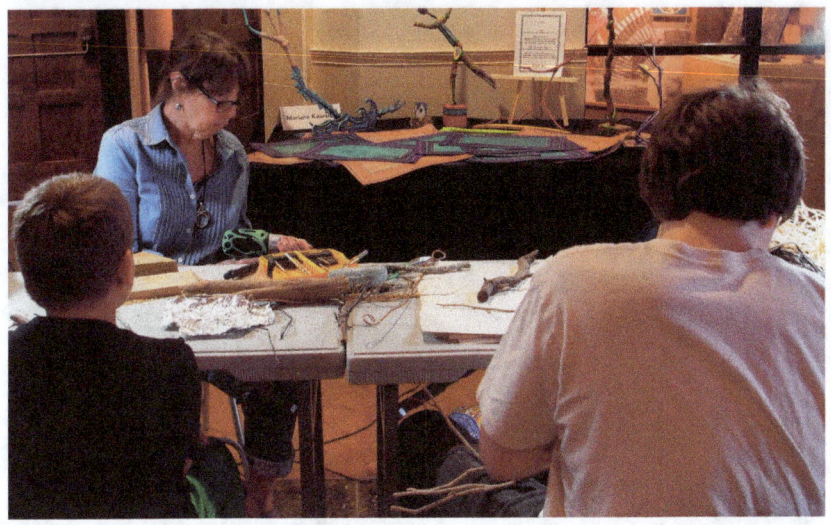

Courtesy: Marcia S. Meale.

exhibition of artworks at the FSU MoFA which were painted, sculpted, or otherwise produced by the co-curatorial committee educators themselves with samples of art-work by their students. Titled *In Our Steps*, the exhibition was touted on the show's poster as "the passing of skills through art from teachers to students." During the workshop, teachers, students, and families were invited to a reception with hands-on make-and-take activities. A presentation with catalogue signing by Faith Ringgold, a former K-12 teacher and the internationally known inventor of story quilts, followed the reception. Three of her story quilts were hung in the *In Our Steps* exhibition. Her *Ancestors Quilt* also appeared in the *Generations* exhibition eight months later.

The second workshop event, billed as a teacher institute titled *Working with Generations Artists*, extended over two days and featured hands-on sessions with seven of the artists from the *Generations* exhibition. A final session of the institute featured an in-person visit to the bronze sculpture studio of a father and son artist team whose work also appeared in the exhibition. The Leon County School District approved teacher attendance at the Weissberger event, *In Our Steps*, and the *Working with Generations Artists* institute to assist teachers in the accumulation of credits toward recertification.

During a *Generations* Teacher Workshop, teachers visited the studio of Bradley Cooley, Sr. and Jr.

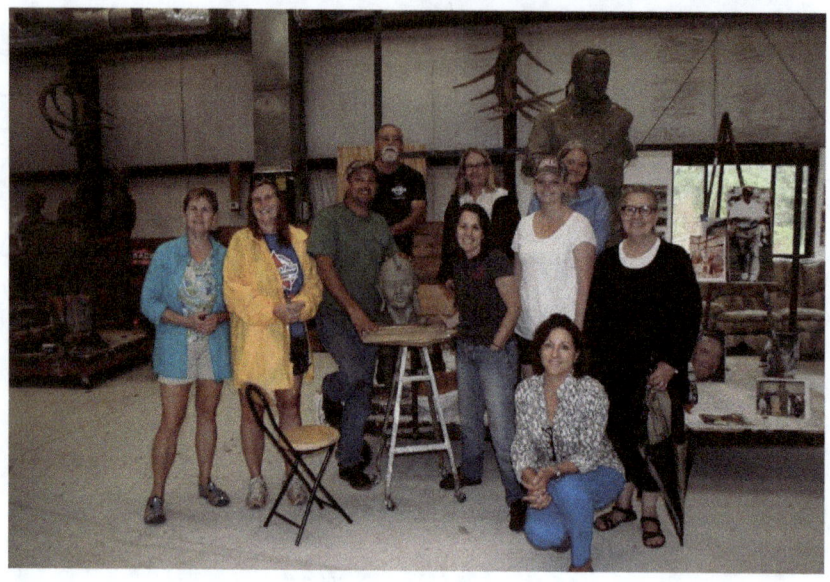

Courtesy: Marcia S. Meale.

Not listed in the catalogue was a workshop presentation given in October of 2013 after the *Generations* project was completed. Co-curatorial team members presented an overview of the project at the Florida Art Education Association Conference. During the Conference workshop, they gave special focus to the Weissberger event as well as methods to use with students for the analysis of works during tours. Also not listed in the catalogue was recertification credit given to co-curatorial team members through arrangement with the county school district for their participation in the *Generations* project.

Exhibition artist interactions were a planned and integral part of all five co-curated projects. As the team of co-curators suggested and selected works for exhibitions, they considered potential interactions by teachers and students with the artists of those works. These interactions took multiple forms. Often they occurred at schools, but on occasion artists travelled on field trips with students. Other formats included artists meeting students at a local historical site, interacting at the FSU MoFA during tours or other scheduled events, or making contact via email. From a school standpoint, field trips cost both money and time which are generally in very short supply. Through the years grant money often financed buses for students' visits to the FSU MoFA for tours and other events. But the impact on students of a visit to the class or school by their "very own artist" (that is how the students feel) usually cannot be replicated in another way. Artists' visits to schools magnified the number and kind of interactions students experienced with the artists they studied, and in many cases an artist's visit to a school was the only way an interaction was possible.

Planned artist interactions provided exciting experiences for students and frequently for teachers and parents as well. As described, during *The Story* project the artist Mark Fletcher accompanied elementary students to a state park to prepare for writing and illustrating narrative poetry. Carrie Ann Baade, a *Generations* project artist, who visited a high school and an elementary school, also set up a station in the museum during the opening reception of *Generations* to sell prints of her work for an inexpensive price with proceeds, in part, donated to a school to help offset their cost of art supplies. During the sale she talked with students and their parents informally one on one. At times artists invited classes to join them at the FSU MoFA during the setup of installation work. Caroline Madden, an artist featured in *Visions of the North Florida Environment* project, even invited students to help her place her materials in one of her installations. As part of the *Generations* project the curatorial team arranged for teachers, their students, and parents at five schools to meet Aletha Butler, a second-generation Florida Highwayman. At this event, which took place on a Saturday on the grounds of the *Generations* partner museum, the Mission San Luis historical site, the audience heard her talk about her work, explain her relationship to the Florida African American artist group the Highwaymen, and demonstrate her plein air painting style. After her presentation students were invited to ask questions and paint with the artist. Supplies were provided and placed ready for use on a nearby table. Parents were asked to assist their children, and art teachers circulated among the working students as did the artist, and unexpectedly as did her artist father, Robert.

When Ms. Butler arrived in Tallahassee, her mother and her father, Robert Butler, a first-generation Highwayman, traveled with her. Curatorial team member Dr. Marcia Meale remembers the Butler family's interactions with teachers, students, and parents as they unfolded.

> The night Aletha Butler arrived I joined her, another teacher, the museum educator, and several others for dinner. The others were Aletha's father Robert Butler and her mother Dorothy. They decided to join Aletha at the last minute. Robert Butler

Second generation Highwayman artist, Aletha Butler, assisted students in a plein air artist interaction.

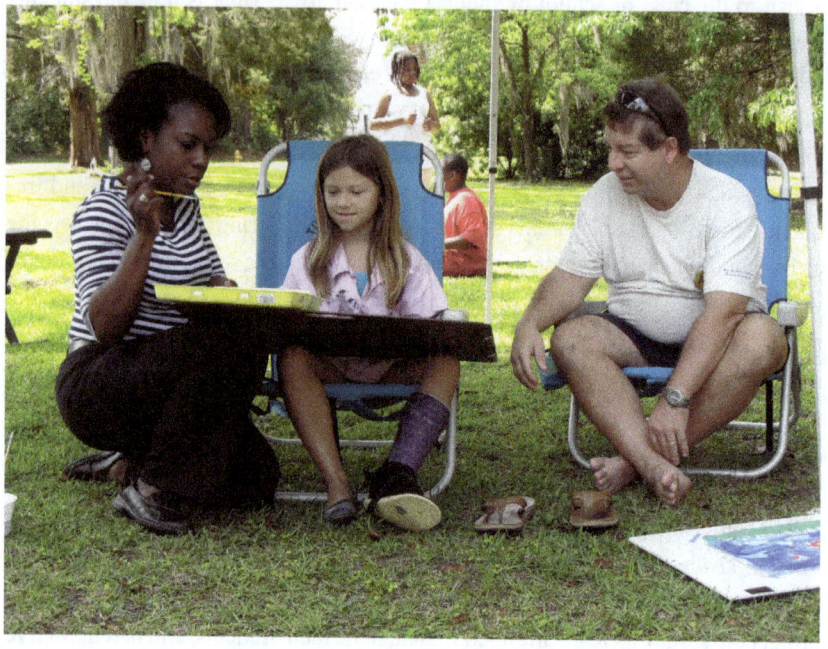

Courtesy: Marcia S. Meale; and the artist, who wishes to dedicate the memory of her participation to her father, Robert Butler (1943-2014).

was an internationally known artist and one of the original Florida Highwaymen. That evening he told me his story, the way he became a professional painter. He grew up in the Lake Okeechobee area working in the orange groves and later at a hospital. "One evening I was mopping the floors in the hospital hallway and I looked out the window. There was the most beautiful sunset. I knew I needed to paint it, that I needed to be a painter." According to Robert he went home and talked to his wife Dorothy. She agreed to give him six months to work as a painter. If at the end of six months he could at least match the money he earned working in the hospital she would accept a permanent career change. He did, and a number of his nine children followed in his footsteps, including Aletha who was the eighth child.

That evening Robert Butler described the Highwaymen's way of working. During the week they would work as fast as they could often sharing ideas and techniques for painting faster or better. They developed a system to speed things along. They sold paintings from the 1950s to the 1980s along the roadside on the weekends often for as little as $25 each. Butler described also going door to door to doctor's offices. He stated his most popular painting had a green sky. In answer to my surprise, he gave me the formula for the painting. His wife provided an envelope on which I wrote as he spoke. That evening I went home and painted two versions of his formula, one mathematically accurate and the other more intuitively, using his 1/3rd formula for the sky.

On Saturday, the following day, art teachers, students, and parents from five elementary schools, including my school, met at Mission San Luis for the plein air painting session featuring Robert's daughter Aletha. I brought my acrylic paints, brushes, and my two versions of the green sky on canvases and asked Robert, in concert with the other host art teachers, what was next. He chose the intuitive canvas and proceeded to work on down the painting surface to demonstrate his techniques. The painting was almost completed when students started to arrive. From there the focus of the day naturally switched to the students.

Aletha Butler gave a short presentation and demonstration to the students followed by a student plein air painting session. Her father joined in as well. Both artists, one representing the first-generation Highwaymen art movement and the other representing the second-generation Highwaymen art movement, worked side by side with the students. One of the African American families from my school was particularly moved by the experience, stating how meaningful it was to them to have the "real artists" working side by side with the children.

Aletha's and Robert's presentation had directly touched students from five schools. But after the Saturday event, we rotated the green sky painting along with fan brushes among classes in the county. The story of the green sky painting continued the Butlers' impact for both art teachers and students as the work passed from school to school. (M. Meale & V. D. T. Wylder, personal communication with a co-curatorial committee member from J. Michael Conley Elementary School at Southwood, M. Meale, July 10, 2020)

As with *The Story* exhibition, to further facilitate student interactions with the art during the *Generations* exhibition the FSU MoFA financed a number of buses

First generation Highwayman artist, Robert Butler, demonstrated to a curatorial member during a plein air artist interaction.

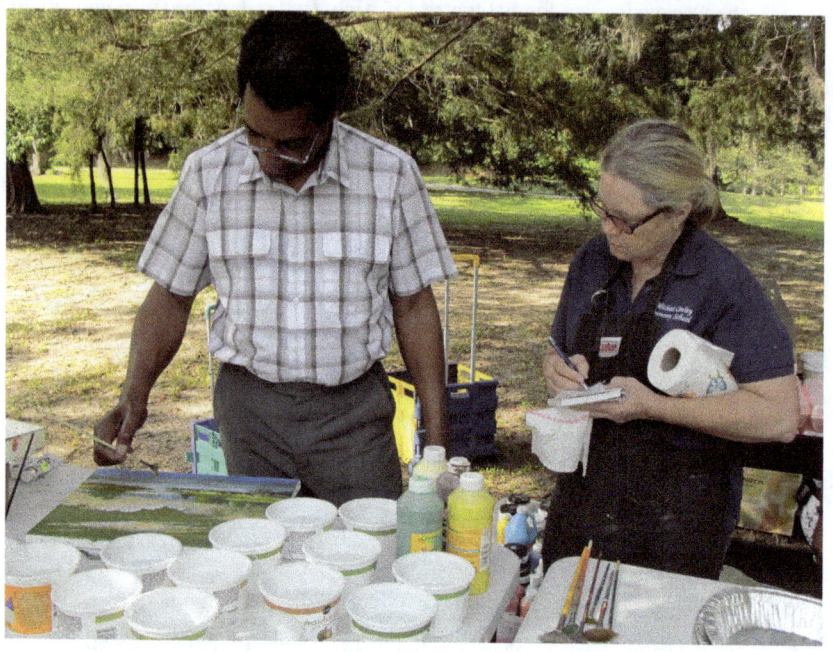

Courtesy: Marcia S. Meale.

through grant funds to bring students to the museum for tours. These hands-on and minds-on museum visits offered some especially enjoyable moments. After a discussion of the generational implications within an image by Eluster Richardson coupled with discussion of the artist's generational relationship to other artists in the exhibition, a tour for elementary students featured a kinesthetic reenactment of the artist's image which showed a trio of young African American girls playing jump rope. Two girls in the image twirled the rope while the third girl, with legs pulled up high in the air, skipped the rope as it touched the ground. Numerous photos were taken as trios of students on the tour pantomimed the image. Afterward, the students talked about the experience of reenacting the action of the painting and the way it affected their relationship to the image and the artist. Photos were sent to teachers digitally to share with their students.

The *Generations* student display at the FSU MoFA featured response work by 622 students from 14 schools. During tours, students particularly liked seeing

Students experienced a painting through kinetic reenactment of a work by Eluster Richardson titled *Double Dutch* during this *Generations* tour.

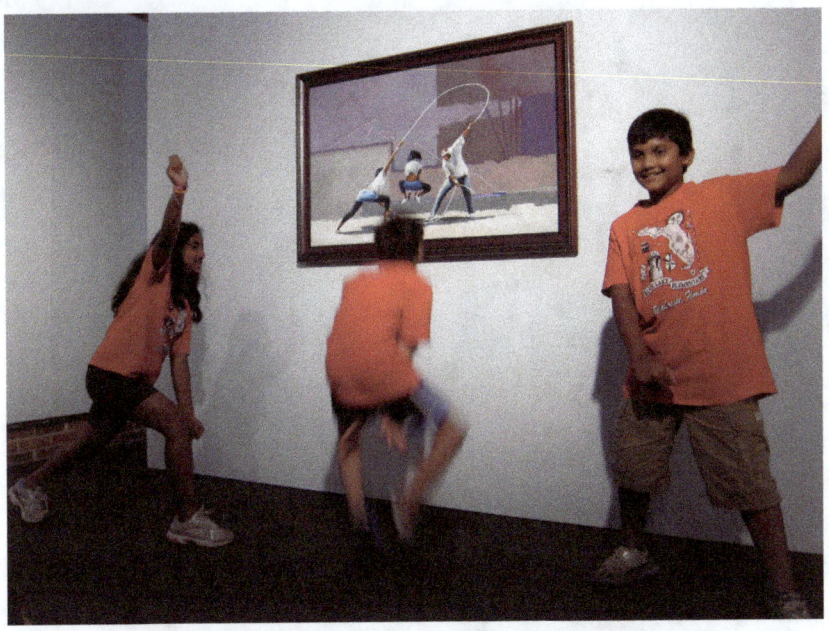

Courtesy: Florida State University Museum of Fine Arts. Photo: Yi Wen Wei.

the work of other students. For the *Generations* tours, the work by a group of Pineview Elementary students under the direction of art teacher Kathryn Jones became a highlight. Jones focused on cultural heritage with her students by reading and discussing a Hawaiian legend in her classroom. To memorialize the legend and introduce it to the audience of the exhibition, her students made large papier mâché puppet heads on sticks of the main characters and painted a modest mural-sized setting for the puppetry action. These were displayed theatrically in the FSU MoFA with the puppets occupying a large, stage-like pedestal placed in front of the mural. Jones, however, had taken the project a step further. A video was recorded as her students acted out the story using the puppets and the painted mural-sized setting. During tours, students would sit on the floor to discuss the legend and its relationship to *Generations*, identify and describe the puppets and setting, and watch the video.

For the *Generations* Student Display, students at Pineview Elementary built puppets and a background setting for the production of a video in which they performed the retelling of a Hawaiian legend.

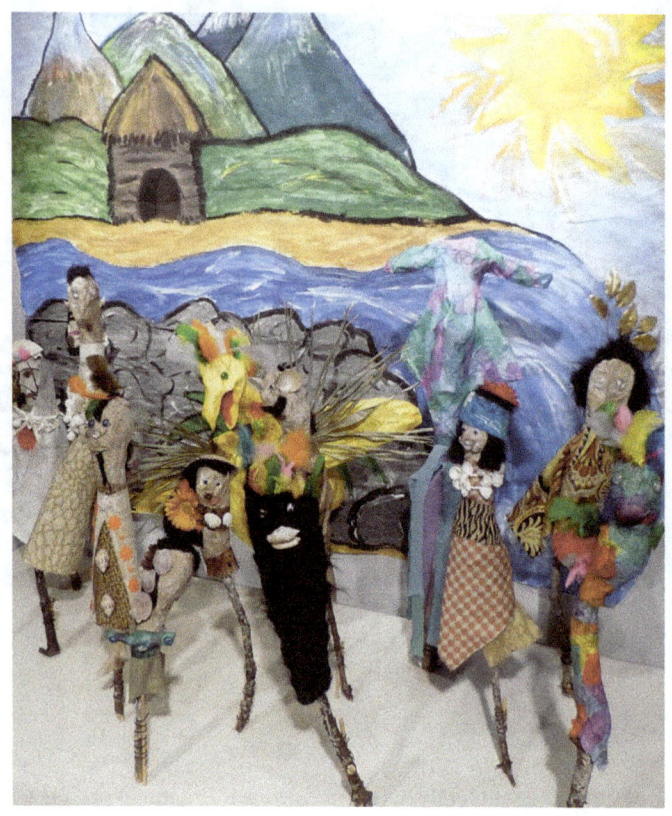

Courtesy: Florida State University Museum of Fine Arts.

The "Big Idea" Approach and *Generations*

Generations easily fell into the "Big Idea" (Stewart & Walker, 2005) philosophy and was approached as such. Certification literature by the National Board for Professional Teaching Standards and Stewart and Walker's book, as mentioned in conjunction with *The Story* project, stress building instructional units using "Big Ideas" or "enduring ideas" that span time, place, and cultures and emphasize the connection of lessons within those units to gain deeper understanding. Projects such as *Generations* facilitated making connections between and among lessons that in the past would have been taught individually unrelated to previous or following instruction. The expansion of Discipline-Based Art Education (DBAE) by Stewart and Walker in their book did not preclude their recommendation of continued use of the core DBAE elements—artmaking, art history, art criticism, and aesthetics. The state standards and thereby art teachers' instructional practices also continued to incorporate DBAE elements, but due to the influences of the National Board process and Stewart and Walker's approach, the DBAE elements became part of an expanded perspective that emphasized understanding and meaning making.

The aforementioned "Big Idea" or "enduring idea" of "legacy" connected all lesson plans contained in the teachers' packet for this exhibition. All lesson plans also followed a format which utilized a related and more complexly stated "Big Idea" as well as "Enduring Understandings" found in Florida's Next Generation Sunshine State Standards.

- The *Big Idea*: Historical and Global Connections: Experiences in the arts foster understanding, acceptance, and enrichment among individuals, groups, and cultures from around the world and across time.
- The *Enduring Understanding 1*: Through study in the arts, we learn about and honor others and the worlds in which they live(d).
- The *Enduring Understanding 2*: The arts reflect and document cultural trends and historical events and help explain how new directions in the arts have emerged (Florida Department of Education, 2014).

The "Big Idea" garnered from the New Generation Sunshine State Standards was applied consistently across all *Generations* lesson plans published in the teachers' packet while the choice of an Enduring Understanding varied between the two listed above. Benchmarks were individualized to distinct lessons, and specific essential questions were written for each lesson to focus and inspire instruction.

Art teachers used the "Big Idea" of "legacy" within the *Generations* project to connect lessons over the course of a semester or an entire school year. In the past, such a time frame often produced unrelated or random lessons. Although the expansion of the meaning of the term "legacy" or "generations" contributed to the variety of artworks included in the final show, the expansion of the term also facilitated making connections in the art classroom between various art media and artists. Dr. Marcia Meale's plans for her fifth-grade class at Conley Elementary demonstrated this connectivity.

> One of the highlights of the year for my 5th graders is using clay. I introduced them to the work of Lucy Martinez, a San Ildefonso Pueblo potter featured in the show, and the related history of her style of pottery. Lucy is known for her black on black ceramics made famous in the 1920s by Maria and Julian Martinez, Lucy's reported in-laws (relationship unverified). Some accounts indicate that Lucy's husband and partner ceramicist, Richard, was the adopted son of Maria and Julian. Maria and Julian invented a way to create patterns on their outdoor fired pieces using a matte and gloss black finish. Maria was one of four southwest potters recognized for keeping alive the traditional Native American ways of making pottery.

> The focal enduring understanding chosen for the lesson—to learn about and honor the traditions and culture of others, in this case Native American culture/heritage and its preservation—provided an example of the expansion of the meaning of "legacy" or "generations," that is the passing of legacy from a specific culture or tradition to the society or culture-at-large. Other objectives, of course, focused on using clay to make a vessel. Fire laws required the use of an electric kiln and other elementary school limitations dictated an imitation of the black on black process using a black underglaze on the whole pot with a clear gloss glaze painted over specific areas to create a design. Students, however, studied the traditional San Ildefonso way of forming the pottery and achieving the black on black effect during firing of which manure was a key and memorable ingredient.

> Students studied historic San Ildefonso designs but also examined their own rituals, traditions, and heritage so that their designs involved the choice of personal symbols or Native American motifs or both. This proximity of cultural choice for designs deepened meaning and made the work created more relevant to each student. By the end of the unit, students held a broader understanding of a specific culture that inspired them to respect and keep aspects of their own cultural heritage alive. About 10 percent of my students and their parents hailed from other parts of the world and represented a cross-section of cultures including: South American, Mexican, Puerto Rican, East Indian, Pakistani, Chinese, Korean and African. The lesson plans of the unit connected artmaking to the history of Native American art and aesthetics and to the lives of students who inhabit a diverse

> contemporary society and who create using multiple, rich, multi-cultural forms, emblems, and influences. (Meale & Wylder, personal communication, 2020)

In the next lesson Dr. Meale switched to painting, but she continued exploring the "Big Idea" of "legacy" or "generations." The teachers' packet, distributed at the beginning of the school year, contained both lesson plans and a CD with images of all the artworks in the exhibition. By using the Florida Highwaymen images on the CD and the Florida Highwaymen website, students were again able to explore the idea of generational legacy, this time from the first generation of an art movement to the second generation of an art movement. The original Highwaymen, as already described in the description of Robert and Aletha Butler's trip to Tallahassee, were a group of African American men and one woman, Mary Ann Carroll, who primarily sold colorful landscape paintings to tourists along Florida's roadways. James Gibson was an original or first-generation Highwayman represented in the *Generations* exhibition and Aletha Butler represented the second generation of the art movement.

The final two lessons for Meale's fifth graders included a collage and a collaborative large-scale crocheted piece. Based on Nancy Youdelman's mixed media relief collage, *Wooden Valentine*, students explored an essential question through Youdelman's chosen medium of collage: How does our heritage live on through ourselves? Students learned that Youdelman studied under Judy Chicago, so her work reflected a teacher-to-student relationship. The last essential question addressed the passing of legacy from a specific culture or tradition to the culture-at-large and asked: How can we create unique art pieces while using and interpreting established processes? This question emanated from the study of the circular piece by Robin Lewis-Wild, spanning 10' in diameter, done in bobbin lace. The study resulted in a cooperative work by these fifth graders done in crochet, an alternative textile tradition. This series of fifth-grade lessons focused on diverse artists, used a wide variety of materials, and examined three of the four pathways of generational legacy highlighted in the exhibition.

By the opening of the *Generations* exhibition, 26 schools had participated in the overall project in some way. The *Generations* Student Display at both venues—the FSU MoFA and the Tallahassee Community College Gallery—included the work of 818 K-12 students. The 3 teacher workshop events brought a total of 252 participants. Artist interactions reached about 450 students, and public *Generations* receptions brought a total of approximately 1,000 attendees. During the first weeks of the exhibition until school closed for the summer, tours averaged over 400 students per week. This audience composed of students, teachers, and parents explored and experienced the four pathways of the "Big Idea" of generational legacy—from family member to family member, from teacher to student, from the first generation of an art movement to the second generation of an art movement, and from a specific culture or tradition to the society or culture-at-large. They interacted with the multiple programs of the *Generations* project to construct personal interior understandings of the topic and to conclude their own meanings, all in accordance with Hein's dictum for a constructivist museum.

Flyer to advertise a teacher workshop during the *Generations* project, registration page.

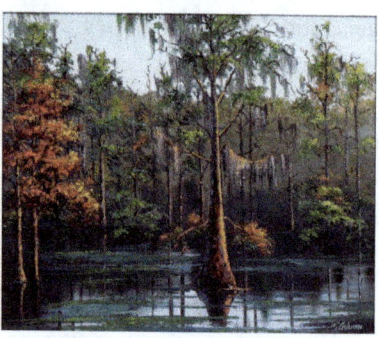

To Register: Send by Friday, May 31

You must fill out the following form and send it via United States Post Office mail or fax to the following address. No e-mail registration will be accepted.
    Attn: Viki D. Thompson Wylder
        FSU Museum of Fine Arts
        Room 250 FAB, 530 West Call Street
        Tallahassee, FL 32306-1140
        Fax: 850-644-7229

I plan to attend the Teacher Institute, *Working with Generations Artists*.
Name: _____
School: _____
Day 1 (6/5): _____ Day 2 (6/6) : _____
Phone #: _____
E-mail: _____

Minimal supplies needed: registered teachers will be notified about the supplies needed for these sessions by Saturday, June 1.

Cosponsors in alphabetical order: Council on Culture and Arts (COCA), Holocaust Education Resource Council (HERC), Mission San Luis, Museum of Fine Arts (MoFA) at Florida State University.

Reverse: Mark Fletcher, *Swamp Music*; Eluster Richardson, *Double Dutch*; Maria Balingit, *Homer*, Ananda Balingit Le-Fils, *Olivia and Her Father*; Mariann Kearsley, *Meditation #2, Holiness Reconsidered*, Kathleen Wilcox, *Sun Heron House*, Valerie Goodwin, *Lake Ella*, Bradley Sr. & Bradley Jr. Cooley, *Mortar and Pestle*. Cover: James Gibson, *Lake Bradford*, Collection: Tallahassee Museum, Courtesy: Tallahassee Museum.

Working with *Generations* Artists

sessions with
Maria Balingit & Ananda Balingit-LeFils
Bradley Sr. & Bradley Jr. Cooley
Mark Fletcher
Valerie Goodwin
Mariann Kearsley
Eluster Richardson
Kathleen Wilcox

This institute is just for you! Have fun! Be an art student again.

Free/TEC Credit Available
Questions: Viki D. Thompson Wylder

Courtesy: Florida State University Museum of Fine Arts.

Hand-out for parents to advertise a *Generations* plein air painting artist interaction with Aletha Butler.

Painting with
Aletha Butler
A Second Generation Highwayman

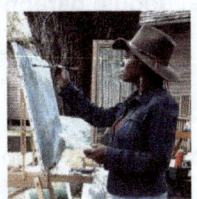

What is this activity?
Aletha Butler, a second generation Highwayman artist, will talk about her artwork, her relationship to the famous and historical Florida Highwaymen artists of the 1950s to 1980s, and will demonstrate her painting style.

In addition, she invites students to ask her questions, but also to paint with her! Paints and other materials will be provided.

This is a wonderful opportunity to personally experience the work of an artist and a connection to history!

Right: Aletha Butler, *Blue Heron*,
         2011, oil on canvas, 10" x 20".

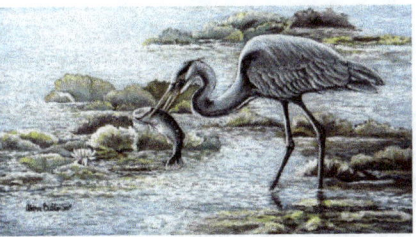

Where will this happen?
- Place: Mission San Luis
- Directions: Head west on Tennessee Street; go through the intersection of Ocala and Tennessee; Mission San Luis is on the right.

When will this happen?
- Saturday, April 27
- First, meet the rest of the school group in the main building at 9:30 am.
- The group will then move to an outdoor location for painting.
- Painting with Aletha Butler will take place from 10:00 am - 12:00 noon.

What will parents do?
Parents will act as painting assistants to their children:
- to encourage children
- to provide supportive words to children (no matter the results!)
- to get more paint
- to get water as needed

- to get paper towels and other supplies
- to assist with clean-up at the end

What should parents and children bring and wear?
- bug spray/repellent if desired
- comfortable clothes for the weather and outdoor space
- clothes on which you and your child don't mind paint marks or stains
- blankets and/or folding camp stools

Is there a fee or is the activity free?
Mission San Luis requires:
- that you stay with your children to avoid the charge of an entry fee
- that you and your children stay in the activity area to avoid the charge of an entry fee

Who were the Highwaymen? Who is Aletha Butler?
The Highwaymen were a group of 26 Florida artists, all African American, who painted the Florida landscape, particularly its wetlands. From the 1950s to the 1980s they sold their work on the side of the road or went door to door. Together it is estimated they painted a total of about 200,000 works.

Eventually critics noticed they had captured iconic or symbolic images of the tropical quality of the state. Highwaymen work is now featured in documentaries and collected by individuals and museums. All have been inducted into the Florida Hall of Fame. Some critics say they participated in the last American art movement.

Aletha Butler's father, Robert Butler, was one of the 26 Highwaymen. Aletha remembers that she and her siblings used to go with their father on "excursions" outside to paint. She notes that he supported nine children as a painter and all the children in her family grew up to be artists in their own right.

Aletha wrote, "like my father, I draw inspiration from Florida's unique landscapes, flora and fauna." Aletha Butler's work can be seen in the *Generations* exhibition at the Florida State University Museum of Fine Arts to open on May 10.

Who are sponsors for this event?
This event is part of the larger *Generations* project which includes an exhibition, catalogue, reception, field trips, and interactions with artists in the exhibition. The project is sponsored by:
- Florida State University Museum of Fine Arts (FSU MoFA)
- Mission San Luis
- Council on Culture and Arts (COCA)
- Holocaust Education Resource Council (HERC)

Courtesy: Florida State University Museum of Fine Arts; and the artist, who wishes to dedicate the memory of her participation to her father, Robert Butler (1943-2014).

Selected pages from the *Generations* catalogue.

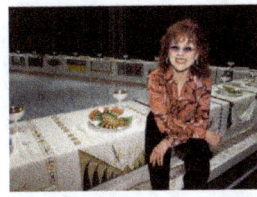

Judy Chicago's role as teacher is important. She established the first feminist art programs in the United States in the 1970s; teaching and art were interwoven during segments of her career. Her pedagogy ranges from the development of feminist methods for the studio classroom to larger community interactions such as her work in 2003 in Pomona and Claremont, California. Chicago taught at several institutions including Duke and Vanderbilt.

Her impact as a teacher was shown with the creation of Womanhouse in 1972. The female student/ teacher installation explored women's roles during a time of limited feminist scholarship. Chicago revisited the Womanhouse concept thirty years later with At Home: A Kentucky Project, a female/male student installation which reflected evolving feminist theory. Her autobiography, Through the Flower, My Struggle as a Woman Artist, demonstrates Chicago's insistence on professional work by her students, work which carries a strong message. Chicago's art itself is instructive. Her Through the Flower image is iconic, symbolizing Chicago's process of self-actualization as a female which suggests a potentially similar process for other women.—KDC (Kimber D. Chewning)

Judy Chicago maintains a studio in New Mexico near Albuquerque. She is represented by ACA Galleries in New York City, www.acagalleries.com, David Richard Contemporary, Santa Fe, New Mexico, www.davidrichardcontemporary.com, and Nye+Brown, Los Angeles, California, www.nyeplusbrown.com.

Selected Awards/Exhibitions: 2012/2013 – Judy Chicago: Upsetting the Applecart, Solo Exhibition, Ben Uri, The London Jewish Museum of Art, London, UK; 2012 – ReViewing Powerplay, Solo Exhibition, David Richard Gallery, Santa Fe, NM. 2009 – Dinner Party Curriculum created by the artist in collaboration with Constance Gee, art educator and Through the Flower Board Member, recently gifted to Pennsylvania State University to maintain online and with Chicago's art education archive to be integrated into teaching and research; developed after the permanent housing of the Dinner Party in 2007 as part of the Elizabeth A. Sackler Center for Feminist Art at the Brooklyn Museum, NYC. 2004 – Lion of Judah Award, Washington, DC (one of numerous grants and awards). 2000 – Honorary Doctorate in Fine Arts, Smith College, Northampton, MA (one of five honorary doctorates).

[above] Judy Chicago with The Dinner Party. Photo © Donald Woodman. [below] © Judy Chicago, Through the Flower, 1991, serigraph, 31 x 30.5 inches. Photo © Donald Woodman.

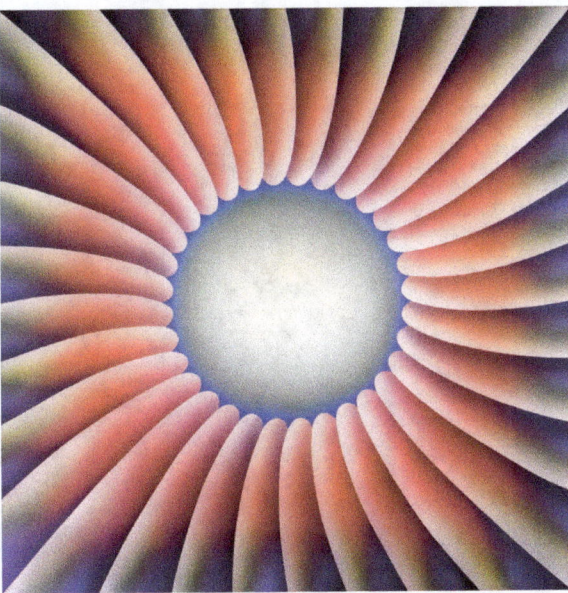

Courtesy: Florida State University Museum of Fine Arts.

James Gibson

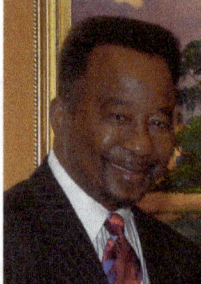

Photo credit: Courtesy of the Florida Division of Cultural Affairs.

In the 1950s James Gibson and other teens did odd jobs for Florida painter A.E. "Bean" Backus in exchange for art lessons. Backus encouraged them saying "talent was talent, no matter what color the artist" recalls Gibson. "It was probably the nicest thing anyone has ever said to me." Several of Backus's students were among the original Highwaymen, selling colorful landscapes to tourists along Florida's roadways.

As working artists, Mr. Gibson and other Highwaymen shared tips and "would get together and paint for days, inspiring, motivating, and laughing with each other." Of his friends Alfred Hair and Harold Newton, he remembers, "Alfred wanted to paint with Harold Newton because Newton could paint better. Harold wanted to paint with Alfred because Alfred could paint faster. I painted with Harold and Alfred to learn from them. They painted with me because I was the best salesman."

Mr. Gibson continues to share his knowledge, teaching young artists through summer camps, the federal Weed and Seed program, and as a visiting scholar at the university level.—GW (Gwendolyn Waldorf, Assistant Curator, Tallahassee Museum utilizing Florida Highwaymen, James Gibson, www.highwaymenjamesgibson.com)

James Gibson is a full-time artist and maintains the James Gibson Studio at 4604 Matanzas Avenue in Fort Pierce, Florida 34946. http://www.highwaymenjamesgibson.com; jg@highwaymenjamesgibson.com.

Selected Awards/Exhibitions: 2008 – May-October, Exhibition, Florida House, Washington, DC. 2007 – Arts Recognition Award, Florida Department of State, Division of Cultural Affairs, Tallahassee, FL. 2005 – Chosen as Ambassador of the Arts, by Florida First Lady Columba Bush in collaboration with Arts for a Complete Education/Florida Alliance for the Arts. 2004 – Induction into the Florida Artist's Hall of Fame. 2000 – Exhibition, Supreme Court, Tallahassee, FL.

James Gibson, *Lake Bradford*, oil on canvas, 25.9 x 29.5 inches. Collection: Tallahassee Museum. Photo courtesy of the Tallahassee Museum.

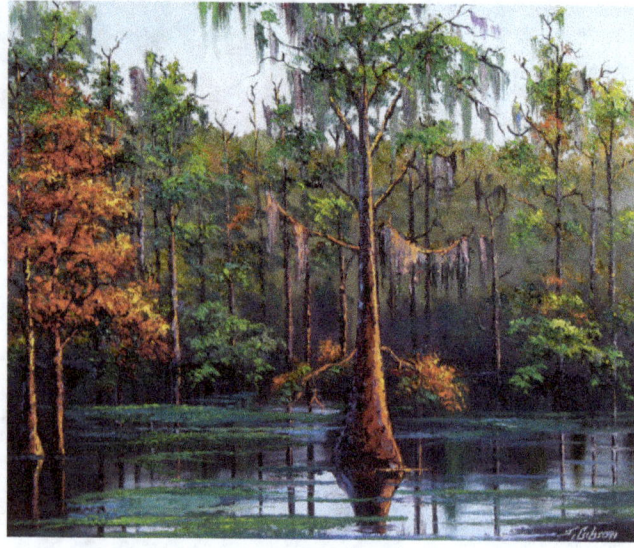

Generations ──   **20**

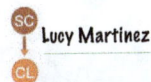

Lucy Martinez

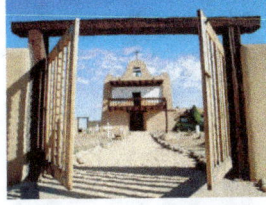

Lucy Martinez lived her life as a potter at the San Ildefonso Pueblo in New Mexico creating black-on-black ceramics made famous by Maria Martinez in the 1920s. Due to her reputation as an excellent potter, Dr. Edgar Lee Hewett, director of the Museum of New Mexico, enlisted Maria Martinez to "recreate" pre-historic ceramics discovered during an archeological excavation in 1908. Throughout several years of experimentation, Maria, in partnership with her husband Julian, who painted the ceramics that Maria shaped, perfected the now famous San Ildefonso black-on-black ceramic style. Maria and Julian invented the technique that allowed black-on-black ceramics to have both a matte and glossy finish. Lucy Martinez continued in this tradition until her death in the 1980s, also working in conjunction with her husband, Richard, who is said to be the adoptive son of Maria. Today, their legacy endures with Lucy and Richard's daughter, Alice, and Alice's son, Ruben, who continue to produce black-on-black ceramics in this traditional manner at San Ildefonso.—*ARMJ (Amber R. M. Jones)*

Lucy Martinez was artistically active from 1930 until her death in the 1980s. Traditional San Ildefonso pottery uses the coil method and is fired in outdoor kilns. Located just north of Santa Fe, the San Ildefonso Pueblo runs along the Rio Grande. Apparently inhabited since about 1300 A.D., it is one of the smaller pueblos in New Mexico. Records show a population somewhere between approximately 500 and 1500. It is, however, one of the most well-known due to the renowned signature black-on-black pottery produced there.

Private collectors throughout the country own most of the work by Lucy Martinez although some objects can be found for purchase at online art auction sites, such as http://www.liveauctioneers.com.

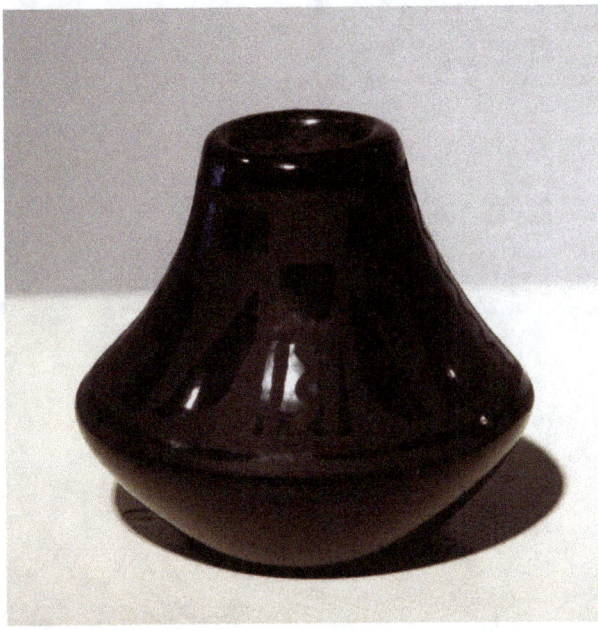

[top left] San Ildefonso Pueblo Mission. [left] Lucy Martinez, *Black Vessel*, 20th century, ceramic, 3.75 inches high x 11.75 inch circumference. Collection: Florida State University Museum of Fine Arts.

Courtesy: Florida State University Museum of Fine Arts.

Paths of Legacy

These artists have been listed under the *path of legacy* for which they were chosen for this exhibition. A number of these artists could be listed in other capacities. The Meaders Family, for example, could be considered under *Specific Culture/Tradition to Culture-at-Large/Society* since they have kept alive a specific folk tradition in pottery. Brent Kington could be listed in this same way since he reintroduced traditional blacksmithing techniques into contemporary art. Faith Ringgold and Grace Matthews could be considered for the designation, *Teacher to Student*, since Matthews was Ringgold's student at the University of California in San Diego in the early 1990s.

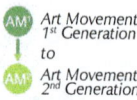

Art Movement 1st Generation to Art Movement 2nd Generation

James Gibson — Aletha Butler

Family to Family

Maria Balingit — Ananda Balingit-Lefils
Préfète Duffaut — Dufo (Jean Charles Duffaut)
Margarete Lalak & Hans Fuchs — Mark J. Fletcher
Mariann Kearsley — Lisa Kearsley Cowling
Henry Lin — Maya Lin
Arie Waldrop Meaders — Whelchel Meaders

Teacher to Student

Carrie Ann Baade — Jim Graham
Trevor Bell — John Hathorn
Judy Chicago — Nancy Youdelman
John Edward Cogswell — Tom McCarthy
William Harper — Peggy Simons & Kathy E. Wilcox
Brent Kington — Jim Wallace
Samella Lewis — Hodges and Rogers Glenn — Eluster Richardson

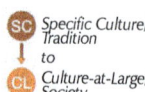

Specific Culture/ Tradition to Culture-at-Large/ Society

Bradley Sr. & Bradley Jr. Cooley
Linda Freeman
Valerie S. Goodwin
Robin Lewis-Wild
Lucy Martinez
Grace Matthews
Faith Ringgold
Aminah Brenda Lynn Robinson

Selected content from the *Generations* Teachers Packet.

Florida State University Museum of Fine Arts.

Generations Education Packet
Table of Contents

All images in this packet are for one time educational use only.
Edited by Alexandra Mumford, Angela Manescala, Ashlyn Eldridge, and
Margaret Swain.
For exhibition tours contact Viki D. Thompson Wylder at 850-644-1299.
Cover Image: Jim Graham, *The Romantic Trout*, 2012, diptych, oil on
canvas, 59" x 72".

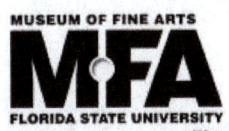

Introduction:
Three Types of Legacy

All works in the *Generations* exhibition will indicate legacy in some way. Artworks and artists were chosen to represent three types of legacy— from one family member to another, from a teacher to a student, from a specific culture to the culture-at-large. This exhibition is one means to encourage a deep and lasting engagement with the arts for people of all ages. Through the study of artists and their work today we can teach and inspire knowledge to pass on to future generations.

Art historically there are many artists who have passed their skills to other family members. For instance, Tuscan painter Orazio Gentileschi taught his eldest daughter Artemisia Gentileschi to draw and paint. Artemisia later went on to be one of the best female painters of the Baroque period. *Generations* provides a number of examples of this personal legacy, such as Maria Balingit passing down her fascination with art and portraiture to her daughter Ananda Balingit-LeFils.

Likewise art history documents an abundance of notable teachers and students. As a student Giovanni Angelo Montorsoli studied the art and painting of master Michelangelo from whom he gained inspiration for his critically revered work *S. Cosmas*. Montorsoli was considered by Michelangelo to be one of his most successful students. Brent Kington, a *Generations* artist, pursued exploratory work using blacksmithing processes and materials within contemporary sculpture. As an inspired student of Kington's, metalworker Jim Wallace would develop his own blacksmith oeuvre creating and developing patterned steel.

In the diverse and multi-cultural society of the 21st century, materials, forms, and techniques from specific cultures and traditions now pass their legacy into the mainstream. Native American artist, Maria Martinez, examined the once lost Pueblo black-on-black pottery tradition to reestablish it as an available artistic form. She reintroduced this legacy of the San Ildefonso Pueblo to the culture-at-large. *Generations* artist Valerie Goodwin uses, preserves, and furthers a traditional technique of women, quilting, further adapting it to western artistic practices by using it to indicate her love of architecture and cultural spaces.

Ashlyn Eldridge   Angela Manescala

Alexandra Mumford   Margaret Swain

Using the Lesson Plans to Form Units of Instruction

"Generations" as a concept for a museum/public school collaboration began one afternoon as two art teachers shared painting tips after a morning of plein aire painting. In the spirit of collaboration a team of teachers working together and individually with the museum education director became the curatorial team. They have chosen a wide variety of artists and artisans for inclusion in this show with the goal of helping students understand the way artists impact current and future generations in order to preserve and perpetuate culture, skills and techniques.

It is the curatorial team's hope that as teachers you will be able to use the lesson plans in this booklet to form a cohesive, meaningful unit of instruction. With that in mind we have included the big ideas, enduring understandings and benchmarks from the New Generations Sunshine State Standards (NGSS) for visual arts. To facilitate creating a unit every lesson plan has a common enduring idea: "There is a desire in the human heart to impact current and future generations in order to preserve and perpetuate culture." This enduring idea, the three approaches to legacy, or the enduring understanding from the NGSS, either separately or combined, can be rewritten into a unit goal or question depending on your preferred format. From there we encourage you to take the lesson plans provided and fine-tune them to enhance your program.

For Leon county teachers the new I-observation system requires that we work at multiple levels, not just the lesson level. Goals written that include both what the student will know and do often fit art lessons well. What do we want our students to know and understand and what will they be able to do by the end of the unit or at the end of each lesson? We are adding a layer on top of what we have often done in the past. The unit goal is a broader understanding of what we want students to know/do/understand and each of the lessons helps build that knowledge.

The unit rubric then tells what students will know and do after finishing all the lessons in the unit. The lesson rubric is often used for grading, for summative assessment, as well as for formative assessments as the students work on their projects. The lesson rubric is specific to that particular lesson and each level of the rubric describes specifically what is expected.

The curatorial team is excited and looking forward to the exhibition of both the professional artists and our own student artists.

Marcia Meale, PhD, J. Michael Conley Elementary

General Elementary Rubric for Art Lessons

Art Lesson	Work shows strong use of all skills and concepts	Making good use of skills and concepts	Work shows some need to improve use of skills and concepts	Work shows a very little use of skills and/or concepts
A. Understanding -Lesson objectives & goals - Applications to life - Cultural & historical Connections	4 The artwork is planned carefully; understanding of most concepts and procedures is shown.	3 The artwork is planned adequately; understanding of some concepts and procedures is shown.	2 The artwork shows little evidence of understanding the concepts and/or procedures.	1 The artwork shows no evidence of understanding the concepts and/or procedures.
B. Skills & Techniques - Craftsmanship - Use and care of tools and materials	4 Students applied all of the skills required and paid close attention to detail.	3 Students showed most of the skills required and the artwork shows average attention to detail.	2 The student applied some of the skills required and paid little attention to detail.	1 The student applied few of the skills required and no attention to detail.
C. Creations & Communication - Application of Elements of Art and Principles of Design - Creativity - Originality	4 The artwork demonstrates some personal expression, logical problem solving skills and application of Art Elements and Principles of Design.	3 The artwork demonstrates an average amount of personal expression, problem solving & application of Art Elements and Principles of Design.	2 The artwork demonstrates little personal expression, problem solving & application of Art Elements and Principles of Design.	1 The artwork lacks evidence of personal expression and little or no evidence of problem solving & application of Art Elements and Principles of Design.
D. Effort - Performance - Time management - Behavior	4 The student put forth the effort required to complete the project well; used class time well, worked independently.	3 The student put forth the effort required to finish the project; used class time adequately	2 The student put forth the effort required to finish the project; used class time adequately; required some redirection or support from the teacher.	1 The student put forth no effort or the project was not completed; class time was not used well; required consistent redirection or support from the teacher.

3

Heritage Through Pottery
With a concentration on the works of Lucy Martinez
By Marcia Meale and Amber Jones

Sunshine State Standards
Big Idea(s): HISTORICAL and GLOBAL CONNECTIONS: Experiences in the arts foster understanding, acceptance, and enrichment among individuals, groups, and cultures from around the world and across time.
SKILLS, TECHINIQUES, and PROCESSES: Through dance, music, theatre and visual art, students learn that beginners, amateurs, and professionals benefit from working to improve and maintain skills over time.
Enduring Understanding(s) VA.4.&.5 H.1.: Through study in the arts, we learn about and honor others and the worlds in which they live(d).
VA.4&5 S.1.:The arts are inherently experiential and actively engage learners in the processes of creating, interpreting, and responding to art.
Bench Mark(s): VA.4.&.5 H.1.1: Examine historical and cultural influences that inspire artists and their work.
VA.4&5 S.1.3. Create artworks to depict personal, cultural and/or historical themes.

Enduring Idea: There is a desire in the human heart to impact current and future generations in order to preserve and perpetuate culture.
Essential Question(s): In what ways did Lucy Martinez contribute to the continuation of (perpetuate) her cultural heritage? Who influenced her pottery making? What do you think this means for future generations? What have you learned from your parents/family members?

Historical Information:

1. Maria Martinez began working with black-on-black ceramics because she was attempting to recreate objects of the past. Maria was asked to replicate some pre-historic pottery styles that had been discovered in an archaeological excavation of an ancient pueblo site near San Ildefonso. These excavations of 1908 and 1909, led by Dr. Edgar Lee Hewett (who was also the director of the Museum of New Mexico), produced examples of many pre-historic pottery techniques. Dr. Hewett asked Maria, who already had a reputation in the pueblo for being an excellent pottery-maker, if she could make full-scale examples for the museum of

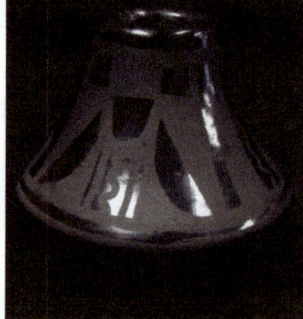

Lucy Marinez
Black Vessel
20th century
Ceramic
3 ¾" high x 11. 3/4"

11

the polychrome ware.

-In this way, Maria learned from the past and attempted to replicate past masters, much in the way that Renaissance artists attempted to replicate ancient Greek and Roman works. Students can "replicate" an idea of the past in someway. Or perhaps brainstorm other examples of the use of replication or copying the past.

2. Maria Martinez not only revived black-on-black pottery but also reinvented the method. She figured out a way to create both a shiny and matte finish. In this way, she preserved the past San Ildefonso style of pottery as well as perpetuated a new form for current and future generations. Her peers, such as Lucy Martinez, continued the tradition, passing it among generations. Lucy's daughter, Alice Martinez, along with Alice's son continues the tradition to this day.

   - Students can discuss the idea of family legacy. What have you learned from your parents/family members?

   -As Maria and Lucy Martinez preserved and perpetuated San Ildefonso culture of the past, ask students in which ways they preserve and perpetuate their various cultures' pasts, whether a larger culture with which they are involved, or a personal family culture. Have they learned any skills, traditions or rituals from family members? This can range from a family gathering, at a holiday or birthday for example, that occurs every year or a cultural celebration or ritual that every family member has experienced, such as bat mitzvah. Students will be forced to think deeply as many aspects of culture may not be immediately evident or obvious.

3. Collaboration – Lucy Martinez, as well as Maria Martinez, most often worked in collaboration with family members when creating an object. In most cases, women created the ceramics while men painted the objects. In the case of Lucy Martinez, Lucy created and fired the ceramics and her husband Richard Martinez painted the objects. Richard was actually a painter by trade. This influenced his designs on the ceramics, as he was known for his recreations of traditional San Ildefonso symbols and motifs. Maria worked in a similar manner, having several family members paint her objects throughout the years.

   -Students can work together to create a single piece of work, whether in pairs or larger groups. Each creator's culture/personal perspective will influence the end result. Students can discuss this collaboration and the effect on the final work. They will discuss the object they made, the shapes they used and the designs created and the reasons they did this. The value of introspective analysis will vary depending on age of artists (students).

12

Grade Level: 4th and 5th

Objectives:
1. Students will examine the cultural and historical significance and influences that inspired the pottery of Lucy Martinez.
2. Students will share verbally or in writing skills, rituals or traditions they have learned from their families.
3. Each student will create a hand built pot based on Native American pottery.
   a. If you are brave, students can pair and share; one student builds then they switch pots and glaze each other's pottery.

Resources: Websites: Maria Martinez, Lucy Martinez and current San Ildefonso potters.
http://www.mariapottery.com/ ; http://www.sanildefonsopottery.com/ /http://www.mariajulianpottery.com/ancestry.cfm?personalID=156

Materials: Clay, clay tools, cloth for tables, water or clay slip, black underglaze, clear transparent gloss glaze.

Activity Procedures:
1. Examine, question and explore pottery by Lucy Martinez, Maria Martinez and modern San Ildefonso potters.
2. In small groups create Venn diagrams of skills or traditions students have learned from members of their families.
3. Sketch design ideas for the pottery decoration based either on historical Native American motifs or personal designs or symbols.
4. Create either clay plates or clay pots. For the clay pots use a pinch pot or coil or combination of both methods. For the clay plate use a small Chinet paper plate and a slab technique.
5. Press lines (do not draw/drag tool to make lines) lightly into the clay to create the borders for the design motifs sketched earlier.
6. Bisque fire.
7. Glaze whole pots/plates with black underglaze, let dry.
8. Apply clear/transparent gloss glaze to some areas of the designs to achieve the black on black style of the San Ildesfonso pottey.
9. Fire again.

Evaluation:
> Objective 1: Informal assessment, teacher observation, student pair and/or share, individual short answer.
> Objective 2: Whole group chart/list or individual/small group notes.
> Objective 3: Art Making Rubric and student self-evaluations.

Couplets of Generations

With a concentration on the works of Mark Fletcher, Hans Fuchs, and Margarete Lalak
By Sara Chang

Big Idea: HISTORICAL AND GLOBAL CONNECTIONS
Experiences in the arts foster understanding, acceptance, and enrichment among individuals, groups, and cultures from around the world and across time.
Enduring Understanding 1: Through study in the arts, we learn about and honor others and the worlds in which they live(d).
Benchmarks:
VA.2.H.1.1 Identify examples in which artists have created works based on cultural and life experiences.
RL.2.4. Describe how words and phrases (e.g., regular beats, alliteration, rhymes, repeated lines) supply rhythm and meaning in a story, poem, or song.
RL.2.7. Use information gained from the illustrations and words in a print or digital text to demonstrate understanding of its characters, setting, or plot.
W.2.3. Write narratives in which they recount a well-elaborated event or short sequence of events, include details to describe actions, thoughts, and feelings, use temporal words to signal event order, and provide a sense of closure.
W.2.5. With guidance and support from adults and peers, focus on a topic and strengthen writing as needed by revising and editing.
SL.2.5. Create audio recordings of stories or poems; add drawings or other visual displays to stories or recounts of experiences when appropriate to clarify ideas, thoughts, and feelings.

Enduring Idea: There is a desire in the human heart to impact current and future generations in order to preserve and perpetuate culture.

Essential Question: How is the artist's work influenced by his grandparents' work?

Grade Level: 2nd—5th

Time Needed: minimum 4 class sessions

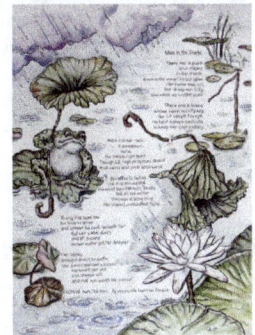

Mark Fletcher,
Maid in the Shade
2008
watercolor and ink
16" x 12"

20

Materials: portraits of Mark Fletcher, Margarete Lalak and Hans Fuchs, images of Mark Fletcher's artwork: *Swamp Music* and *Maid in the Shade*, images of Margarete Lalak's artwork: *Princess Sunshine* and *Bee Maja*, Hans Fuchs' poem: *Helmut*, samples of couplet poems, writing papers, drawing papers, pencils, crayons, markers

Objectives:
1. VA.2.H.1.1/ RL.2.4/ RL.2.7: Students will view, read and comprehend the artwork and poems of Mark Fletcher, Margarete Lalak and Hans Fuchs. They will understand the connection between Mark Fletcher's work and his grandparents' work by comparing their images and poems.
2. W.2.3/ W.2.5 : Students will study the poem format: couplet. They will compose their own poems using multiple couplets about their grandparents or elder relatives. They will also revise, edit and publish their poems.
3. SL.2.5: Students will illustrate their poems and present their poems orally in front of their classmates.

Activity Procedures:
1. Teacher will present brief biographical information about the artist Mark Fletcher and his maternal grandparents, Margarete Lalak and Hans Fuchs.
2. Teacher and students will examine and compare Mark Fletcher's artwork and Margarete Lalak's artwork. They will notice Mark Fletcher created artwork based on his grandmother's theme, e.g. frog at the pond with lily pads and insects dancing in nature.
3. Teacher and students will read, analyze and compare Mark Fletcher's poems and Hans Fuchs' poem. They will notice the theme of family connection since the poem is about Mark's uncle, *Helmut*. Teacher and students will also discuss the rhyming words and rhythm in Mark Fletcher's poem.

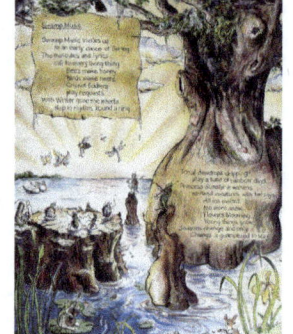

Mark Fletcher
Swamp Music
2009
watercolor
and ink
16" x 12"

4. Teacher will explain the couplet poem format to students. Teacher will guide students to brainstorm ideas or details about their own grandparents or elder relatives. Students will jot down their ideas on paper.
5. Teacher will also guide students to brainstorm rhyming words. Students will also jot down rhyming words.
6. Students will compose couplets about their grandparents or elder relatives.
7. Teacher will guide students to revise, edit and publish students' poems.
8. Students will illustrate their published poems.
9. Students will present their poems in front of the class.

Evaluation:

21

Teacher will score students' poems based on a 3-point rubric:
capable—developing—beginning

For information about Mark Fletcher:
www.markfletcher.embarqspace.com
www.turtlehill.blogspot.com

Biographical information about Margarete Lalak and Hans Fuchs:
Margarete Lalak and Hans Fuchs were Mark Fletcher's maternal grandparents. They
lived in Austria. Margarete was an artist. Hans was an office clerk. During World War II,
Margarete and Hans, along with their two children (Eva and Helmut, mother and uncle
of Mark) were forced to flee Austria. Unfortunately, Hans was killed in a concentration
camp and Margarete died after the war ended. Since Eva and Helmut were orphaned,
they had to move to the U.S. and settled in Ohio. That is where Mark was born in 1963.

HELMUT
by Hans Ernst Fuchs

May you be of bright courage,
You bright child
who entered the circle of the sun's beaming rays,
and drink the spring of your new world
so full of love, as it was presented to you.

May you be of bright courage,
you child of deepest love,
and be strong and handsome
as at that moment when youth married strength.
It goes forth
to create the worth of eternity,
and you, our child.

Be of bright courage
You son of fortune,
live clear and bright,
true to your name,
which will guide you through life,
you who are the desire of our love.

Family Heritage and Ourselves

With a concentration on the works of Nancy Youdelman
By Ashlyn Eldridge

Florida Sunshine State Standard
Big Idea: Historical and Global Connection
Enduring Understand 1: Through study in the arts, we learn about and honor others and the worlds in which they live(d)
Benchmark: VA.4.H.1.3 – Describe artworks that honor and are reflective of particular individuals, groups,events, and/or cultures.

Enduring Idea: There is a desire in the human heart to impact current and future generations in order to preserve and perpetuate culture

Essential Question: How does our heritage live on through ourselves?

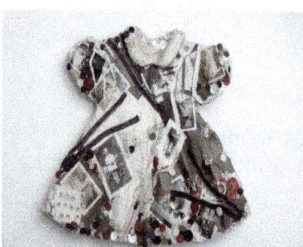

Nancy
Youdelman
*Wooden
Valentine*
2005
Mixed Media,
17½" x 20" x
2½"

Session Activity: Based on Nancy Youdelman's piece, *Wooden Valentine*, students will create their own collages, using family photographs and found objects. Nancy Youdelman is known for using old dresses and shoes, and collaging elements to illustrate the past but using materials from the present. As a class, discuss this idea of the past and the present with relation to families and the way they live on through us now. Each student will bring in photographs from grandparents or parents and other found objects to make an overall collage of both past and present. As a class, discuss the reasoning for choosing these items. Discuss the significance of the photos they have brought in. After their work is complete, as a class the students will hang the projects around the room allowing them to see everything together. Viewing this together will show individual histories and emphasize the past affecting the future. Examples of questions will be: Why is family important to you? Do you know the origin of your family? Why do you think your parent's and grandparent's history is important for you? Addressing similar questions will help the student's become aware of the past.

Grade Level: K-5

Time Needed: Over 3 class sessions

Objectives:
1. Student's will understand more about their heritages and family backgrounds.
2. Student's will gain an understanding of the history that came before them.

Materials: Students provide found clothing, photographs, and any found items they desire to include – buttons, paper, markers, crayons, colored pencils, glue, any string or thread. Anything found outside can be incorporated.

Activity Procedures:
    Class 1:

1. As a class, discuss together the importance of family and the way family history affects us. Ask the following questions:
    a. Why is family important?
    b. What do you know about your grandparents, and their jobs?
    c. Do you know your family origin? Ex: English, Italian, African.
    d. Have you heard stories about the first immigrants in your family?
2. As the teacher, bring in photographs of yourself as a child and your family. Give examples of the way the assignment relates to you.
    a. Where is your family from?
    b. Tell a story about the first immigrants in your family, and describe any accomplishments or challenges they faced.
    c. Why is their history important for you?
3. Show examples of Nancy Youdelman's work and explain her overall idea of giving tribute to the past and the way her art has developed from that.
4. Allow for class discussion.

Class 2:

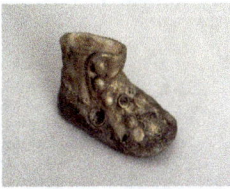

Nancy Youdelman Precious 2008 Mixed Media, 3" x 4½" x 2"

1. Students will bring in photographs, at least one piece of clothing, and found objects.
2. Go outside and explore the natural elements to possibly incorporate in the project.
3. Inside – lay out each student's items. Each student will describe his/her photos and items and the reasons they were chosen.
4. Each student will explain the potential content of his/her picture or the significance of the potential arrangement.

Class 3:

1. Begin the collage project. Use the idea that Nancy Youdelman suggests, using the form of the clothing to be the structure and form of the design.
2. Taking the photographs and found objects, have the students use glue to apply the items, creating designs individual to the students.
3. Be sure to copy the photographs so the students do not ruin the actual hard copies.
4. Allow for an extra class to finish and display, if needed.

Evaluation:
Rubric for Family Heritage and Ourselves

Art Lesson	Work shows strong use of all skills and concepts	Making good use of skills and concepts	Work shows some need to improve use of skills and concepts	Work shows a very little use of skills and/or concepts
A. Understanding -Lesson objectives & goals - Family history - Importance of the past in a personal way	4 The artwork is planned carefully; understanding of most concepts and procedures is shown.	3 The artwork is planned adequately; understanding of some concepts and procedures is shown.	2 The artwork shows little evidence of understanding the concepts and/or procedures.	1 The artwork shows no evidence of understanding the concepts and/or procedures.
B. Skills & Techniques - Craftsmanship - Use and care of tools and materials -Collage	4 Students applied all of the skills required and paid close attention to detail.	3 Students showed most of the skills required and the artwork shows average attention to detail.	2 The student applied some of the skills required and paid little attention to detail.	1 The student applied few of the skills required and no attention to detail.
C. Effort - Performance - Time management - Behavior	4 The student put forth the effort required to complete the project well; used class time well, worked independently.	3 The student put forth the effort required to finish the project; used class time adequately	2 The student put forth the effort required to finish the project; used class time adequately; required some redirection or support from the teacher.	1 The student put forth no effort or the project was not completed; class time was not used well; required consistent redirection or support from the teacher.

Our Florida Heritage: How Would You Sculpt It?

Concentrated on the works of Bradley Cooley and Bradley Cooley Jr.
By Evelyn Pender

Big Idea: Historical and Global Connections: Experiences in the arts foster understanding, acceptance, and enrichment among individuals, groups, and cultures from around the world and across time.
Enduring Understanding: Through studying the arts, we learn about and honor others and the world in which they live.
Benchmark: VA.4.H.1.1: Identify Historical and cultural influences that have inspired artists to produce works of art.

Enduring Idea: There is a desire in the human heart to impact current and future generations in order to preserve and perpetuate culture.
Essential Question: In which ways do sculptures record our history?

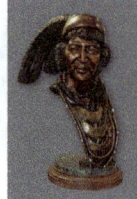

Cooleys
Osceola
2012
bronze
20" x 8" x12"

Session Activity: Based on the works of Bradley Cooley and Bradley Cooley Jr., students will learn about the traditions, dress, tools, symbols, and tribal ways of the Seminole and Miccosukee people and legends. They will create their own sculptures out of clay using the pinch, poke, and pull method. Their sculptures will show persons doing something in the daily life of the tribe and will be adorned in tribal costume with tools or accessories. Details will be added with texture and drawing in the clay. Bases can be applied if needed. After drying and bisque firing, students will glaze their sculptures to resemble bronze using a low fire bronze glaze. After students have finished their sculptures they will write short paragraphs explaining their ideas and design.

Grade Level: 4th

Time Needed: Four class sessions.

Objectives:

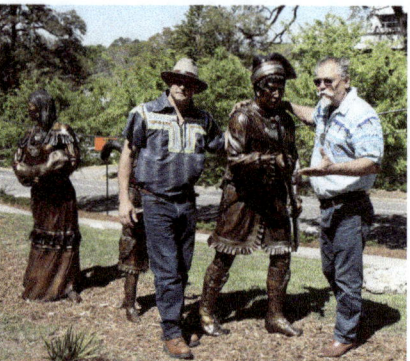

Bradley
Cooley Sr.
and Bradley
Cooley, Jr.

1. Students will learn about the Seminole and Miccosukee tribes by looking at the works by the Cooleys and researching and hearing about the Native American tribes of Florida.
2. Each student will draw an illustration about tribal life that demonstrates what it was like to be part of a community with traditions, tools, and dress.
3. Students will finalize their drawings of the persons they will model with clay using gestural drawings to plan body movements and placements.

67

4. Students will then model their personal sculptures using the pinch, poke, and pull method adding textures and drawing in the clay to add fine details. Details that depict the tribe's dress, tools, or accessories will be added. Edges will be smoothed and details finalized. A base can be added if the sculpture needs support.
5. After drying and bisque firing, students will use a special glaze on their sculptures so they resemble bronze sculptures like the Cooley's work.
6. Students will then write about their work and connections to the Seminole or Miccosukee people.

Materials: Ceramic clay, texturing tools, pencils, paper, glaze.

Activity Procedures:
1. Show slides of the Cooley's Native American sculptures by accessing their web site:
   http://www.bronzebycooley.com
2. Students can research the native tribes of Florida if accessible, or the teacher can share information about the tribes, their dress, tools, tribal ways, and symbols.
3. Follow the procedures outlined in the objectives above.

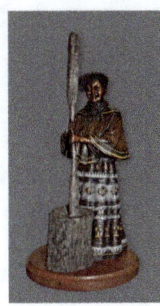

Cooleys
Mortar and Pestle
2011
Bronze
20"x 8"x 12"

Evaluation: Teacher will use the General Elementary Rubric to monitor student progress and understanding.
Students will use a rubric to self-assess their work.
1. Did I pre-plan my idea with a drawing?
2. Did I finalize my sculptural process with a gesture drawing?
3. Did I use the pinch, poke, and pull method in creating my sculpture?
4. Did I add details and texture to my sculpture?
5. Did I finish my sculpture with glaze?
6. Did my writing reflect connections to the Seminole and Miccosukee people?
7. Did I do my best work? Explain why or how.

CHAPTER 8

Project #5: The Influence of Social Justice Art Education

Project Title: *Waging Peace!*
Planning and Program Implementation: Spring 2016–Spring 2018
Exhibition Year: 2018
Co-curatorial Team:
Tallahassee, Florida K-12 inter-school art educators
- Bond Elementary School—Dr. Michele Davidson
- Canopy Oaks Elementary School—Leslie Anderson
- Conley Elementary—Dr. Marcia Meale
- Deerlake Middle School—Linda Kaye Johnson
- DeSoto Trail Elementary School—Kim Salesses
- Florida State University Schools—Barbara Davis, Eileen Baum-field Lerner
- Godby High School—Althea Valle
- Lincoln High School—Shannon Takacs
- Montford Middle School—Dr. Donald E. Sheppard
- Ruediger Elementary School—Katharyn Jones

Tallahassee Homeschool Group Cooperative
- Cooperative Educator—Lisa Girard
- Cooperative Educator—Melinda Stuart-Tilley

Anderson-Brickler Gallery and Collaborative Art Projects (CAP)
- Chief Curator and Director of Educational Programs—Kabuya Bowens

Council on Culture and Arts
- Assistant Director, Education and Exhibitions Manager—Amanda Karioth Thompson

Florida State University Museum of Fine Arts
  •   Curator of Education—Dr. Viki D. Thompson Wylder
Holocaust Education Resource Council
  •   Executive Director—Barbara Goldstein
The Plant on Gaines Street
  •   Board Member—Jennifer Hamrock
Artworks: 49
Artists: Hannah Smith Allen, Bradley Arthur, Leon Bedore (Tes One), Sara C. Chang, Du Chau, Hank Feeley, Allison Finn, Mark J. Fletcher, Raquel Fornasaro, Carmen Rojas Fines, Richelle Gribble, Marcia Haffmans, Mariann B. Kearsley, Dan Kurland, George Lorio, Cecelia Lueza, Stephen Marc, Roberta Masciarelli, Sean S. McGraw, Maria Mijares, Bernie M. Molaskey, Joe Norman, Dan Noyes, Luisa Padro (Artysta LuLu), Ashlyn Pope, Orly Ruaimi, Natalie Sassine, Judy Lipman Shechter, Regina Silvers, Susanne Slavick, Linda Stein, Jason Stout, Anika Toro, Ani Tung, Patricia Anderson Turner, Jackie Weaver, Eva Weingarten, Anita S. Wexler, Ashley P. Wilson, Lori Hope Zeller

Beginnings

The doors for the *Waging Peace!* reception opened at 6:00 p.m., but I waited until 6:05 p.m. to start the formalized installation of the *Peace Puzzle*. The gallery was packed. A low hum filled the space while elementary and middle school children with their parents, relatives, and teachers watched the installation progress. During the proceedings I called individual children forward to carefully position pieces onto a round puzzle blueprint laid on a low pedestal, approximately 10 feet square, which formed the centerpiece of the K-12 section of the exhibition. Children's renditions of animals, plants, forests, waters, and other environmental scenes covered each of the puzzle pieces. Occasional peace symbols, or the like, interspersed the finished composition which included 37 mini-works organized in three adjacent concentric expanses curving around a middle section to form an overall circle shape. As they added pieces to the puzzle installation, a few children made public statements about the meanings of their imagery and/or the overall

Multi-school *Peace Puzzle* project: mid installation during the *Waging Peace!* opening reception.

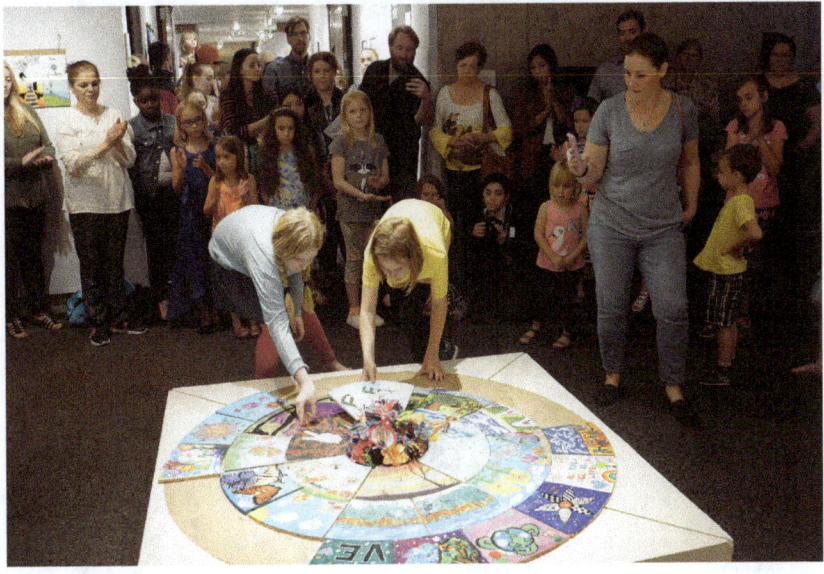

Courtesy: Marcia S. Meale.

work. After the alignment of each wedge-shaped, painted, wooden puzzle piece, the audience clapped.

Katharyn Jones, a co-curatorial team member from Ruediger Elementary School, suggested this cooperative installation project. Elementary and middle school students, 119 in total, under the supervision of their teachers from 15 schools, created the positive imagery on these puzzle pieces. The work was produced with the intent of participation in this assembling ceremony and the larger aim of bringing attention to the importance of healthy world ecological integration. Co-curatorial team members saw current detrimental changes to an interconnected world environment as producers of global inequity and therefore a challenge to social justice and sustained peace. A work by California artist Richelle Gribble titled *Land–Sea–Air*, selected by the co-curatorial team for the *Waging Peace!* exhibition, provided the inspiration for this multichild, multiteacher, and multischool work.

—VDTW

For this multi-school *Peace Puzzle* project, a student read her statement aloud to explain the meaning of her contribution to visitors attending the *Waging Peace!* opening reception.

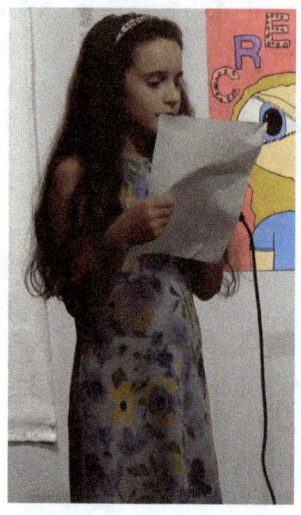

Courtesy: Marcia S. Meale.

Multi-school *Peace Puzzle* project: fully installed during the *Waging Peace!* opening reception.

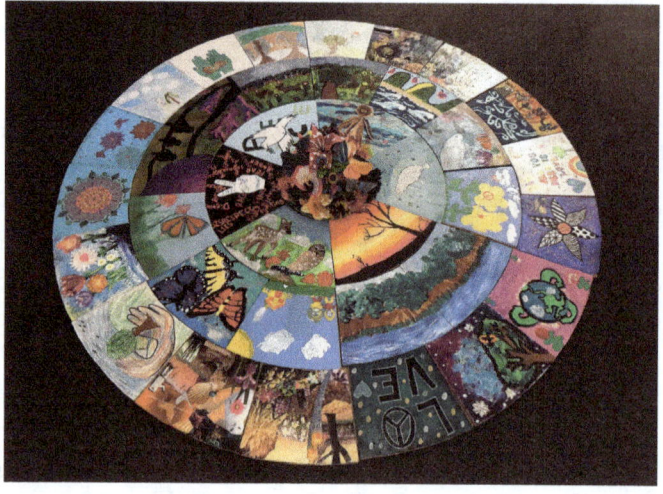

Courtesy: Marcia S. Meale.

The Project Backstory

An *International Peace Mural Project* titled *Kids' Guernica* had engaged teachers in Leon County in various ways since 1995. By 2016 and the advent of the *Waging Peace!* project, groups from at least 40 different countries associated with *Kids' Guernica* had produced several hundred peace murals. All murals adhered to the dimensions of Picasso's famous visual antiwar statement. All were painted on canvas and all were movable. In 1995, the original mural for this international effort was painted by "kids" in Tallahassee as part of an exchange with a Japanese commemorative program marking the 50th anniversary of the bombing of Nagasaki at the end of World War II. The Florida State University Museum of Fine Arts (FSU MoFA) hosted a 15-year celebration of *Kids' Guernica* in 2010 with an exhibition of approximately a dozen peace murals from across the globe.

The FSU MoFA exhibition included a second Tallahassee peace mural which was planned collaboratively by the education program of the museum with art teachers from 14 Leon County schools and painted by their students. The *Kids' Guernica* effort also engendered an FSU MoFA student display titled *Peace!* which featured additional work by students from 20 Leon County schools to accompany the international mural exhibition (Anderson, 2009, pp. 18–19). Over time, these exhibitions further precipitated the production of local student peace murals and other peace-focused artwork as part of community events organized by Leon County teachers.

Description of the Project and Exhibition

A new FSU MoFA peace project and exhibition was first suggested by teachers at the end of the 2015 school term following a local peace mural project. Several teachers wanted to continue the local project's themes in a way that resulted in greater impact and a larger audience. A year later the suggestion was solidified and planning began.[1] For *Waging Peace!* the accompanying catalogue explained the thesis and title of the exhibition. "The term, 'waging,' was chosen to convey

---

[1] Dr. Teri Abstein acted as Curator of Education from the summer of 2014 till the summer of 2016. The idea for the exhibition emerged during her stewardship of the curatorial position. Dr. Abstein authored the original *Waging Peace!* Call for Entries.

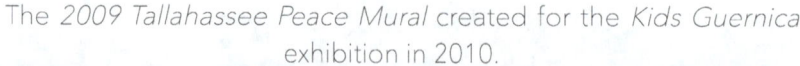

The *2009 Tallahassee Peace Mural* created for the *Kids Guernica* exhibition in 2010.

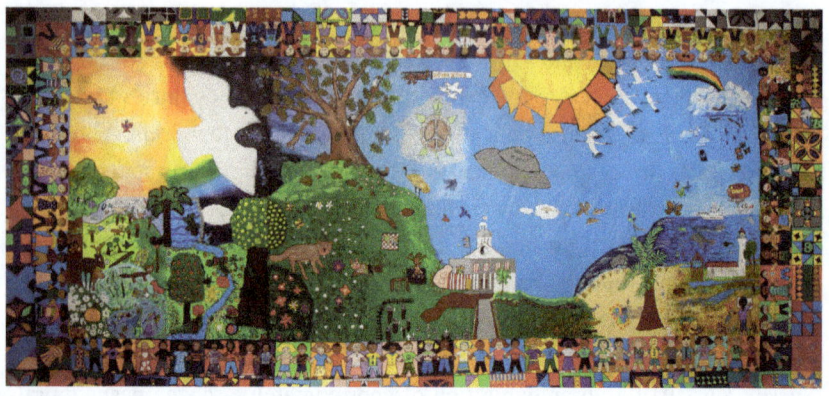

Courtesy: Florida State University Museum of Fine Arts.

an underlying conception of peace as 'active.' " The catalogue statement further clarified:

> [Peace] does not mean merely the absence of violence or war. Rather peace means the constant challenge or struggle to construct ethical balance among individuals and groups in society. It means preserving and promoting the natural ecology of the earth with the aim of a fair sharing of its sustained resources.
>
> (Thompson Wylder, 2018, p. 6)

As work on the project and exhibition proceeded, two team members discovered the Jimmy Carter Center used the term in its "precept-like motto, 'Waging Peace. Fighting Disease. Building Hope' " (Thompson Wylder, 2018, p. 6). These two team members were especially excited by this discovery of an overlap of social justice aims and phrasing. Since these two team members and the students they represented were not part of the public school system, but belonged to a home-school cooperative, they were eventually able to organize field trips for their students with visits to the Carter Center in Atlanta and to Plains, Georgia where the past president spoke at his church most Sundays.

Gribble's *Land–Sea–Air*, the work used as impetus for the exhibition reception installation event, had been chosen from a national call for entries. In a reflection of the inspiration for the production of the international peace murals, the call for entries stated the *Waging Peace!* project was developed with the spirit of Picasso's *Guernica* in mind. It asked for

> artworks which would convey one or more of the following: 1) a response to, solution towards, or consequences of peace or its absence, 2) active progress towards or analysis of the nature and possibility of peace, 3) overcoming conflict, and 4) promoting, striving towards, seeking, investigating the journey of, and achieving peace. Works could address multiple levels of the possibilities mentioned through personal, spiritual, regional, cultural, geographical, or worldwide concerns.
>
> (Thompson Wylder, 2018, p. 6)

The call for entries garnered submissions of approximately 300 artworks by artists who hailed from fourteen states as far afield as Arizona, California, New York, and Maryland. Other regions like the Midwest were represented and, of course, Florida.

The team chose 49 pieces by 40 artists with the intent of representing a range of social justice topics. When looked at in total, the selected exhibition imagery presented an interwoven and complex peace message which included a myriad of subtopics. Much of the work centered on the recognition and respect for the interdependence of all life inclusive of both culture and nature. Some work acknowledged the tension that exists between creation and destruction with the historical human pattern of eradication and renovation. Other messages included: the recognition of the consequences of war and violence; the power of words and imagery in their ability to bring messages, even with a small voice or fleeting or shadowy image; the necessity of questioning; the hope for collaborative action to honor and mend the past yet move forward for just and fair access to opportunity; and the need for actuating a balance between societal and natural forces to produce an equitable and sustainable life on the planet. In an elegant work, the message of the artist, Du Chau, a Texan who migrated from Vietnam as a child, simply stated that peace requires a backbone. In his work titled *Foundations*, he "nestled [a] set of 44 porcelain doves," which he organized linearly through a "descending" and "diminishing scale" to "transform" them "into a backbone like structure" nearly 40 inches long and thus well over life-size (Chau, 2018, p. 14).

The content for this project took form during one of the shorter planning time frames for the five projects discussed in this book. Planning and fulfillment of the project took just two years, from the spring of 2016 to the spring of 2018 when the exhibition opened. Although each of the previous co-curatorial teams included inexperienced team members, most also counted the return of experienced members. For *Waging Peace!* over half the team members fell into the experienced category which facilitated a speedy project development and production. The range of backgrounds for the team members for this last project, however, exceeded the previous four co-curatorial teams. Two parents representing a homeschool cooperative joined school art educators from all grade levels—elementary, middle school, and high school. Past co-curatorial teams featured participants from the community, but this co-curatorial team somewhat exceeded the scope of its community antecedents. The *Waging Peace!* team included: the chief curator and director of educational programs for the Anderson-Brickler Gallery, a space emphasizing African American contributions; the assistant director, education and exhibitions manager from the Tallahassee Council on Culture and Arts (COCA); the executive director of the Holocaust Education Resource Council (HERC); and a board member from The Plant, a nonprofit do-it-yourself inclusive community space. The Plant, in accordance with its mission statement, works to empower free expression by encouraging individuals to organically organize, research, and experiment in any of the arts (Hamrock, 2018, & V. D. T. Wylder, personal communication with board member of The Plant, Jennifer Hamrock, April & May, 2020). After selecting the works for exhibition, the co-curatorial team planned the plethora of other programs to accompany the *Waging Peace!* project. They envisaged a student display, an education packet of lesson plans, interactions between artists and students, a catalogue, an all-day teacher workshop, events at several schools as well as at the Anderson-Brickler Gallery and The Plant, an opening reception with performances and activities, and interactive tours extended throughout the eight weeks of the exhibition.

The student display for this project followed a distinct format. The FSU MoFA set aside one gallery for student work. To emphasize the collective nature of much activism and to encourage widespread student participation, all student artwork shown in the FSU MoFA student display was required to be cooperative or collaborative. Due to space limitations, only works by students of the co-curatorial team members were displayed here. By the time of exhibition installation, eight schools submitted cooperative/collaborative artworks by 626 students for the student display. Lincoln High School students, under the direction of art instructor Shannon Takacs, submitted a work inspired by a Linda Stein tapestry. Stein's work titled *Ten Heroes* "depict[ed] fierce females during the time of the Holocaust juxtaposed with…selected pop-culture and religious icons of protection." Stein used the "blending of fantasy and reality figures [to] prompt conversations about everyday heroism and brave upstanding against bullying and bigotry" (Stein, 2018). Stein's work featured photographic head portraits of each of these ten women printed on material surrounded by sewing and stitch-ery accoutrements such as pieces of leather, snippets of myriad fabric designs, zippers, sections of decorative cord, snaps, occasional buttons, and jewelry-like curios. The *Ten Heroes* tapestry hung as a rectangular piece 56″ × 62″. Instead, the Lincoln High School students transformed an old wedding dress with train by using Stein's process. They covered the dress in portraits and the other types of material used in the inspiration piece. For the *Waging Peace Gown* well over a hundred students, female and male, participated.

> Each student created a small sewn work of art that included layers of fabric, embellishments, and an image(s) of a strong female who promotes/promoted peace. The strong female could be from history, popular culture, or the student's life (mom, grandmother, sister, friend, themselves). All of the small sewn works of art were then joined to cover [the] dress and create a single…sculptural piece.
>
> (Takacs, 2018)

Waging Peace! Gown: collaborative work by Lincoln High School students for the *Waging Peace!* Student Display.

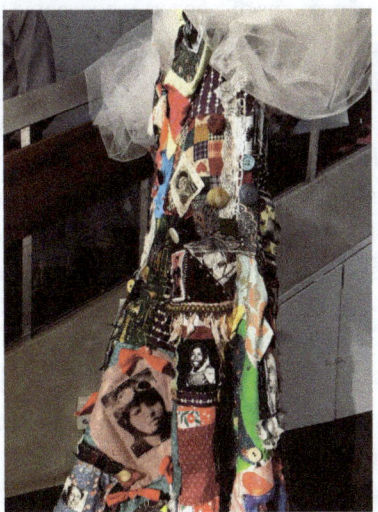

Courtesy: Florida State University Museum of Fine Arts.

During this tour, students interacted with the high school work in the *Waging Peace!* Student Display titled *Waging Peace! Gown.*

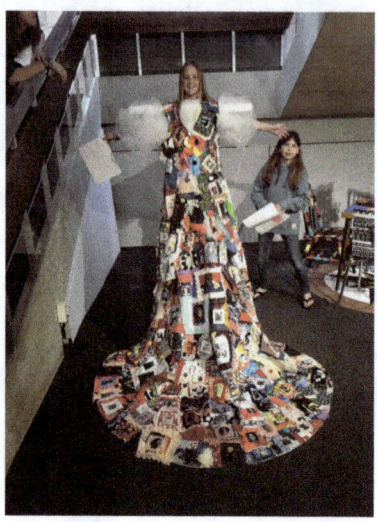

Courtesy: Florida State University Museum of Fine Arts.

As in past projects, additional exhibition space was arranged for the display of student work from the classrooms of teachers who wanted to participate but were not on the co-curatorial team. The education manager for the Tallahassee Council on Culture and Arts, who sat on the co-curatorial team and curated a gallery space in the Tallahassee City Hall, reserved a place in the City Hall schedule for this "spill-over." The student display at City Hall allowed the exhibition of work by 300 additional students from 13 more schools. In contrast to the exhibition at the FSU MoFA, the exhibition at City Hall allowed works completed by individual students as well as works that were cooperative or collaborative. Each student display, at FSU MoFA and City Hall, hosted its own reception on separate evenings.

In concert with the social justice theme of the project, lesson plans in the education packet written by teachers on the co-curatorial team and FSU MoFA interns emphasized and mirrored social justice concepts found in the artwork chosen for the exhibition. In a plan written by Katharyn Jones, she referenced Jacqueline Weaver's installation of two tents titled *The Border Projects: In Conversation* in which the artist set aside space for talking, listening, and sharing either through conversations begun by viewers sitting inside the tents or by listening to provided recordings. Jones, an elementary art teacher, constructed a plan in which the students would view and learn about Weaver's tents and then build their own tent art installations in the classroom using common materials like blankets, sheets, curtains, and the like. Though the lesson mimicked common play, Jones designed the experience as a stimulation for talking, listening, and sharing about tents themselves, their potential relationships to displaced persons, and the connection between adequate shelter and peace. In her procedure Jones wrote:

> Students will work together in groups of 4 or less to create their own art installation tents…After the builds, students will pick up a survey, a pencil, and a light source (flashlight). Once inside their structures students can talk with one another to complete the experience surveys. After completing and turning in the surveys, students are invited to explore other builds.
>
> (Jones, 2018, p. 31)

The survey asked questions such as "What would you need to live in this tent?" (Jones, 2018, p. 32).

In a second session Jones' plan called for showing photographs of tents used in refugee camps or used by displaced people during the Great Depression accompanied by questions such as "What is a reason someone might not have a place to live? Why is having a place to live important? Would you feel comfortable living in a tent?" (Jones, 2018, p. 31). After this discussion Jones' plan directed students to create sketches expressing their experiences with this project. Throughout Jones' plan she peppered the students with prompts for drawing relationships between their activities/discussion and "waging peace." A final evaluation of each student's work included his or her comments, and thus understanding, of the relationship of this project to the concept of peace.

Jacqueline Weaver's *The Border Projects: In Conversation* also became an inspiration for a collaborative effort by teachers on the team to produce student-level discussion-starter questions for use within the tent conversation spaces of Weaver's artwork. Many team members directed their students to note on index cards questions consequent to the theme of the exhibition. Students were further encouraged to accompany those questions printed on the cards with illustrative sketches. Students' questions centered on their concerns, for example, ways to counteract bullying by posing questions to each other that would establish friendship connections. At the opening reception, with the artist Jacquelyn Weaver's permission, the cards were placed on a pedestal just outside the tents. Viewers were encouraged to take a card or cards into the tents to use as stimuli for conversation.

During the opening reception, visitors used a student prompt card to converse while sitting in the tent installation titled The *Border Projects: In Conversation* by Jacqueline Weaver.

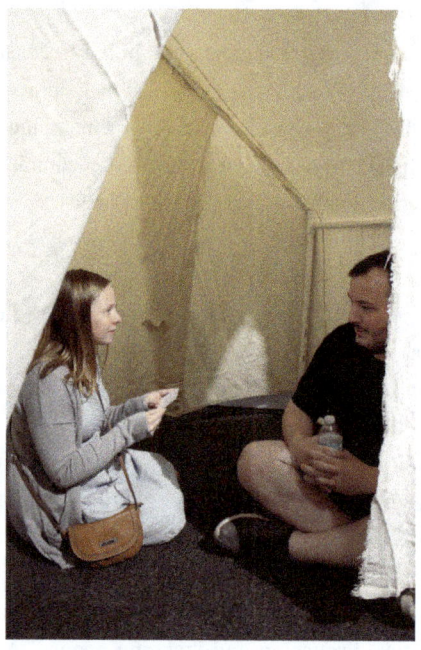

Courtesy: Florida State University Museum of Fine Arts.

Written by two interns in consultation with Dr. Marcia Meale from J. Michael Conley Elementary School, another lesson plan in the packet evolved in stages into a multischool traveling project. The lesson plan, titled *All People Have a Place on Earth*, referenced a work by Judy Lipman Shechter titled *Boots on the Ground*. Shechter's installation featured rows of pairs of shoes in a gridlike formation or matrix. Many pairs in the rows were bronzed baby shoes, and occasionally in a row Shechter placed an imprint of bare feet in plaster turned upside down. She placed all on the floor on a spread of soil, 56 feet square in size. In her artist's statement Shechter explained her message, "I'm presenting our troops as children, because in reality each serviceperson is someone's child, and everyone can understand the tragic loss of a child" (2018, p. 37).

With Shecter's permission, the lesson plan provided an alternate interpretation of the work. Though bronzed baby shoes appeared dispersed throughout Shechter's installation, the work also included other styles and sizes of shoes in addition to the bare plaster feet. Ultimately, the lesson plan focused on respect for "people from all walks of life" (Zhu & Mendoza, 2018, p. 52) and pointed to the fact that the people symbolized in Shechter's work are all "standing on the same ground" (p. 51). The plan tasked students with bringing old shoes to class to paint and/or decorate to symbolize "people they know or know about" (p. 50). Through analysis and discussion of Shechter's installation as well as discussion of the shoes prepared in class, students were charged with determining a potential change from Shechter's shoe placement design, a matrix, to an alternate formation that would also communicate/symbolize the concept of peace.

The interpretation and adaptation of Shechter's work, under Dr. Meale's direction, found its final form in a multischool traveling installation project. Dr. Meale and her elementary students began the project by gathering and preparing shoes and in so doing tweaked the plan to ease the circumstances of traveling. The collection of shoes in a variety of styles and sizes—ballet, golf, dress shoes, sneakers, high heels, East Indian wedding shoes, flip flops, and baby shoes—were painted gold to symbolize equality among all occupations and all cultures.

Three additional teachers at three other schools participated—one elementary, one middle school, and one high school. Each of the schools used the installation in distinct ways. The Lincoln High School class designed a series of shoe formations which they photographed in different settings on school grounds. The students cast themselves as integral players in the designs, posing in these photographs in sync with the various formations of the shoes. The students then photographed the formations a second time but without the class present. The final work became a series of pairs of haunting documentary photographs. The first photograph of each pair provided a record of the seriousness of endeavor with this project as well as a sense of the cooperation and solidarity among the diversity of students present. The second photograph revealed the legacy of the

Gallery view of *Boots on the Ground* by Judy Lipman Shechter: the work was used as an inspiration for a traveling project titled *All People Have a Place on Earth.*

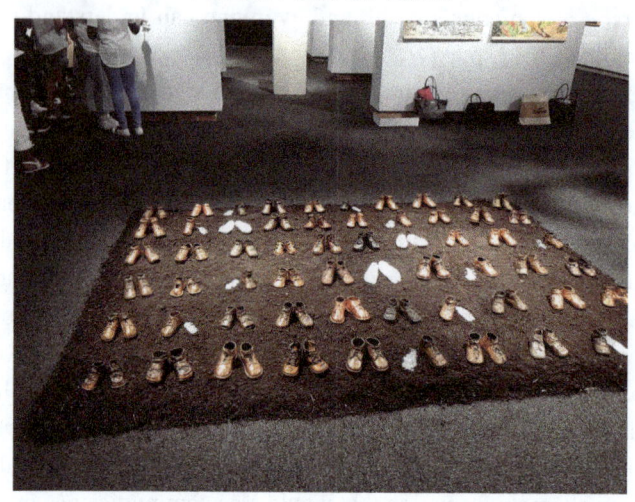

Courtesy: Florida State University Museum of Fine Arts.

All People Have a Place on Earth: students at J. Michael Conley school worked with an elementary version of this traveling project inspired by Shechter's work.

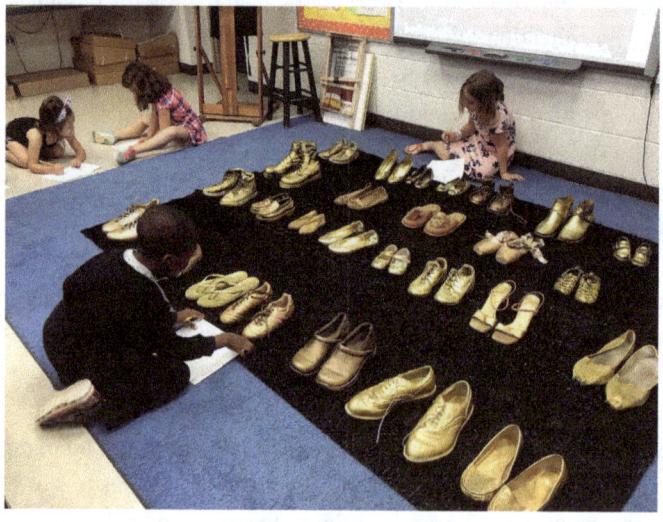

Courtesy: Marcia S. Meale.

All People Have a Place on Earth: Lincoln High School Version #1 of
the traveling project inspired by Shechter's work.

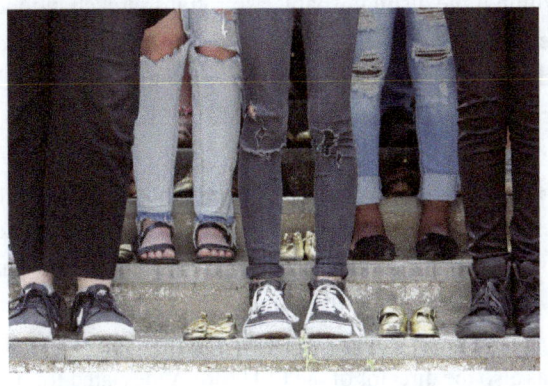

Courtesy: Shannon Takacs.

All People Have a Place on Earth: Lincoln High School Version #2 of
the traveling project inspired by Shechter's work.

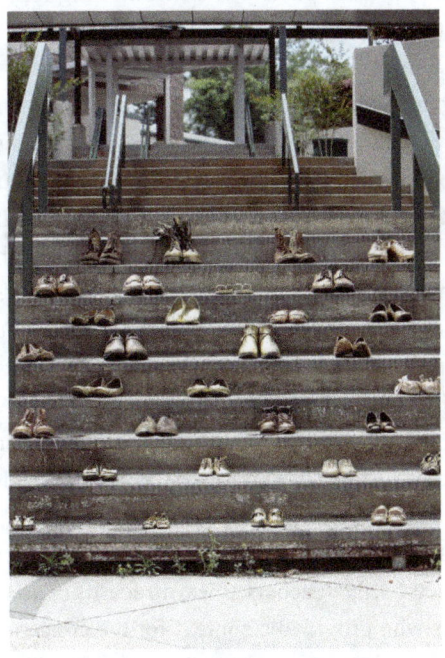

Courtesy: Shannon Takacs.

students through the symbolism of the shoes alone. After the students were gone, the shoes still in formation suggested the students' respect for the diversity of society and within it the distinguishable aspirations of each individual communicated by the distinctness and contextual location of a pair of shoes. After the four-school itinerary, a fifth iteration of the installation was installed as part of the student exhibition at Tallahassee City Hall.

The catalogue for *Waging Peace!* was developed in a time frame parallel to the development of the education packet of lesson plans. Much of the catalogue followed a generally accepted catalogue format with a section devoted to the artists and a smaller separate section devoted to the curators. Images of the artwork were accompanied by artists' statements. The curator section included an individual profile of each member of the co-curatorial team. The catalogue editor, who was also the director of the FSU MoFA, deviated from usual practice by also publishing in the curator section excerpts of several of the lesson plans written for the education packet. The FSU MoFA distributed catalogues and the education packet of lesson plans months prior to the exhibition as resources to use in classrooms. Catalogues were distributed in hard copy to teachers while the education packet of lesson plans was distributed digitally and posted on the FSU MoFA website. When the exhibition opened, the FSU MoFA offered all viewers free catalogues.

As teachers began to work with students to prepare them for the *Waging Peace!* exhibition, they interacted with exhibition artists themselves or arranged for interaction between their students and artists. Although co-curatorial members received workshop credit from the local school district for their general curatorial participation in *Waging Peace!*, as they had for the previous *Generations* project, members planned a distinct workshop for teachers inclusive of those not on the committee and not necessarily engaged in the art field. New York artist Linda Stein, whose work *Ten Heroes* profiled women of courage related to the Holocaust, visited the FSU MoFA to participate in an all-day teacher workshop as the featured speaker. Financial support from the Tallahassee Holocaust Education Resource Council and the Florida State University Schools made Stein's visit possible. In addition to Stein's lecture, the workshop offered a number of additional facets: 1) official school system credit for attendance by art teachers toward recertification requirements, 2) additional speakers who provided a context for the concepts of Linda Stein's work, and 3) presentation by teachers from the Florida State University Schools who were already working in their K-12 classrooms on the issue of

At the *Waging Peace!* Teacher Workshop featuring Linda Stein, teachers enjoyed a moment of levity.

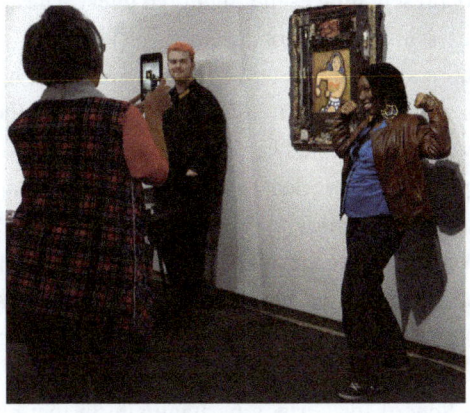

Courtesy: Florida State University Museum of Fine Arts.

The *Waging Peace!* Teacher Workshop featured artist Linda Stein.

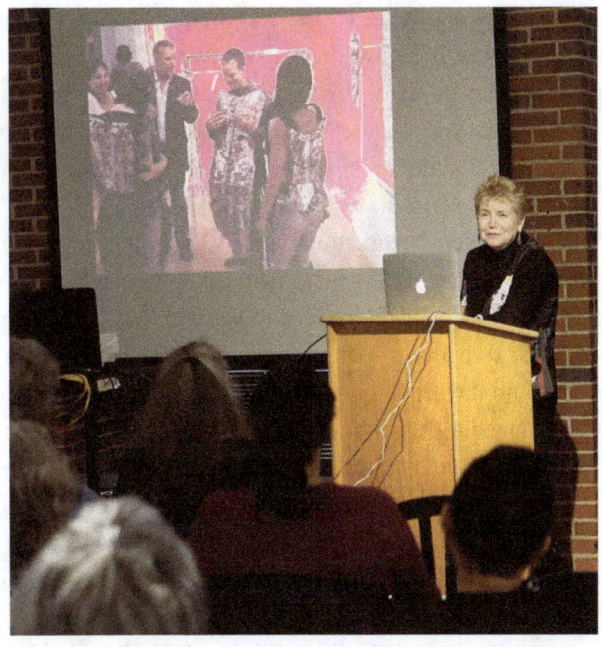

Courtesy: Florida State University Museum of Fine Arts.

the Holocaust and an all-school presentation of that Holocaust work in the school auditorium and school gallery. The school invited Linda Stein to the evening all-school presentation as their honored guest. The artist spoke briefly to the audience after an introduction.

During preparations for Linda Stein's visit she outlined her usual protocol for presentations at workshops. In addition to speaking about her artwork, Stein customarily also highlighted her imagery interactively using local dancers. For this *Waging Peace!* workshop, to honor that portion of Stein's usual format an FSU dance professor and choreographer, Hannah Schwadron, was tapped to join Linda Stein at the workshop. Schwadron screened her 2015 film titled *Klasse* (directed by Malia Bruker, FSU Assistant Professor of Communication). In her film Schwadron cast German middle school students from the Ida Ehre School in Hamburg as dancers. Performed and filmed at the historical Jewish School for Girls, a heritage site in that city, Schwadron's *Klasse* documented the dance she choreographed in collaboration with the Ida Ehre School students. Through dramatic movement performed within the frame of authentic desks and chairs of a preserved Jewish School for Girls classroom, the dancers symbolized the story of the gradual disappearance of Jewish pupils from their classes as they left their country for safety reasons just prior to World War II. Schwadron also saw the dance as an ode to her grandmother's Holocaust history in Hamburg. The dance communicated a remembrance of the caring of students for each other and for themselves, their sorrow, their bravery, and their resilience. The message of the dance mirrored Stein's message in *Ten Heroes*.

In addition to the teacher workshop with Stein, four local/regional artists were formally contracted to meet with students at schools. The artists informed students about their media, techniques, and *Waging Peace!* messages and led hands-on sessions. Two artists focused on two-dimensional media—the first on digital media and the second on ink and paper. The other two focused on three-dimensional media—the first on stone (using subtractive processes) and the second on natural found materials with paint (using additive processes). Together these four artists visited thirteen classrooms and interacted with over 250 students. A fifth local artist curated into the exhibition, who happened to be a teacher in an elementary classroom and worked in digital media, was also contracted. She completed a video interview based on questions solicited from various students in elementary and middle school classes who had been introduced to her work. Typical questions covered the inspiration for her work, her media, and the message of her imagery. "How did you get inspired from places all over the world? What editing software do you recommend? What do you mean when you say 'a state of inner peace?'" (V. D. T. Wylder, personal communication with an artist from *Waging Peace!* exhibition, Sarah Chang, March 23, 2018). The finished "homemade" video was recorded on the artist's phone by directing her own students to ask the submitted questions. It was sent digitally to teachers and posted on the FSU MoFA website.

Several community partners extended the opportunity to both students and the greater community for collaborative participation with the project. Kabuya Bowens joined the co-curatorial team as Anderson-Brickler Gallery's chief curator and director of educational enrichment programs. The Anderson-Brickler space focused on the contributions of African American artists. Bowens targeted and directed students at the James S. Rickards High School in Tallahassee who built a public space sculpture emphasizing the theme of *Waging Peace!* A range of influences inspired the sculpture from the work of African American artists like Romare Bearden to the public space art of people like Alexander Calder. The finished collaborative piece was placed outside the gallery and could be viewed by the public as they drove past the site.

Another local partner generated a complex program of community *Waging Peace!* workshops that culminated in an additional exhibition for the project. Jennifer Hamrock as a member of the co-curatorial team and Board Member of The Plant, a do-it-yourself community art center run by volunteers, devised a collaborative process for her institution that paralleled the more extensive co-curatorial process for *Waging Peace!* Hamrock advertised a call to local and regional artists to participate in a meeting at The Plant to develop a series of workshops and a final exhibition of the artworks created during the workshops called *Waging Peace at the Plant.* During successive meetings, artists proposed their ideas, processes, and materials. Aspects like scheduling, publicity, and funding were also discussed and determined.

> As far as the Plant's involvement, I envisioned art, education, and community collaboration...My hope was to connect artists, have people make art together, and showcase the Plant as a community space[,]...an inclusive creative space, where individuals could use the space for meetings, as a studio and workshop,

The *Chronicle* article detailed collaboration with a local partner, The Plant, for the *Waging Peace!* project.

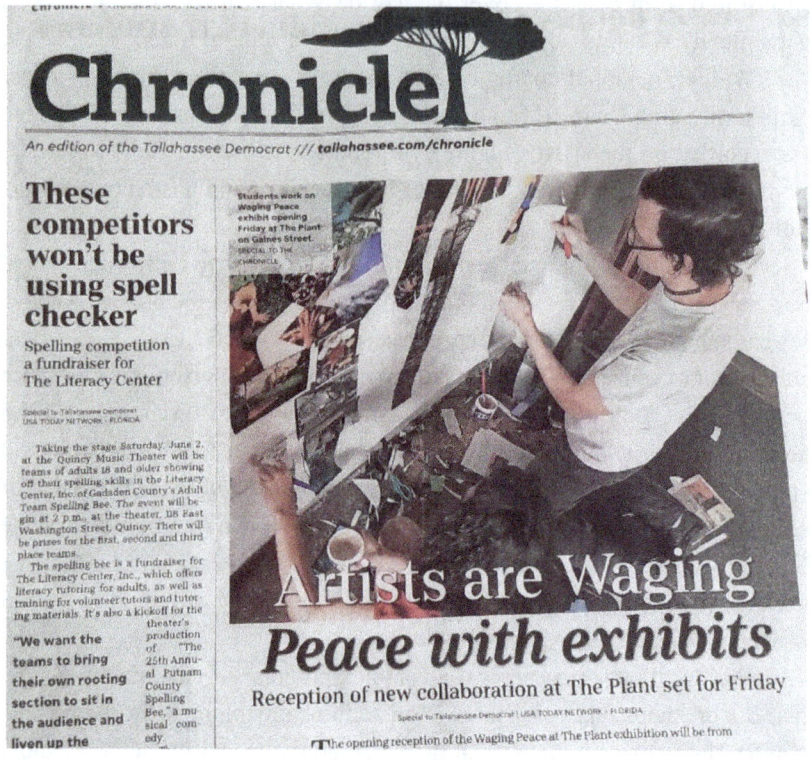

Courtesy: Florida State University Museum of Fine Arts; article photo courtesy of Jennifer Hamrock and The Plant on Gaines Street.

for exhibitions, for performances, etc.... The theme of waging peace, and the exhibition of artwork, spoke to the mission of The Plant.

(V. D. T. Wylder, personal communication with board member of The Plant, Jennifer Hamrock, April & May, 2020)

Planning took place during meetings in the fall of 2017. The Plant, in collaboration with the hosting artists, offered nine workshops by arranging approximately two workshops per month during the spring of 2018. An exhibition of creations made by workshop participants opened on May 11. Workshops covered an assortment of concepts and processes from *Draw or Doodle: What Would a Peaceful World*

Look Like to YOU to *Building a Community Together: A Collaborative 3-d Art Project*. The *Draw or Doodle* workshop was conceived as

> a visual conversation between two community spaces, The Kearney Center and The Plant. Clients from the Kearney Center [drew]/and doodle[d] on designated days on mural paper. The mural [was] then…installed at The Plant…for anyone to respond to. The mural [was] taken back and forth between spaces over a six-week time span to create layers of dialogue between various community members.
>
> (The Plant, 2018b)

The Kearney Center is a "a one-stop-shop for individuals experiencing homelessness or economic hardship in the North Florida region" (The Kearney Center, 2015). In the *Building a Community* workshop

> participants create[d] their own models of parts of peaceful neighborhood streets…houses, schools, community gardens, storefronts, parks or anything else one might find in a neighborhood. Each participant [was] given a 12″ × 12″ foam board base on which [to] build using found materials. Each base [had] a road and sidewalk section along the front edge.
>
> (The Plant, 2018a)

The models "lined up as a neighborhood street" (The Plant, 2018a) and the mural of doodles joined other artworks in the *Waging Peace at the Plant* exhibition in May.

Workshop participants varied—parents and their children, people off the street, college students, friends of the artists, people who saw publicity for the program in the local newspaper, and so on. Hamrock observed that most participants seemed to experience "the pure enjoyment of making art" and "making art together" in particular. "There wasn't a wave of crowds, but it had a pulse… We did accomplish what we set out to do. [At] the opening…there was a nice crowd." Hamrock summarized the experience, "To provide programming for 5 straight months to the community for free was waging peace all on its own" (Wylder, personal communication, 2020).

The week following the reception at The Plant and after the doors had already opened for the *Waging Peace!* exhibition, the FSU MoFA hosted its own reception. As for previous exhibitions outlined in this book, the FSU MoFA reception provided an array of events within an event. Musical performances by school

Elementary student violinists from the local school system performed during the *Waging Peace!* opening reception.

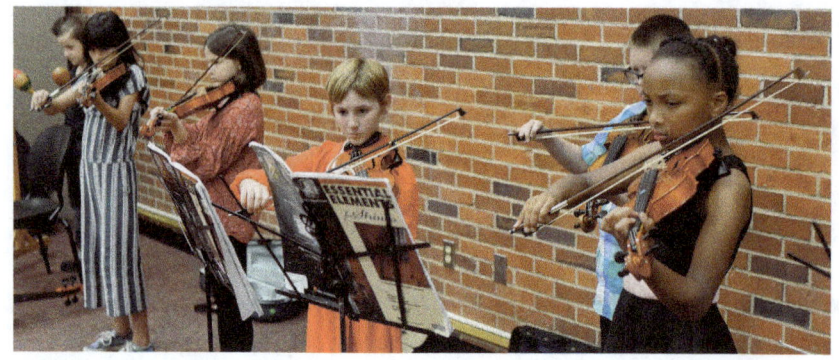

Courtesy: Florida State University Museum of Fine Arts.

Make & take activity tables were ready when the doors opened for the *Waging Peace!* reception.

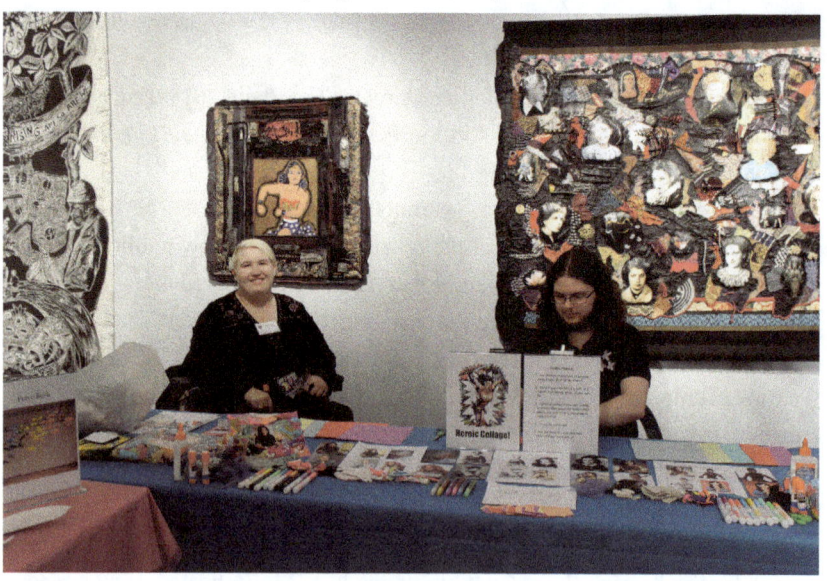

Courtesy: Florida State University Museum of Fine Arts.

Students interacted with the *Parkland Memorial Installation* during the
Waging Peace! opening reception.

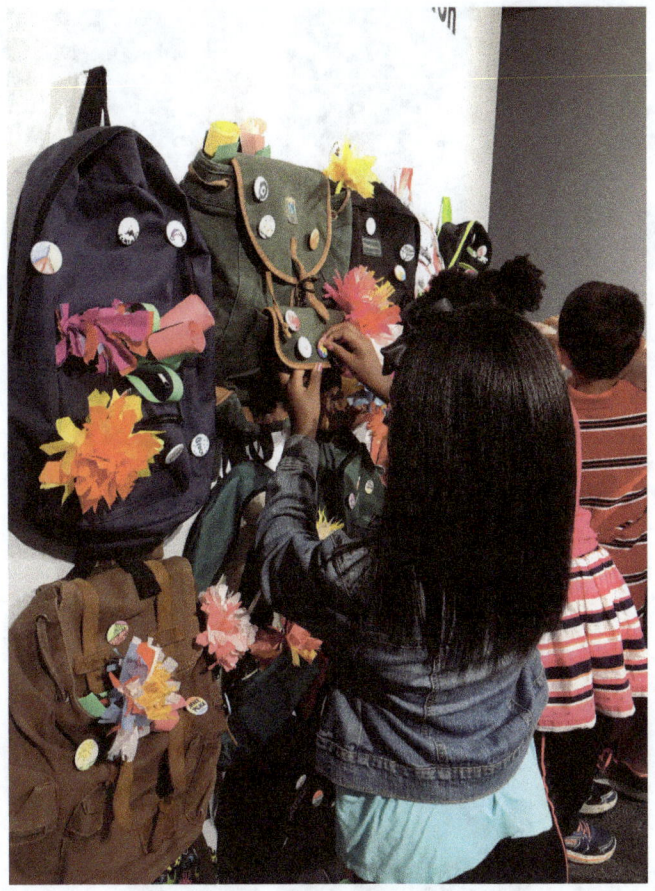

Courtesy: Florida State University Museum of Fine Arts.

groups and multiple "make and take" tables based on the exhibition artwork
engaged the audience. Viewers put together "Heroic Collages" while looking at
Linda Stein's tapestry titled *Ten Heroes*. They worked on an "Ecosystem Drawing" while observing Richelle Gribble's multipaneled painting titled *Ecosystems*
accompanied by a temporary didactic of the meaning of the environmental
term. The ceremony for the *Peace Puzzle* installation, the sharing and listening

Students and parents enjoyed make & take activity tables during the
Waging Peace! opening reception.

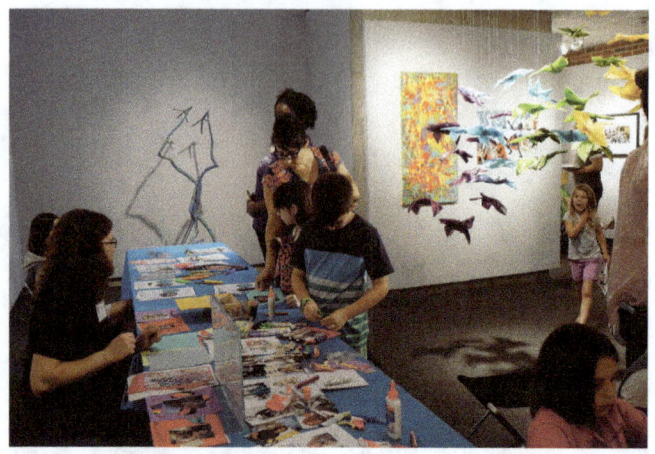

Courtesy: Florida State University Museum of Fine Arts.

During a *Waging Peace!* tour activity, students were eager to discuss
the work by Leon Bedore (Tes One) titled *Brace for Impact.*

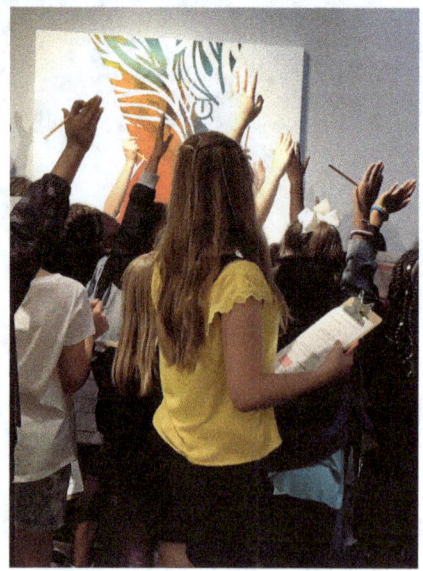

Courtesy: Marcia S. Meale.

During a *Waging Peace!* tour activity, a student interpreted for other students the work by Suzanne Slavick titled *Reconstruction (Magenta Beirut)*.

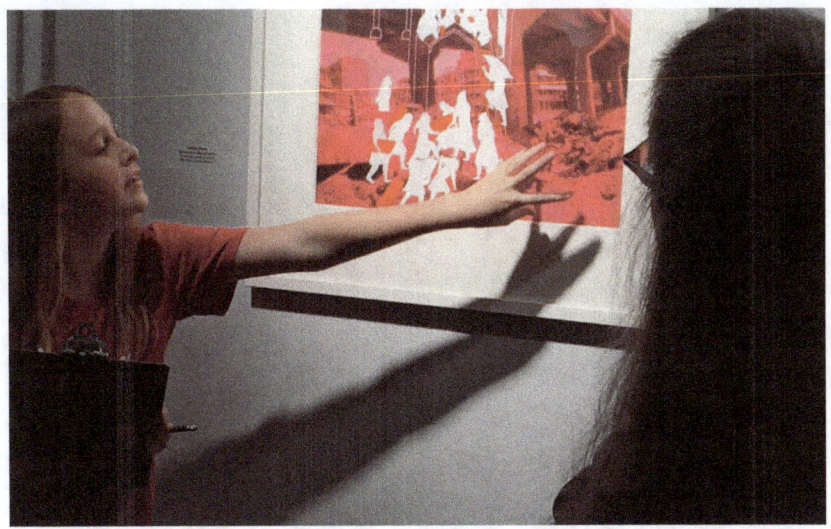

Courtesy: Florida State University Museum of Fine Arts.

encouraged within Jacqueline Weaver's installation, *Border Projects: In Conversation*, and the *Parkland Memorial Installation* activities provided a deeper connection with and understanding of those works. For the *Parkland Memorial Installation*, depicted in more detail in Chapter 1, the audience added to the installation by making paper flowers and messaged buttons to attach to the teachers' satchel, gym bag, and 15 backpacks arranged on the wall. Each symbolized and honored a teacher or student victim of the shooting at the Stoneman Douglas High School in 2018 in Parkland, Florida. A pair of teachers on the co-curatorial committee quickly designed the installation to address the recent tragic event. They intended for the installation and interactions with it to allow the audience to mourn, empathize, and feel urgency toward contributing to a peaceful societal solution for the epidemic of school shootings in the country.

Grant monies to assist with the cost of K-12 student transportation to the FSU MoFA buttressed the number of school tours prior to and after the reception for the exhibition. School groups participated in interactive "minds on" and "hands on" tours given multiple times per day. After the end of the school year summer camp tours took their place. "Minds on" school tours often began with group

For this tour, students broke into small groups to discuss works in the
Waging Peace! Student Display.

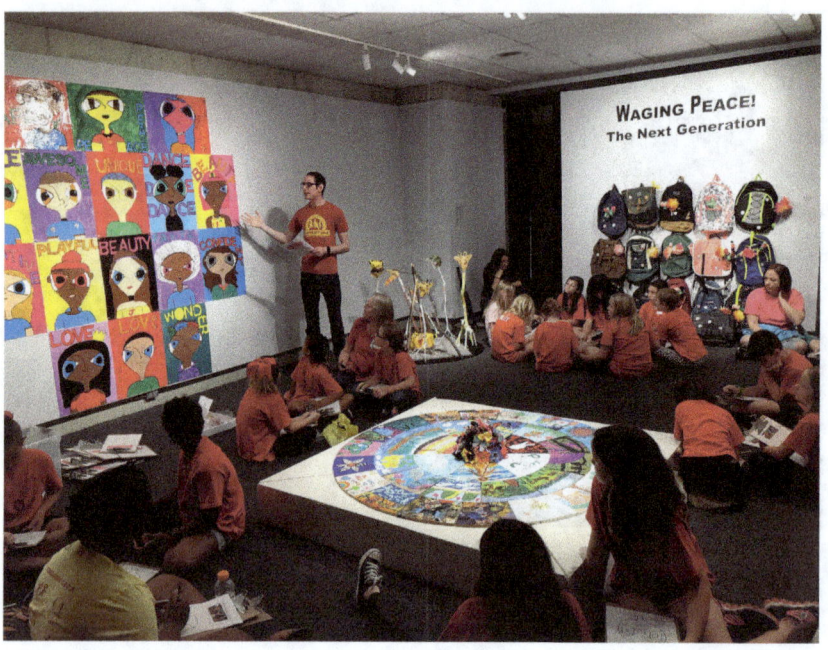

Courtesy: Florida State University Museum of Fine Arts.

discussions of the meaning of the exhibition title *Waging Peace!* as well as
ways students (and adults) might wage peace daily within their own schools and
neighborhoods. Taking grade level into account and utilizing a scavenger hunt
format, students then walked through the exhibition with partners discussing and
determining the peace messages within individual artworks. As a culmination to
this tour, the class as a group listened to individual students who volunteered to
explain their reasons for selecting works of art during the scavenger hunt. This
explanation-and-listening process required the class to move from one work to
another as individual students stood in front of chosen works and pointed out
visual components of the works that affected their comprehension of the works'
peace messages. The class, after listening, was encouraged to further comment
or discuss the work at hand. Individual verbal comments and class discussion
were promoted by telling students that all ideas and choices were acceptable
when backed by thoughtful reasoning.

During a *Waging Peace!* tour activity, a student contemplated the work
by Luisa Padro (Artysta Lulu) titled *Wun Luv.*

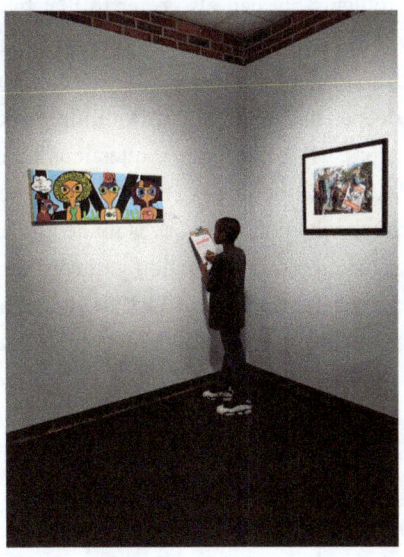

Courtesy: Marcia S. Meale.

Social Justice Art Education and *Waging Peace!*

Although the *Waging Peace!* project and exhibition is an example of the use of
Stewart and Walker's "Big Idea" approach, concepts within social justice art
education provided an additional and important influence for this last project
and exhibition mounted in 2018. Social justice art education normally refers
to pedagogical practice in the classroom, but social justice art education here
refers to ways the ideas for that practice affected the curatorial efforts of the
committee for W*aging Peace!* including selection of work and the development
of accompanying activities. Unlike the "Big Idea" approach, Discipline-Based
Art Education, or traditional formalistic practice, social justice art education
primarily consists of fostering the classroom application of a group of concepts
with little formula for their implementation. A few writers like Marit Dewhurst,
a proponent of social justice art education, do begin to identify specifics. She
proposes three characteristics necessary for its practice: connecting, questioning,
and translating. For Dewhurst, "connecting" means artwork needs to be the result

of an artist's "exploration of the ways injustice plays out in the world and in relation to the artist's own life." Her idea of "connecting" refers to work done in the classroom by students but can also refer to that by professional artists. "Questioning" for Dewhurst pertains to "a deeper understanding of the issues of injustice" on which artwork in this genre is based. "Investigative and analytic questions" fuel this deeper understanding of "multiple social, cultural, political, and economic factors." Two summative questions to ask include: "What's happening?" and "Why is it happening?" The third characteristic, "translating," is the mechanism through which the artwork is made into an "activist" artwork that is the aesthetic translation of information gathered during connecting and questioning. "In the act of translating, activist artists negotiate the concurrent goals of creating an aesthetic object and achieving their intended activist aims" (Dewhurst, 2010, pp. 8–9).

The selection by the co-curatorial committee of a work by Florida artist Bradley Arthur demonstrates Dewhurst's process in action within the context of the development and implementation of the *Waging Peace!* exhibition. Arthur's work titled *WMD's* fused visual symbol and medium to "create an aesthetic object" with "activist aims." The artist molded steel nails into a calligraphic message in the configuration of a $4'' \times 17'' \times 4''$ hanging bas relief. The artist's work consisted entirely of minimal text. Through manipulation of focused lighting on the sculptural script, the viewer read the term "WORDS" spelled out in metal text which unexpectedly appeared to cast a shadow that read "WEAPONS."

Arthur wrote in his artist statement, "Words are visual symbols we are taught and learn to believe. In any language these symbols describe, compare, label, name and identify everything in the world including ourselves and each other" (Arthur, 2018, p. 11) Arthur's statement explained his relationship to his own artwork, but his statement also indicated reasons co-curatorial teachers felt a sense of connection to the piece and selected it for the exhibition. In addition, the artist's statement hinted at a basis for students' attraction and connection to the work during exhibition tours. Frequently, students selected this work as a piece they wanted to introduce to their classmates, and it was a piece that inspired comments and discussion by a large number of students during these introductions.

Dewhurst's main questions about injustice ("What's happening?" and "Why is it happening?") shed further light on the connections made with this artwork and a resultant deeper social justice understanding of it. Teachers and students both

During a tour of the *Waging Peace!* exhibition, students figured out the mechanics of the work by Bradley Arthur titled *WMD's*.

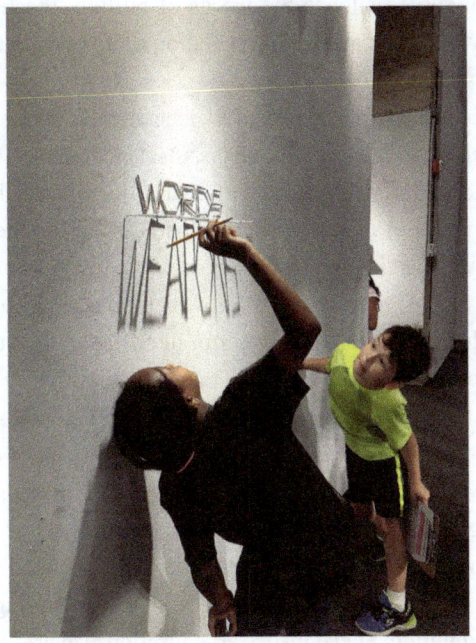

Courtesy: Marcia S. Meale.

appreciated the artist's acknowledgement that words could be used as weapons, powerful weapons of mass destruction as the title *WMD's* indicates. Words used as weapons through injurious name-calling of others with internalization of such labelling by victims form the backbone of bullying in schools today. Many of these teachers and students had participated in programs to prevent the occurrence and spread of bullying, particularly by nurturing respect for contemporary culture's increasing personal, group, and community diversity and by making bullying unacceptable within school culture. The artist's title with its indication of monumental destruction emphasized the seriousness of his work's content.

As students viewed the work during tours, they admired the aesthetics of the spare construction of the object with its ability to convey a "get-to-the-point" message important to them. Invariably from one tour to the next, students voiced similar observations about words that might be spoken and heard in a moment but would carry shadowy and lingering deleterious effects long after they were spoken and heard. With deep insight a number of students understood further meaning—that words, ironically, can also be used to "combat" the use of words as weapons, to silence the words of bullies. Teachers and students understood this work as an aesthetic translation of an essential message within antibullying activism.

Generally, the concepts of social justice art education fall under the umbrella idea of nurturing social consciousness through the arts. Under that umbrella idea, social justice art educators approach the arts with two major and overlapping concerns in mind: 1) the exposé of inequality and unjustness, and 2) the construction of social connection. Social justice art educators see both as avenues toward social justice reform. Much of the content of artwork in the social justice realm acts as an exposé in the hope of affecting reform, like Bradley Arthur's aspiration to eradicate the practice of discrimination in the form of bullying. Social justice art education works toward reformist art practice through methods like advocating personal research into social justice issues, the examination of the strategies and media involved in the making of work addressing these issues, looking at factors impacting artists and their artwork, and encouraging critical inquiry of the content of social justice artwork. Students demonstrated the use of these methods through their analysis of Bradley Arthur's work during the tours of the *Waging Peace!* exhibition. Social justice art education also uses processes such as these to encourage the production of exposé work by students themselves. These processes tend to align with Marit Dewhurst's approach. Despite the importance of the concepts and methods utilized by this part of social justice art education pedagogy which focus on the exposé of inequality and unjustness, it seems that most of the concepts within social justice art education pedagogy center on the construction of social connection through the arts.

Social justice art education encourages the building of social connection through a myriad of strategies. This form of art education embraces collaborative processes through group planning, decision-making, and implementation. All perspectives, voices, and interests of participants are welcomed in all parts of teaching and artmaking processes. This pedagogy seeks active, not passive, involvement and leads to collective projects with the collective process seen as fostering democratic forces. This collaborative and collective attitude extends to contexts beyond the school setting as exhibited within the co-curatorial process for the exhibition *Waging Peace!* Certainly, the exhibition's co-curatorial approach demonstrated the advocacy of active collaborative engagement and the adoption of collective projects as delineated by proponents of social justice art education. In addition, all artwork shown in the student display section of *Waging Peace!* required teachers to plan for some form of collaborative or collective completion of student artwork for the display.

Related to this espousal of collaboration or collectivity is the respect within social justice art education for the ever-widening reaches of the community and the use of art to communicate the goals of empathy, engagement, ethical practice, and other social justice values to shape a hopefully ever-improving community at every level from the classroom to the globe. The artmaking process is multifocal. The communication aspects of artmaking or art object, or the transmission of meaning by the artmaking process or the art object, are deemed as important as the completion and existence of the end product. The social connection role of artmaking and art object is paramount.

A lesson plan in the exhibition education packet titled *Waging Peace by Bridging Communities* contributed by Lisa Girard and Melinda Stuart-Tilley, co-curatorial members from the Tallahassee Homeschool Group Cooperative, demonstrated these social justice art education practices. An exhibition work by New York artist, Lori Zeller, titled *Love & Tolerance = Change*, provided inspiration for the lesson plan. Girard and Stuart-Tilley expressed a generalized vision for the plan in a lesson section titled "Session Activity."

> The artist repeats the title three times on the surface of her painting in three different languages. Participating students will write at least three letters to "PeacePals" in other countries. The students will then create a collaborative work of art that reflects the connections made through this letter writing and will reflect their knowledge gained of the various countries of the PeacePals… Ultimately the students will be challenged to learn and understand the point of view of people from another culture, a means to waging peace. They will create a book to include letters written to/received from PeacePals. Students will create artworks to accompany the letters. Each artwork will encapsulate aspects of the PeacePals' culture or cultures learned during the course of the project. In addition, a large poster will be displayed with the book. The poster will include artwork done by the participating students superimposed with statements, reminiscent of Lori Zeller's statement written on her artwork, about peace gleaned from the letters written to/received from PeacePals.
>
> (Girard & Stuart-Tilley, 2018, p. 81)

Girard and Stuart-Tilley devised questions to provoke students' thinking about "waging peace by bridging communities" throughout the several months of the project. For example, as a group they discussed:

> "What did you share about American/Floridian culture?…How can you build a
> sense of community with your PeacePal and his/her culture/country? Do you think
> your PeacePal feels a sense of community with you? What makes you think that?"
>   (Girard & Stuart-Tilley, 2018, p. 83).

Despite the focus on meaning, understanding and knowledge of media and aesthetic aims are deemed important within social justice art education. To emphasize these factors, co-curatorial members selected work to show expertise in a wide range of materials, style, and technique. Co-curatorial members also selected artwork to show the extended scope of topics and themes within the realm of social justice. This pedagogy seeks to use art to create a new world vision, one that promotes: diversity of persons and cultures; balance among civilization, other living species, and the environment; participatory process; and within the art field, regard for a range of artwork. The range of work and the range of topics within the *Waging Peace!* exhibition featured: paintings like that by Leon Bedore titled *Brace for Impact* showing two clasped hands of people from different ethnicities/races, stylized and silhouetted against an otherwise open compositional space; the untitled digitally stitched panoramic photograph by Stephen Marc showing the singular focus of a celebratory crowd who participated in a ceremony in which the governor of South Carolina "sign[ed] the bill to remove the Confederate battle flag…from South Carolina Statehouse grounds" (Marc, 2018, p. 26); and environmental pieces like the oversized abstracted woodcut image by Natalie Sassine, *Gulf South Rising*, which addressed the crisis of climate change on the Gulf of Mexico.

Social justice art education approaches the artwork itself, if installed, as a symbol of values or knowledge to share with the current community or the community of the future. The co-curatorial committee did select work with values and knowledge in mind, with the idea of communicating those values and knowledge to their students and to the community-at-large. They also knew a catalogue would be published to accompany the exhibition and selected work with the idea of sharing the catalogue with the community of the future. Social justice art education proponents believe artwork can act as a place of community observances where meaning is ritualized. For an exhibition like *Waging Peace!*,

Waging Peace! exhibition: installation view of works by Linda Stein, Leon Bedore (Tes One), Mariann Kearsley, Eva Weingarten, and Patricia Anderson Turner.

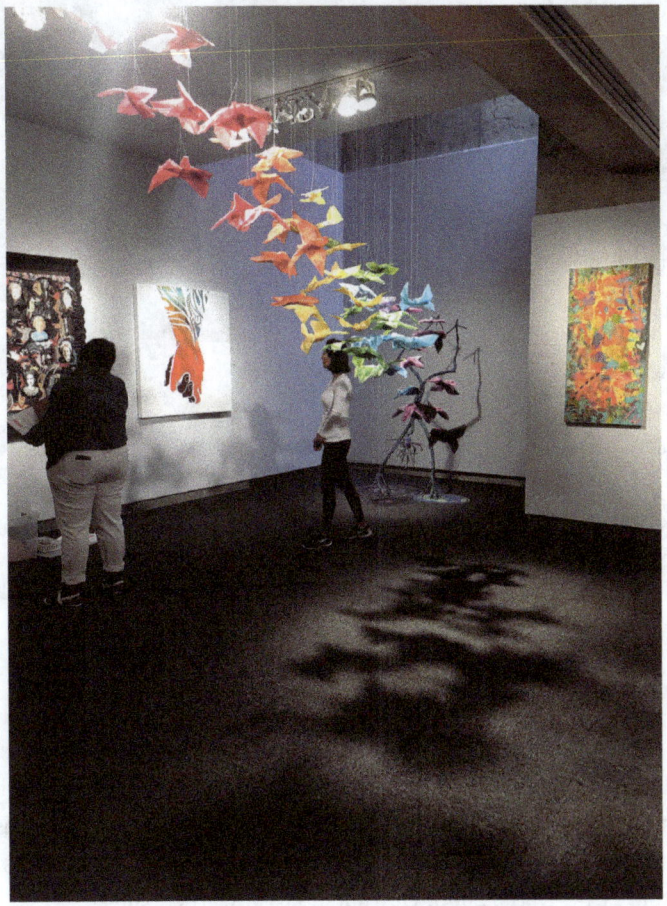

Courtesy: Marcia S. Meale.

reception activities and tours acted as rituals where meaning was revealed through formalized and open-ended discussion and other forms of participation. The *Peace Puzzle* installation ceremony which inaugurated the reception for *Waging Peace!* provided an opportunity for K-8 students to symbolically dramatize the meaning of their art in front of their peers, family, friends, and the public-at-large. Thus, in social justice pedagogy, art performs for a broad audience, not just for

During a tour of the *Waging Peace!* Student Display, students discussed the multi-school *Peace Puzzle* project.

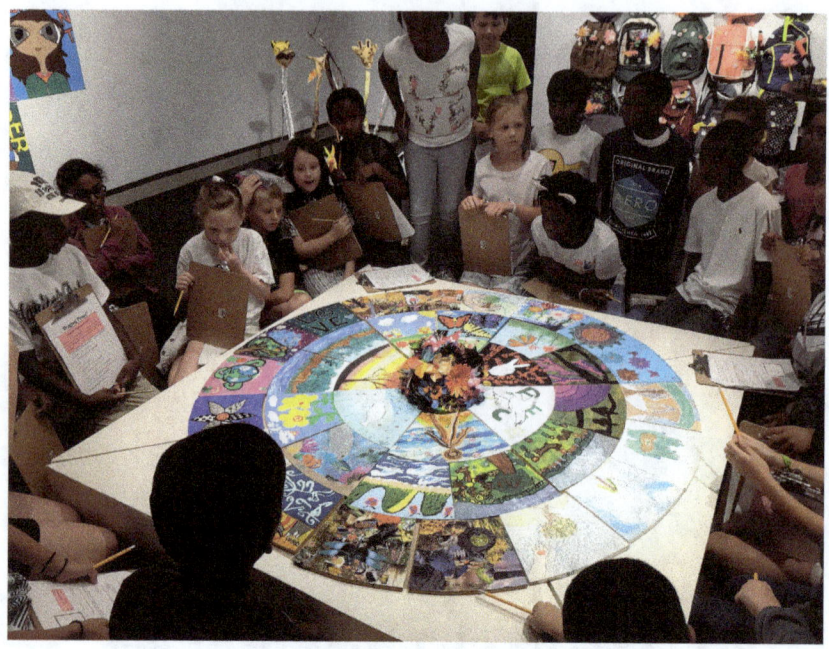

Courtesy: Marcia S. Meale.

the individuals of the art world who carry specific art attitudes, "sophistication," and preference. Creating social connection through interaction and relationship between the artwork and a wide public becomes the goal, a means to assist in the creation of a community who lives social justice values (Blatt-Gross, 2017; Buffington, 2014; Darts, 2006; Dewhurst, 2010; Garber, 2004).

As usual the museum totaled numbers of participants for all events within this project. Like the evolution of interaction with *The Story* and *Generations*, eventually 25 schools joined *Waging Peace!* in one way or another. Over 900 students created response artwork to the works curated into the exhibition. As already stated, these were displayed at the FSU MoFA and at Tallahassee City Hall. Over 400 people attended *Waging Peace!* receptions. Over the course of the last five months of the project, between offsite participation at schools and community organizations and onsite participation at the FSU MoFA, the tally for participation reached over 3,000.

For this project three art education professionals, Jennifer Hamrock, Rachel Fendler, and Anna Freeman, also conducted a qualitative analysis and published their results in 2019 in an article in *The International Journal of Arts Education* titled *Waging Peace! An Art Museum as a Resource for Partnerships*. The authors acknowledged the prevalent usage of quantitative tabulations by museums to evaluate such programs but felt these assessments ignored program richness, strength, depth of commitment to collaborative engagement, and openness to participation. During their research they interviewed 21 persons involved including the museum educator, an administrator, a gallery director, teachers in the school system, homeschool teachers, artists, community organizers, and interns. They conducted two interviews per person, one toward the beginning of the project and one after the exhibition opened. A final focus group included eight participants. Their interview topics covered areas like involvement, objectives, and impact.

The authors noted a strengthened museum/school relationship. Educators cited the expansion of their professional resources which influenced curriculum planning. They liked the opportunity to meet with other art teachers monthly to jointly generate ideas, and they felt the process positively impacted their students, citing a sense of genuineness and earnestness in their students' work. Community membership in the project was judged by this study to provide advantageous outreach between the museum and participating local organizations. By working together, both the museum and involved community organizations enhanced their outreach to local artists and to a larger city audience.

The authors cited a sense of empowerment, creativity, camaraderie, and satisfaction felt by the members of the co-curatorial team. The educators on the committee indicated this satisfaction transferred to their students. The authors described the project as a "network" that was "horizontal and decentralized" (Hamrock, Fendler, & Freeman, 2019, p. 8). The museum education program's invitations to "professionals, such as educators and artists, to participate [yielded] them authorship of the project in the process" (p. 8). This brought a "sense of ownership" (p. 4) to all on the committee which the authors commended for yielding a positive effect to the outcome. The *Waging Peace!* project was appraised as "unique" (p. 2), but it was also appraised as a "model" (p. 3) for the building of connections and relationships into larger networks by museum education programs or other such entities due to its "multifaceted" (p. 2) quality and strong valuation by its participants.

Selected pages from the *Waging Peace!* catalogue.

WAGING PEACE!

TABLE OF CONTENTS

3

Courtesy: Florida State University Museum of Fine Arts.

BRADLEY ARTHUR

My work is intended to bring awareness to our inner world. I chose simple construction nails, not to build something utilitarian, but to create an object to contemplate. Words have tremendous power and we interpret them subjectively. Although words usually occur outside us, they enter our deep inner thoughts and register meanings. Words are visual symbols we are taught and learn to believe. In any language these symbols describe, compare, label, name, and identify everything in the world including ourselves and each other.

Besides offering actual words, this piece from the Shadow Thoughts series invites the viewer to interact in a multi-level process. First the viewer sees. Next the viewer ponders the seen juxtaposed with its shadow. The gallery light, acting almost as an individual actor, reveals a deeper insight to the viewer who shares the revelation with the light in real time. This process happens within us and that is where Peace abides. —BA

The artist is a sculptor and Amrit Yoga instructor. He maintains his studio in Land O Lakes, FL (PO Box 2028, 34639) where he is self-employed but also works at various yoga studios. Website: www.BradArthur.com. Contact information: ba@bradarthur.com.

Selected Awards and Exhibitions: 2014—*Feel Herd*, Ybor School of Visual Arts Gallery, HCC, Tampa / Ybor City, FL; 2007—*Kol Ami Star Memorial Sculpture & Garden*, Congregation Kol Ami, Tampa FL; 2006—*Word Sculpture*, Kotler Art Gallery, J.F. Germany Public Library, Tampa, FL; 2002—*Components of Public Safety I & II*, Hillsborough County Public Art, Tampa FL; 1990—*Generations*, Miami Jewish Home and Hospital for the Aged, Miami, FL.

▼Bradley Arthur, *WMD's*, 2004, paint on welded steel nails, light and shadow, 4 x 17 x 4 inches (without the shadow).

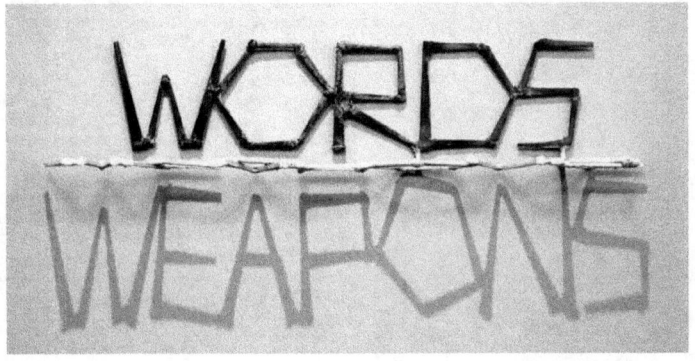

11

Courtesy: Florida State University Museum of Fine Arts.

WAGING PEACE!

DU CHAU

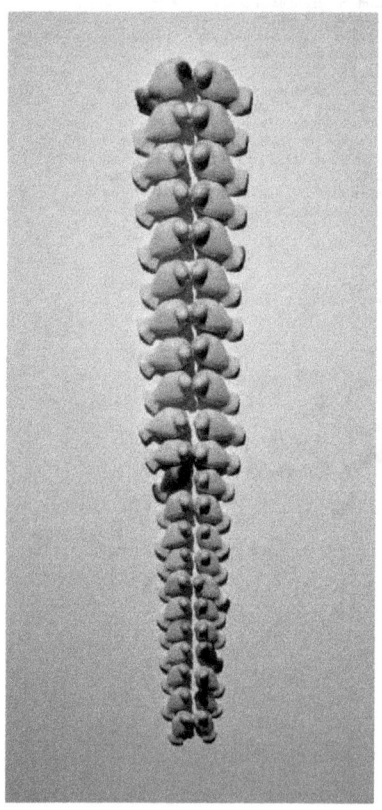

My work medium is predominately porcelain. Some of my pieces combine ceramics and wire elements to create a quiet and contemplative charged space. My current artworks evoke early childhood memories in Vietnam and repetitive daily activity to visualize different parts of myself.

I am passionate about duplicating forms using a mold making and slip casting technique. This process reveals my fascination with clay replication with subtle variations. Constant permutation is the core of my creative process.

Foundations is a nested set of 44 porcelain doves, descending into diminishing scale and transforming into a backbone like structure. Formed by the reiterative slip casting of porcelain into molds initially made, the successive casts shrink in firing. The progressive diminution of scale into each iteration becomes a metaphor for the dissolution of the birds into space. Their soulful calls and coos bring many people hope in a chaotic world. —DC

The artist is an adjunct professor at Brookhaven College in Dallas, TX. He is represented by Liliana Bloch Gallery and also maintains a studio at 2271 Monitor Street, Dallas, TX 75207. Website: www.duchauwebsite.com. Contact information: duchau@mhd.com.

Selected Awards and Exhibitions: 2017—NCECA International Residency at Curaumilla Art Center in Chile; 2016—*Intensity*, Brazos Gallery, Richard College, Dallas, TX; *Qui E Ora*, CRETA Rome, Rome, Italy; *Hanging On 2*, ArtSpace, Dallas, TX; 2015—*Part of a Continuum*, Liliana Bloch Gallery, Dallas, TX.

◄Du Chau, *Foundations*, 2012, porcelain, 39½ x 7½ x 2½ inches.

14

LUISA PADRO (ARTYSTA LULU)

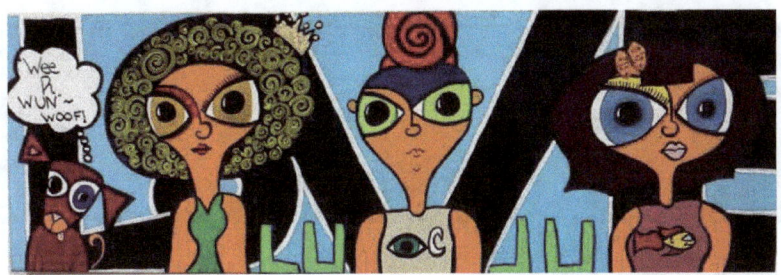

Four characters, Fiona the Dog, Queen, Vik, and Veronika, are featured in Wun Love. *Fiona is seen thinking "Wee R Wun" (translation: we are one), alongside a diverse group of characters, because dogs understand unconditional love. The center character, Vik, could be male or female and was intentionally created that way to include the LGBTQ+ community. All of the human characters are painted the same orange as an indication of their designation as one species. The word "Love" was purposely painted in a way that would require time for the viewer to notice. Art has a way of subliminally affecting the viewer. When viewers read these words while trying to understand the painting, they will have said "we are one" in their minds or out loud. Maybe it's implanted by the time they walk away with that very profound and simple statement. —Lulu*

The artist is a full-time artist / painter and maintains a studio at 319 West Curtis Street, Tampa, FL 33603. She is represented by The Wandering Eye Art Gallery in Ybor City. Website: www.ArtystaLuLu.com. Contact information: Luisa@ArtystaLuLu.com.

Selected Awards and Exhibitions: 2016—nominated for Best of the Bay, Best Local Artist, Creative Loafing, Tampa, FL; 2015—nominated for Best of the Bay, Best Local Artist, Creative Loafing, Tampa, FL; Selected for ArtPop Tampa, featured on six billboards and a HART bus, ArtPop, Tampa, FL.

▲Luisa Padro (Artysta Lulu), *Wun Love*, 2015, mixed media, acrylic, gold leafing, ribbon, 12 x 36 x 2 inches.

33

Courtesy: Florida State University Museum of Fine Arts.

JUDY LIPMAN SHECHTER

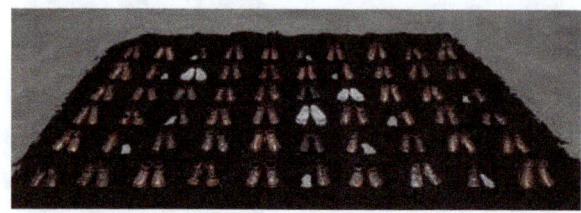

Small But Mighty, Christopher Art Gallery, Chicago Heights, IL; 2016-17—Freeport Art Museum, Freeport, IL; 2016—Honorable Mention, Marin Museum Of Contemporary Art, Novato, CA.

Deaths from war cannot be ignored.

I want to show these deaths are unacceptable and make us question why we are at war. If we could perceive our troops differently, perhaps those making the decision to put them in harm's way may hesitate, re-evaluate, and find other solutions for solving conflicts. I'm presenting our troops as children, because in reality each serviceperson is someone's child, and everyone can understand the tragic loss of a child.

As a child I saw that my friends' and cousins' baby shoes had been magically changed into bronze. I was fascinated. Shoes preserved and now on display had became tributes to love, mementos of a special time shared . . . a time of a child's dependency and of a parent's responsibility.

Children outgrow their dependence, yet a parent's sense of responsibility remains throughout a lifetime, making these deaths a more poignant tragedy worthy of everyone's reflection. —JLS

The artist maintains a studio at 459 West Broadway, New York, NY 10012. Website: www.judylipmanshechter.com. Contact information: judylipmanshechter@gmail.com.

Selected Awards and Exhibitions: 2017—International Exhibition, Masur Art Museum, Monroe, LA; National Exhibition, Armstrong Fine Arts Gallery, Savannah, GA;

▲Judy Lipman Shechter, [and detail below] *Boots on the Ground*, 2016-ongoing, mixed media: bronze, copper, metal, plaster, soil, plastic, 7 x 96 x84 inches.

37

WAGING PEACE!

LINDA STEIN

Tackling oppression—including racism, sexism, classism, ableism, homophobia—through the lens of bullying and gender justice, is the mission that has guided me as activist and artist.

My Ten Heroes tapestry depicts fierce females during the time of the Holocaust juxtaposed with my selected pop-culture and religious icons of protection. The blending of fantasy and reality figures prompt conversations about everyday heroism and brave upstanding against bullying and bigotry.

William Moulton Marston's version of Wonder Woman (1941-1947) represents a moral exemplar for me. I love that she turns around villains and helps the downtrodden by using her magic wrist bracelets, lasso, and invisible plane—without ever killing. In my art, I re-create the graphics of her comics to reflect my own gender justice/anti-bullying proclivities. I change her text-bubbles to reflect my own messages: What is the role of strength in contemporary culture? What defines bravery? What makes a hero? —LS

The artist is Founder and President of Have Art: Will Travel and maintains a studio at 100 Reade Street, New York, NY 10013. Website: www.lindas-tein.com, www.haveartwilltravel.org. Contact information: studiomanager@lindastein.com.

Selected Awards and Exhibitions: 2017—Artist of the Year, NYCATA/UFT, New York, NY; 2016—Artist Honoree for Commitment to Arts and Culture, NAWA, New York, NY; 2016—Artist-in-Residence, Squire Foundation, Santa Barbara, CA; 2015—Financial Grant, MFJC, New York, NY; 2005—Financial Grant, LMCC, New York, NY.

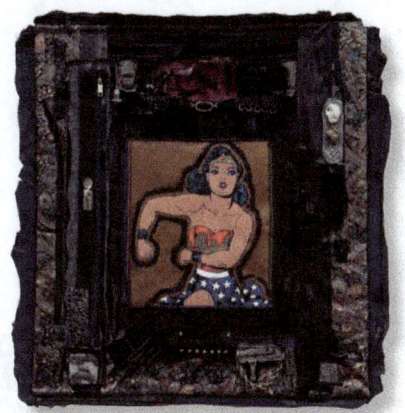

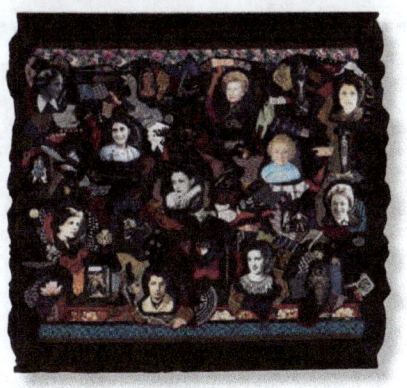

▶[top right] Linda Stein, *Wonder Woman's Mobility 718*, 2011, quilted tapestry of mixed media with acrylic painting on canvas, 33 x 32 inches.

▶[bottom right] Linda Stein, *Ten Heros 859*, 2016, leather, archival pigment paint on canvas, fabric, metal, zippers, 56 x 62 x 2 inches.

40

Courtesy: Florida State University Museum of Fine Arts.

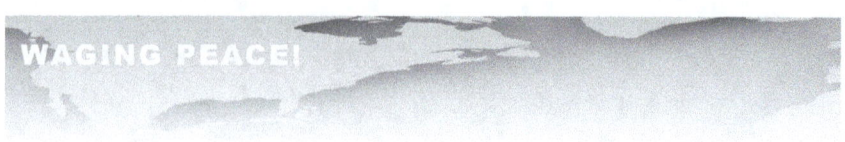

PATRICIA ANDERSON TURNER

Seeking peace is an eternal journey filled with turbulence and joy, a flight made by all creatures no matter their color or size or how they choose to spread their wings. This flight soars upward, whether to meet the challenges of world peace or the personal pursuit of emotional well-being.

I used silk organza for its near weightlessness and the vibrancy with which it takes my dyes. Due to health issues, I was unable to sit at the sewing machine I normally use to create my art. I could, however, stand in my tiny pool to dye the silk and I could stand at an ironing board to shape the silk. Hence, I taught myself origami. Over many weeks, the folding became ingrained in my fingers. The slimmest of wires are entwined in the bodies and wings; they are hung simply using needle and thread.

Enjoy this delicate Flight *toward peace, toward peacefulness.* —PAT

The artist maintains a studio at 1830 Banana Street in Punta Gorda, FL 33980 and is represented by Creations Gallery in Punta Gorda. Website: www.patriciaturnerart. com. Contact information: patriciaturnerart@yahoo. com.

Selected Awards and Exhibitions: 2017—Scholarship Artist Retreat with Fran Gardner at the Atlantic Center for the Arts, New Smyrna Beach, FL; 2016—Honorable Mention, *FL3TCH3R: Social and*

Politically Engaged Art, Reece Museum, Johnson City, TN; 2015—3rd Place, and Best Use of Color, *National Quilt Extravaganza*, Philadelphia, PA; 2011—First Place, *La Vie Della Di Incontrano a Verona*, Museum Modern Art, Verona, Italy.

▼Patricia Anderson Turner, *Flight*, 2016, silk, 90 x 54 inches.

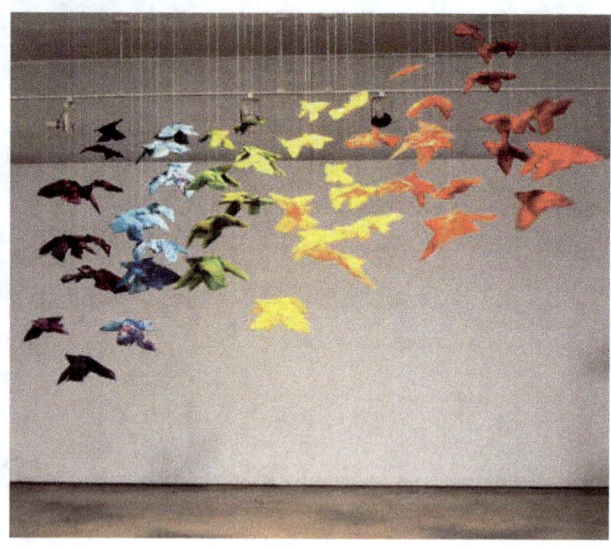

Selected content from the *Waging Peace!* Teachers Packet.

Courtesy: Florida State University Museum of Fine Arts.

Lesson: Public Art Project "A Piece for Peace"

Leslie Anderson, Canopy Oaks Elementary School

*This lesson plan could utilize any work in the Waging Peace Exhibition.

Biography of the Artist:

Although this artwork is originally a 16" x 20" painting, it would translate nicely into a large scale mural due to it's graphic nature and bright, bold color scheme. The peaceful nature of the design would also make it fitting for a meaningful public art piece.

Combining traditional and non-traditional techniques, Leon "Tes One" Bedore creates works of art that contrast nature with technology, allowing him to find beauty in everyday life. These comparisons help create paintings that are symbolic. Bedore aims to add a sense of movement into his artwork to help bring his energy into the piece and emphasize his message to the viewer.
Source: www.tesone.net

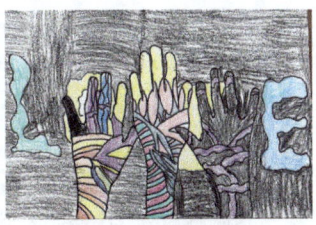

Crayon Drawing by Student based on *Brace for Impact*, Leon Bedore, acrylic on paper, 16" x 20"

Next Generation Sunshine State Standards:
➤   **Big Idea:** Critical Thinking and Reflection
    Enduring Understanding 1: Cognition and reflection are required to appreciate, interpret, and create with artistic intent.
•   **Benchmark:** VA.5.C.1.1 Develop a range of interests in the art-making process to influence personal decision-making.
•   **Benchmark:** VA.5.C.1.3 Examine and discuss exemplary works of art to distinguish which qualities may be used to evaluate personal works.
    Enduring Understanding 2: Assessing our own and others' artistic work, using critical-thinking, problem-solving, and decision-making skills, is central to artistic growth.
•   **Benchmark:** VA.5.C.2.4 Identify examples of constructive criticism and use them to improve artworks and enhance artistic growth.
    Enduring Understanding 3: The process of critiquing works of art leads to development of critical-thinking skills transferable to other contexts.
•   **Benchmark:** VA.5.C.3.2 Use art-criticism processes to form a hypothesis about an artist's or designer's intent.
➤   **Big Idea:** Skills, Techniques, & Processes
    Enduring Understanding 1: The arts are inherently experiential and actively engage learners in the process of creating, interpreting, and responding to art.
•   **Benchmark:** VA.5.S.1.4 Use accurate art vocabulary to communicate about works of art and artistic and creative processes.

17

Lesson: Public Art Project "A Piece for Peace"
Leslie Anderson, Canopy Oaks Elementary School

➤ **Big Idea:** Innovation, Technology, and the Future
Enduring Understanding 2: Careers in and related to the arts significantly and positively impact local and global economies.
▪ **Benchmark:** VA.5.F.2.3 Discuss contributions that artists make to society.
Enduring Understanding 3: The 21st century skills necessary for success as citizens, workers, and leaders in a global economy are embedded in the study of the arts.
▪ **Benchmark:** VA.5.F.3.1 Create artwork to promote public awareness of community and/or global concerns.

Session Activity:
Students will participate in a classroom discussion based on the *Waging Peace!* PowerPoint, and PowerPoint on public art. Students will be placed into small groups and will go over a Public Art Project packet as a class. Each group will pick a challenge from the packet. Students will first sketch their ideas on the worksheet in the packet then complete the rest of the worksheet. Groups will present their ideas to the class. Presentations will help lead students to recognize the significance of public art in the pursuit of waging peace and to realize in which ways we can benefit from public art.

Objectives:
➤ Students will learn, appreciate and experience what public art is.
➤ Students will learn the power of using symbols in art to communicate ideas.
➤ Students will design a piece of art using words, color, symbols and/or images to convey an idea about peace.
➤ Students will work in groups to create, decide, and present a full project.

Grade Level: 5

Time Needed:
4 sessions

Materials:
➤ Technology: *Waging Peace!* PowerPoint, Public Art PowerPoint, YouTube Video on Public Art.
➤ Resources: Visual images, Books on Banksy (and other street artists), Local public art.
➤ Supplies: Paper, Writing utensils.

Activity Procedures:
➤ **Session 1:** Students will be introduced to public art through a PowerPoint presentation, or YouTube video (K-5: https://www.youtube.com/watch?v=MNO14EzuPM4 OR 6-12: https://www.youtube.com/watch?v=yBPm7DWrTbI), that will provide several visual images to promote classroom discussion.
    Using the images from the *Waging Peace!* exhibition, teacher will lead students into a class discussion about how artists use symbols, color, words and images to express their ideas. How can ideas be transferred using other artistic means? How can artists communicate a concept with color or images? How can a thought elicit a personal reaction from the viewer? What is the importance of using symbols, colors, and images as metaphors for ideas?
➤ **Session 2:** Assign students into small groups and provide the project packet/package.
    Review the package step by step providing ample examples.
    Allow students to work together and assist them in answering questions and concerns.
    Each group will have a specific challenge. Depending on the challenge, students will have to use symbols, colors, and images to deliver their final ideas.

18

Lesson: Public Art Project "A Piece for Peace"
Leslie Anderson, Canopy Oaks Elementary School

> ➤   **Session 3:** Students will each sketch an idea on the space provided in the package.
> After they finish their sketches, students will complete the last part of the package.
> ➤   **Session 4:** Students will present their projects and will be required to share one or two questions
> from the package, but teacher will encourage students to share all the questions from the package.
> If camera is available, document images to share with class.

Evaluation:
> ➤   4 - All objectives are met and the work exceeds the criteria.
> ➤   2 - Some objectives are met and the work is incomplete.
> ➤   3 - All objectives are met and the work meets the criteria.
> ➤   1 - Many objectives are not met and the work is incomplete.

Public Art Project
"A Piece for Peace"

Name of your group:_____

Names of group participants:
1._____
2._____
3._____
4._____
5._____
6._____
7._____

19

Lesson: Public Art Project "A Piece for Peace"
Leslie Anderson, Canopy Oaks Elementary School

For this project, you will work with the following theme:
Peace

Think of a piece of art that will express and communicate a peaceful feeling. Use the space underneath to brainstorm some ideas of what peace means to you.

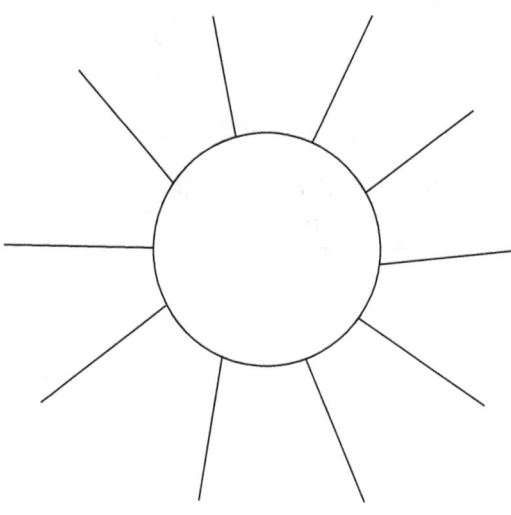

Lesson: Public Art Project "A Piece for Peace"

Leslie Anderson, Canopy Oaks Elementary School

Proposal for the creation of a public art piece for the City of Tallahassee

Art Statement:

1. Describe your artwork.

_____

_____

_____

2. What is the big idea behind your artwork?

_____

_____

3. Overall feeling?

_____

_____

_____

1. Is public art in society important? Why or why not?

_____

_____

2. What can public art accomplish? What can it give us?

_____

_____

_____

If your project could have a name, what would you name it? Why would you name it this?

Example: _Our City in Peace._

_____

_____

_____

21

Lesson: Public Art Project "A Piece for Peace"
Leslie Anderson, Canopy Oaks Elementary School

Use this space to sketch your idea. Please use as much detail as you can.

Public Art Project

Lesson: Public Art Project "A Piece for Peace"
Leslie Anderson, Canopy Oaks Elementary School

Vocabulary you may need to know:

Two-Dimensional
Three-Dimensional
Design
Environment
Form
Installation
Proposal
Plan
Point of View
Site
Edge
Observation
Background
Assemblage
Border
Layer
Mixed Media
Proportion
Recycle
Symbol
Lighting
Structure

Public Art Project Proposal
Challenge #1

You have to design a water feature for a park. The water feature will be installed in the children's area. Safety is one of the most important concerns. The construction area is quite flat.

Required Theme:
Peace

Things to consider:
How safe is the project?
What materials will you use?
Are there any maintenance issues?
How much will it cost (budget)?
Describe your proposal. What will it look like?
How will people react to it?

Public Art Project Proposal
Challenge #2

You have to design a piece of art to decorate the entrance of the Department of Education in Tallahassee, Florida. This piece will be located in the circular lobby of the building. The room you will use is quite large. The height of the lobby is two stories tall.

Required Theme:
Peace

Things to consider:
How safe is the project?
What materials will you use?
Are there any maintenance issues?
How much will it cost (budget)?
Describe your proposal. What will it look like?
How will people react to it?

23

Lesson: Public Art Project "A Piece for Peace"
Leslie Anderson, Canopy Oaks Elementary School

Public Art Project Proposal **Challenge #3** You are going to design a crosswalk at a very busy intersection. The crosswalk will connect state buildings to a small park that is often used during state workers' lunch breaks. **Required Theme:** Peace **Things to consider:** How safe is the project? What materials will you use? Are there any maintenance issues? How much will it cost (budget)? Describe your proposal. What will it look like? How will people react to it?

Public Art Project Proposal **Challenge #5** You are going to design a mural in a part of town that has high crime. The City of Tallahassee wants the mural to change the perception of the neighborhood and promote a sense of peace. **Required Theme:** Peace **Things to consider:** How safe is the project? What materials will you use? Are there any maintenance issues? How much will it cost (budget)? Describe your proposal. What will it look like? How will people react to it?

Public Art Project Proposal **Challenge #4** You are going to design a light feature to enhance a bridge in the middle of the city. The area where the bridge is located is in a run-down part of town. The city wants to enhance it to help promote new businesses and strengthen our community. **Required Theme:** Peace **Things to consider:** How safe is the project? What materials will you use? Are there any maintenance issues? How much will it cost (budget)? Describe your proposal. What will it look like? How will people react to it?

Public Art Project Proposal **Challenge #6** The City of Tallahassee wants to honor a group of firefighters that helped during a catastrophe. They want an interactive and meditative space for families to visit. **Required Theme:** Peace **Things to consider:** How safe is the project? What materials will you use? Are there any maintenance issues? How much will it cost (budget)? Describe your proposal. What will it look like? How will people react to it?

Lesson: Public Art Project "A Piece for Peace"
Leslie Anderson, Canopy Oaks Elementary School

Public Art Project Proposal
Challenge #7

The City of Tallahassee wants to paint a mural in a local high school where gang-related crime occurs. They want the mural to promote school pride, peace, and to help strengthen the school's community.

Required Theme:

Peace

Things to consider:

How safe is the project?
What materials will you use?
Are there any maintenance issues?
How much will it cost (budget)?
Describe your proposal. What will it look like?
How will people react to it?

25

Waging Peace Tent
Katharyn Jones, Ruediger Elementary School

Biography of the Artist:

Jacqueline Weaver is an artist, educator, and curator who currently lives in Chicago. As an artist, she works with a variety of media including videos, drawings and paintings. Her installation work for this exhibition, *The Border Project: In Conversation* asks viewers to think about their own homes and living situations. Her artwork resembles tents that one might associate with camping trips and causes the audience to think about why people might live in temporary spaces. *The Border Project: In Conversation* includes three-dimensional pieces where one can experience "living" in a tent.

Source: http://www.jacquelineweaver.com

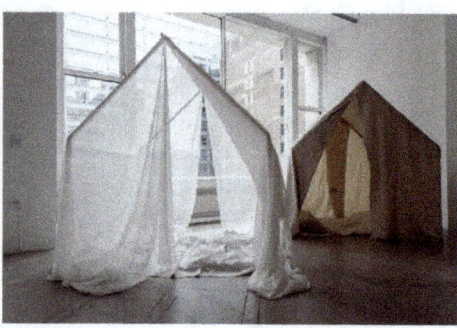

Jacqueline Weaver, *The Border Projects: In Conversation*, 2016

Next Generation Sunshine State Standards:
Big Idea: Critical Thinking and Reflection
Enduring Understanding 3: The process of critiquing works of art lead to development of critical thinking skills transferable to other contexts. (VA.4.C.3)
Benchmark: VA.4.C.3.3 Use the art-marking process, analysis, and discussion to identify the connections between art and other disciplines.

Big Idea: Historical and Global Connections
Enduring Understanding 1: Through study in the arts, we learn about and honor others and the worlds in which they lived. (VA.4.H.1)

Benchmark: VA.4.H.1.1 Identify historical and cultural influences that have inspired artists to produce works of art.

Big Idea: Innovation, Technology, and the Future
Enduring Understanding 1: Creating, interpreting, and responding in the arts stimulates the imagination and encourages innovation and creative risk taking. (VA.4.F.1)
Benchmark: VA.4.F.1.1 Combine art media with innovative ideas and techniques to create two-dimensional or three-dimensional works of art.
Enduring Understanding 3: The 21st century skills necessary for success as citizens, workers, and leaders in a global economy are embedded in the study of arts. (VA.4.F.3)
Benchmark: VA.4.F.3.1. Create art to promote awareness of school and/or community concerns.

Big Idea: Organizational Structures
Enduring Understanding 3: Every art form uses its own unique language, verbal and non-verbal to document and communicate with the world. (VA.4.0.3)
Benchmark: VA.4.O.3.1 Apply meaning and relevance to document self or others visually in artwork.

29

Waging Peace Tent
Katharyn Jones, Ruediger Elementary School

Big Idea: Skills, Techniques, and Processes
Enduring Understanding 1: The arts are inherently experimental and actively engage students in the process of creating, interpreting, and responding to art. (VA.4.S.1)
Benchmark: VA.4.S.1.1 Manipulate tools and materials to achieve effects in personal works of art.

Session Activity:

Based on Jacqueline Weaver's *The Border Project: In Conversation*, students will craft their own art installation tents, challenging students to answer how they might "wage peace" when planning and executing their tents. The lesson will be grounded in historical and cultural context, emphasizing how all over the world, for a variety of reasons, there are displaced people living in temporary shelters. Students will work together to achieve a common goal, form a sense of community in doing so, and gain insight from creating and interacting with their temporary structures. Students will work together in groups of 4 or less to create their own art installation tents with materials organized and ready for the build (blankets, sheets, table cloths, curtains, pillows, etc.). In order to effectively craft their tents, students must work together in a peaceful and cooperative way. After completing their tents, they will each answer one of the four questions pertaining to the descriptions of the tents and the ways in which they wage peace. The second session will include creating sketchbook drawings related to their experiences with the art installation tents in addition to reviewing art vocabulary and asking students to discuss living situations and their corresponding conditions.

Grade Level: 4th Grade	Time Needed: 2- 40 minute sessions

Objectives:
1. Students will discuss tents, the purpose of tents, and their own personal interaction with tents.
2. Students will learn about Jackie Weaver's installation art, *The Border Project: In Conversation*.
3. Students will use creative problem solving and collaboration to form temporary structures.
4. Students will each complete a survey on their experiences with the installations.
5. Students will make connections between art vocabulary and other disciplines.

Materials: Computer projection of artwork, "building" materials (sheets, chairs, pillows), sketchbook paper, pencils, survey, flashlight, coloring media
- **Teacher preparation:** PowerPoint, Examples, Supplies, Survey, Assessment

- **Vocabulary:** Jackie Weaver, Installation Art, *Waging Peace*, Collaboration, Interior, Exterior, Temporary Structures

- **Extensions:** Sketchbook, Jackie Weaver's website and the other resources attached, additional *Waging Peace* lesson plans

30

Waging Peace Tent
Katharyn Jones, Ruediger Elementary School

Procedure for Session 1:

1. Begin the session with the question "What are tents used for?" Students may answer camping, shade, festival booths, school carnivals, car detailing, greenhouses, or even living shelters.

2. Briefly introduce the *Waging Peace* art exhibition and artist Jackie Weaver's image of the installation *The Border Project: In Conversation*. Ask one or more of the following questions: What do you notice in the image? How do the structures differ? What might be the purpose of these tents? How many people do you think would fit inside? How does this wage peace?

3. Read the blurb connected with the image. Present students with the session's challenge. Students will work together in groups of 4 or less to create their own art installation tents. Have materials organized and ready for the builds (blankets, sheets, table cloths, curtains, pillows, etc.) Inform students they will need to "wage peace" by purposefully working together in a peaceful way to complete their builds.

4. Challenge students to answer how they might "wage peace" when planning and executing their tents.

5. After the builds, students will each pick up a survey, a pencil, and a light source (flashlight). Once inside of their structures, students can talk with one another to complete their experience surveys. After completing and turning in the surveys, students are invited to explore other builds (Experience Survey Builds).

6. Conclude the session with clean-up reminding students that sometimes art, especially installation art, is temporary.

Procedure for Session 2:

1. Review the information from the previous session including the art vocabulary.

2. Ask students to each share with a neighbor one positive and one negative about their art installation experiences.

3. Some people do not have a choice about their living situations. Ask students to each list a reason someone might not have a place to live. Ask why having a place to live is important. Ask students if they would feel comfortable living in tents and why.

4. Optional: share some of the information from the websites listed in the additional resources section of this lesson plan.

5. Prompt students to create sketchbook drawings related to their experiences with the art installation tents.

Sketch ideas might include: draw yourself engaging in peace with your art installation; draw the inside of your art installation; draw what you and your partners did to create the installation space; draw yourself waging peace; create a symbol for waging peace.

Waging Peace Tent

Katharyn Jones, Ruediger Elementary School

Student Experience Survey: Choose any four questions to answer
- Is there enough room in the tent for everyone to fit?
- Is the tent comfortable? How does it make you feel?
- How much time would you want to spend inside of the tent?
- What would you need in order to live in this tent?
- Was your team able to work peacefully together?
- Describe the interior of your tent.

Evaluation:

Name: _____ Teacher: _____ Date: _____

4=Excellent   3=Very Good   2=Good   1=Needs Work   0=Did Not Complete

Waging Peace Tent 4th Grade	Student's Self-Assessment	Ms. Jones's Assessment
Collaborated for Build (Participation)	4 3 2 1 0	4 3 2 1 0
Comments:		
Answered Survey	4 3 2 1 0	4 3 2 1 0
Comments:		
Completed Assignment on Time	4 3 2 1 0	4 3 2 1 0
Comments:		
Waged Peace (Behavior)	4 3 2 1 0	4 3 2 1 0
Comments:		
Completed Sketchbook Entry	4 3 2 1 0	4 3 2 1 0
Comments:		
1. What is important for peace?		
2. What was your biggest challenge?		
3. Did you have fun with this project?		
Project Grade: /20		

32

Registration document for *Waging Peace!* Teacher Workshop featuring Linda Stein.

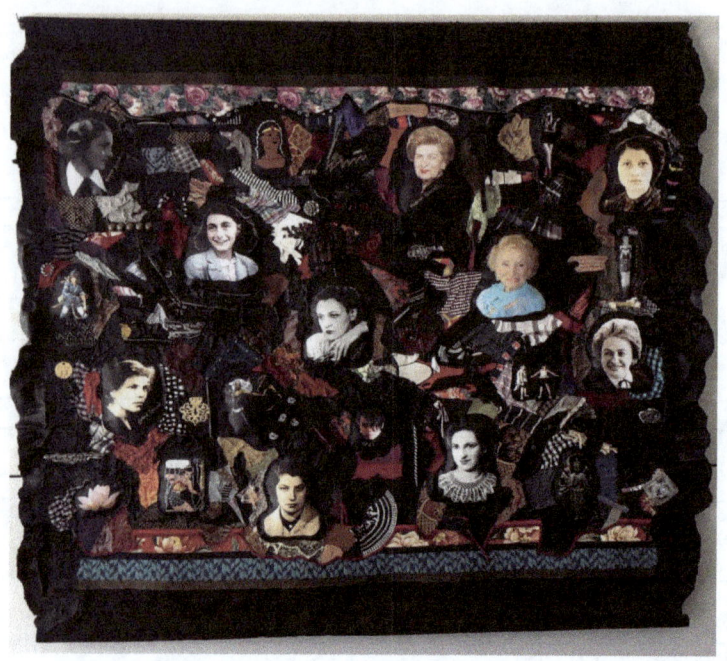

Waging Peace with New York artist, Linda Stein

Ten Heroes (women related to the Holocaust), leather, archival pigment on canvas, metal, zippers, 56 x 61 x 2 in

The *Waging Peace* exhibition, catalogue and events were sponsored in part by an award from the City of Tallahassee and Leon County administered by the Council on Culture & Arts; by a grant from the State of Florida Division of Cultural Affairs; the Holocaust Education Resource Council; and The Peace on Earth Gift. This workshop is also in part sponsored by the FSU Schools.

 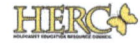 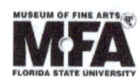

Linda Stein

From the *Waging Peace* catalogue:

"Tackling oppression – including racism, sexism, classism, ableism, homophobia – through the lens of bullying and gender justice, is the mission that has guided me as activist and artist. My *Ten Heroes* tapestry depicts fierce females during the time of the Holocaust juxtaposed with my selected pop-culture and religious icons of protection. The blending of fantasy and reality figures prompt conversations about everyday heroism and brave upstanding against bullying and bigotry."   – Linda Stein

The New York City Art Teachers Association/UFT has honored Stein with their Artist of the Year award. The artist will be giving a keynote address on October 28, 2017. Linda Stein has been honored with the 2016 Artist of the Year Award by the National Association of Women Artists for her "Outstanding Contribution to the Arts." She has also been awarded grants and residencies from Squire Foundation, Memorial Foundation for Jewish Culture, Djerassi Foundation, Lower Manhattan Cultural Council, Hunter College, Virginia Center for the Creative Arts, Suffolk BOCES Arts and Humanities, and the America the Beautiful Fund. Her art archives are at Smith College and the Linda Stein Feminist Art Education Collection will be housed at Penn State University. She currently lives and works in Manhattan and East Hampton.

Friday, January 12, 2018, 10:00 am to 3:00+ pm
Lunch Included; Raffle; Book Signing by the Artist/Author
Florida State University Museum of Fine Arts

Resources: Educational Encounters from Linda Stein's website: http://h2f2encounters.cyberhouse.emitto.net. This workshop will also be part of week-long HERC sponsored activities. Contact Barbara Goldstein for HERC schedule: barbara@holocaustresources.org.

Teachers will need substitutes and will get TEC credit. TEC will pay for 20 substitutes for art teachers. Questions: Contact Shannon Takacs: takacss@leonschools.net.

To Register:
Send Registration Form to arrive by Friday, December 1, 2017

Mail or fill in, scan, and send to vwylder@fsu.edu
Attn: Viki D. Thompson Wylder
FSU Museum of Fine Arts
Room 250 FAB, 530 West Call Street
Tallahassee, FL 32306-1140

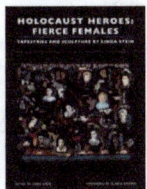

Registration: mail or scan and send.

Name: _____

School: _____

Phone #, easily reached: _____

E-mail: _____

Courtesy: Florida State University Museum of Fine Arts.

Waging Peace!

What does "waging peace" mean?

When we say "waging peace" we mean that we have to show action to bring peace – we must do things to bring peace. We must show respect for ourselves, other people, and nature.

Circle all the things listed below that you can do to wage peace. We will discuss your answers.

1. put your plastic bottles in the recycling bin

2. be friendly to a student who is often teased by others

3. be happy

4. report bullying to a teacher

5. pick up trash when you see it laying on the ground

6. take an injured bird to the wildlife veterinarian

7. welcome a student to your class who is from another country

8. take a meal to a neighbor whose house lost electricity during a hurricane

9. become a pen pal to a student in another country

10. plant a garden with native plants

Waging Peace Messages: Scavenger Hunt

The artists in this exhibition are trying to tell you messages about ways to wage peace. Select any work of your choice with the following messages as a guide and be prepared to explain your answer.

1. We can wage peace by working with others to rebuild cities and highways after destructive things might happen like hurricanes or earthquakes.

Give the name of the artwork and the artist's name:

_____   _____
name of the artwork   artist's name

2. People all around the world receive and send messages through the internet. We can wage peace by showing respect when we send messages.

Give the name of the artwork and the artist's name:

_____   _____
name of the artwork   artist's name

3. We can wage peace by being brave and fighting for others like this woman.

Give the name of the artwork and the artist's name:

_____   _____
name of the artwork   artist's name

4. We can wage peace by reaching to hold hands with others who are different than we are.

Give the name of the artwork and the artist's name:

_____   _____
name of the artwork   artist's name

5. We can wage peace by understanding that all nature (plants, animals, and earth) are connected, that we must take care of each part of nature because it is connected to other parts.

Give the name of the artwork and the artist's name:

_____   _____
name of the artwork   artist's name

6. Select an artwork of your choice. We can wage peace by following this artist's message (be prepared to tell the message of this artist, as you see/understand it).

Give the name of the artwork and the artist's name:

_____   _____
name of the artwork   artist's name

Draw a sketch of the artwork in the box to the right.

CHAPTER 9

Tracing the "Constructivist Co-Curation" Process—Vantage Points and Steps

Beginnings

I am a hybrid. I came to my career as a museum educator from multiple vantage points. I taught English in two middle schools. As a resource teacher, I instructed kindergarten through fifth grade at an elementary school. I moved forward in a zigzag educational direction to earn a Master of Fine Arts in studio art and a PhD in humanities with a concentration in art history. I taught a humanities course as an adjunct at the community college level as well as art education courses at Florida State University as an adjunct. When I taught at the elementary level, I bussed my students to the very museum in which I now found myself to be the curator of education. I wanted a museum program to help my students embrace the artwork and the space in which it was exhibited. I wanted such a program to help each student personally experience the many messages and meanings that hung everywhere on the walls, experience the making of the art they saw, and come to an understanding of a relationship between their visit to a museum, their own lives, and the life of the community in which they lived.

As a curator of education, I brought these experiences to my position. I looked at my role from the artist's and art historian's point of view, and I certainly looked at my role from the teacher's standpoint. I asked teachers for their expectations for a visit to the museum with their students or a visit to the school by museum educational staff. Tours and outreach site activities were tailored to classroom pedagogical needs. I asked teachers for their requests for programs and their expectations of the place of the museum in the lives of their classrooms. In partnership with teachers, programs developed. For example, an eighth-grade class spent a year learning about and selecting artwork from the museum's permanent collection to curate their own exhibition for one gallery space. This was repeated with a group of students at the elementary level. These programs seemed like apt reflections of the invitations to teachers themselves to participate in the curatorial life of the museum.

> In the fall of 1999, I brought the idea of teacher co-curatorial ventures to the Florida State University Museum of Fine Arts (FSU MoFA) director. Soon thereafter, teachers at Buck Lake Elementary joined me to form a co-curatorial committee for the first of the five projects described in this book. Teachers, rather than staff, selected the theme for the project, and as required, the theme was approved by the FSU MoFA director. Of the five projects, three were the result of invitations from the museum, but two projects, the third and the fourth, were requested by teachers themselves. All five project thematic concepts emanated from teachers. This "hands-on and minds-on" co-curatorial process for teachers helped to provide a profound "hands-on and minds-on" experience for their students. Although a step-by-step process moved each of these projects forward, each also unfolded organically. Each project offered specific challenges and surprises. For me each proved intellectually and emotionally stimulating.
>
> *–VDTW*

As an elementary art educator, I yearly taught over 900 students, kindergarten through fifth grade. Needless to say my time was generally filled with instruction, preparing lessons and getting supplies ready. Fortunately, throughout the museum/school co-curation process my focus could remain primarily on my classroom and ways to mesh my pedagogy with aspects of the co-curation projects. I created activities for my students in response to the work the committee selected, publicized the project to other teachers and parents, and the like. The curator of education handled museum organizational aspects such as scheduling co-curatorial meetings, preparing artwork images for review, conducting registrarial (arrangement of artwork loan forms, shipping, condition reporting) and preparatorial duties (laying out and hanging the artworks) for professional and student pieces, and setting up opening nights and other museum events. Potential artist's visits were determined in co-curatorial meetings and the curator of education arranged and scheduled the interactions. Likewise, artist workshops for teachers were determined at meetings and arranged and scheduled by the curator. Tours and financial support for busing were implemented by the curator but were first discussed at co-curatorial meetings. Teachers performed an important evaluative and decision-making role. The expertise of teachers complemented the expertise of the museum educator to form the strength of the partnership.

> From my perspective as an art educator, museum staff undertook many of the jobs that would have overwhelmed me, and they facilitated interactions with artists that enriched experiences for my students. They offered a professional setting for the display of student work and an opportunity for families to interact with artwork by both students and professional practitioners through hands-on activities. The co-curatorial process encouraged the development of new student-related audiences and new regard for the artwork of students. But perhaps most importantly, diverse audiences that included my students and often their extended families experienced the opening nights as noisy occasions in which they shared joy and respect for art.
>
> *—MM*

Show Ideas

Before the start of these collaborative projects, art teachers in the school district experienced a more traditional relationship with museum exhibitions, which originated and were curated conventionally. Once a year, either elementary or secondary art teachers were invited to submit student artwork in response to one museum-curated show. Opening nights for these student displays began to feature student musical performances as well as make and take tables for elementary students. By this time, teachers felt a level of comfort in their relationship with the FSU MoFA and some practices were established that became core to these five collaborative ventures. Not everything had to be invented for the larger, more complex co-curatorial projects.

The first constructivist co-curated show, *Visions of the North Florida Environment*, provided inspiration for art educators in the district. The project not only demonstrated a collaboration between a team of teachers and the museum education staff but also served to raise the bar of possibilities. Art teachers in the district were able to look beyond the usual museum–school relationship in which teachers, if so moved, molded their classroom and field trip activity, often artificially, to utilize museum offerings. Seeing the students at that first show dressed and actively working as docents for art selected by a team of teachers from their school sent a message that more was possible.

As described above and in previous chapters, these various collaborative projects and their exhibitions originated both from the museum's curator of education and from the art teachers in Leon County, although all thematic concepts for these five projects originated with teachers. Thematic concepts evolved from pedagogy being addressed in the classroom or through teachers' discussion with each other of ideas for broad unit plans envisioned for the classroom. After the first project and show, teachers felt empowered to independently approach the Curator of Education with ideas and requests for collaborative projects themselves. Since the early 1990s, an open, positive working relationship between art teachers and the curator has made these approaches plausible. This chapter will focus on the collaborative co-curatorial participants and process, outline procedures or operations, and lay out who did what.

Meeting of the Museum Curator of Education and the Museum Director

After an invitation for participation in a co-curatorial project was forwarded to teachers by the curator of education or teachers made a request for such a project, teachers submitted a thematic concept for the project to the curator of education. The curator then took the overarching thematic concept and its nascent exhibition and program details to the museum director, often in written outline form. At this point, during discussion both reviewed the potential and scope of plans of the project and exhibition chiefly to determine placement in the museum schedule and a prospective museum budget. They identified grant opportunities and organizations to tap for funds and anticipated any accompanying publications such as posters or catalogues.

Meetings with Co-Curation Committees

An important role in the co-curation process is that of committee facilitator. This is the person who maintains organization, keeps the timeline moving along, interacts and communicates with all parties, and calls and chairs meetings. For these five co-curation projects, the curator of education at the museum took on that role. Primarily committee members were teachers either from a single school (*Visions* and *In Print*) or from the district at large (*The Story, Generations, Waging*

Peace!). Most teachers on co-curation committees taught art at the elementary or secondary level, but a number of teachers did not. Two teachers taught English for Speakers of Other Languages or ESOL classes K-12, one teacher taught gifted students K-5, and a number of teachers for the first project, *Visions of the North Florida Environment*, came from the generic elementary classroom. Two "teachers" on the last committee for the *Waging Peace!* project taught as members of homeschool cooperatives.

Committee members joined co-curatorial teams through various methods. District-wide emails sent by the curator of education served as a call or invitation to teachers to serve as members with originator teachers. The curator of education attended art teacher meetings to announce the formation of committees and to invite additional teachers to join. She also recruited in an ad hoc manner dependent on the circumstances. For the second project, *In Print: The Language of Art*, she recruited a local secondary art instructor as a main committee member from a museum studies class she was team teaching. Art teachers also spread the word and invited other teachers to join committees. The two elementary art teachers on the committee for *Visions of the North Florida Environment* recruited the eight other teacher members of their committee from the classrooms of their school. Generally, at co-curatorial meetings members of the community were identified and invited to join committees by the curator of education or other members upon agreement by the committee already in place. For example, an elementary teacher on the *Waging Peace!* co-curatorial committee identified a nonprofit, do-it-yourself community organization called The Plant as a potential organization for representation on the co-curatorial team for that project. Other examples from the projects in this book include representative members from Tallahassee Community College (TCC), the Tallahassee Council on Culture and Arts (COCA), the Holocaust Education Resource Council (HERC), the Anderson Brickler Gallery, and Mission San Luis.

The topics of the first meetings focused on titles of exhibitions (and thus names of projects) as well as content and definition of any terms or concepts. In some cases, early meetings also helped define content and scope for a "call for entries." Once co-curatorial committee members submitted digital images of artwork for exhibition consideration or artists sent digital images due to a "call for entries," the curator of education organized the images for presentation to the co-curatorial committee and potential inclusion of artworks into the show. The co-curatorial committee members viewed each digital image and decided on the basis of consensus if it should be included. Discussion of artwork centered on the appropriateness of the work for the theme of the project; the skill, technique, and use of media displayed; the meaning and/or the aesthetics of the work; the possibilities shown by the artwork for student–artist interactions, events, and teacher workshops; and the works' use for potential lesson plans and student response works in the classroom. Points from these discussions were noted for possible implementation later. The selection process sometimes continued as long as a year since meetings typically lasted for one and a half to two hours and only occurred once a month barring summers and the Thanksgiving/Christmas season (see sample meeting agenda). Once artworks were selected and confirmed, meetings switched focus to the planning of student–artist interactions, in-service workshops for teachers, the planning of events like preview shows if any, the writing of lesson plans for a teacher's packet, and the format, style and writing of the catalogue. Toward the end of each project, co-curatorial committee members began to consider delivery of student artwork for display at the museum and other alternate locations, opening nights with their related activities, the scheduling of tours, and monetary assistance for student busing to the museum.

Workshops for teachers and the writing of lesson plans for the teachers' packet often took place early in summers before teachers dispersed for vacation trips or other personal business. Co-curatorial committee members often came together for a single scheduled day-long lesson plan writing session for each project packet, with lunch served by the museum. Any unfinished plans were handed in later by co-curatorial committee members with a deadline approximately one week after the session. Over the summer months, lesson plans with images were compiled into packets through museum intern assistance directed by the curator of education. Communication with artists, loans for artwork, and catalogue details were also often finalized by the curator of education during summers so that catalogue drafts with artwork imagery could be sent to the museum designer and bids by commercial printers could be solicited. One year to one semester prior to each exhibition, catalogues (or posters for the first two projects) were printed and available for teachers to use in the classroom with the teachers' packets. The curator of education facilitated meetings and work sessions and she advised the co-curatorial committees according to museum protocols. She regularly invited interns she supervised to attend both. She occasionally invited an intern who provided sustained work and services to the committee to become an official co-curatorial member.

Throughout the process a myriad of decisions were made by the committee using informal consensus. As stated, meetings were generally held monthly at the museum with the exception of summers and holidays. These meetings were key to keeping the process moving forward, to adding multiple voices and perspectives, and thus more depth to the final exhibition and the related activities and products of the overall project.

Project Budgets: Museum and School

Museum budgets were cobbled together from multiple sources and via multiple methods. Budgets for these projects were often proposed at their outset or soon thereafter and finalized one to three years in advance of their exhibitions due to grant applications and the solicitation of additional funds or in-kind contributions from other entities like community organizations. For example, for *The Story* the Tallahassee Council on Culture and Arts sponsored an early event with Faith Ringgold attended by art educators and students involved with the project. For the project titled *Generations*, the Holocaust Education Resource Council funded much of the Ela Weissberger workshop. Weissberger had survived the Holocaust and written about her art teacher at the Terezin labor camp. The same organization pledged funds to bring New York artist Linda Stein to Tallahassee to talk about her work during the *Waging Peace!* project. Stein, showing intense interest in this project, reduced her usual fee by half. Linda Stein was the creator of *Ten Heroes*, a tapestry which lauded ten women heroes of the Holocaust Era. One school represented in the *Waging Peace!* project pledged funds to pay for Linda Stein's lodging during her visit to the FSU MoFA. The artist agreed to visit a program and exhibition inspired by the *Waging Peace!* project at their school.

The funds for these projects and exhibitions tended to be "shoestring" budgets. Some aspects of mounting such projects, however, were already built into the overall cost for the operations of the FSU MoFA. For example, all works shown in exhibitions were covered by the FSU MoFA insurance policy. Normal FSU MoFA operating appropriations also paid for such things as lights, refreshments for events, and employees who worked on the projects, including those like the preparator who hung the exhibitions and the publications designer who blocked out and constructed catalogues and exhibition mail-out invitations. Specific project budgets aided by grants tended to support particulars outside the usual operating cost of the institution and ranged between approximately a few thousand and ten plus thousand dollars, while featured exhibitions at many museums can cost in the tens of thousands of dollars and often much more. A budget of $13,500 supported *The Story*, the largest of the budgets for these projects. Though our project budgets utilizing grant funds were small, these specific budget dollars played an important role for details like the shipping of artwork to the FSU MoFA, the sponsorship of artists and speakers for both teacher workshops and student–artist events, busing, and the printing of materials like catalogues. Costs were lessened through several methods. For example, to reduce the cost of catalogues, bids solicited to printing companies with the least costly bid accepted were required by the university. In the case of shipping, the FSU MoFA paid for return shipping and insurance to artists while the artists generally paid for incoming shipping and insurance to the museum. A few exceptions to this practice occurred for high market value works like those by Faith Ringgold which a New York gallery lent to *The Story* and *Generations* projects. In that instance the FSU MoFA paid for shipping both ways covered by wall to wall insurance. By and large artists either hand-delivered artwork if they lived within driving range or artists shipped work by United Parcel Service (UPS) or Federal Express.

For *Generations* the Tallahassee/Leon County Council on Culture and Arts awarded the project $4,500 for honoraria for educational presentations, workshops, lectures, art supplies, and busing. From this money, eight artists gave presentations/workshops for a "Teacher Institute." Each artist was paid for an hour-long segment. These artists lived in the immediate area of the FSU MoFA and did not require travel reimbursements. Two additional artists from the immediate area interacted with classrooms for the same amount of payment. The second-generation Highwayman artist Aletha Butler traveled from central Florida to give a Saturday plein air painting presentation to students and parents from five schools on the grounds of the Mission San Luis historical museum. Her payment covered reimbursement for traveling expenses, overnight food and lodging, and a honorarium. The second-generation Haitian artist, Charles Duffaut who was living in Michigan at the time, visited Tallahassee to give a lecture at the FSU MoFA, visit several local elementary classrooms, and give a painting demonstration at a family day event. His payment, like that for Aletha Butler, included reimbursement for travel and lodging as well as a honorarium. Additional monies supported the busing of students to the FSU MoFA for tours and art supplies for the Aletha Butler plein air event. Most artists and institutions were generous with time and reduced fees for educational events for K-12 students which allowed for greater interaction between artists, teachers, and students for all five projects described in this book. For *The Story* project, one of the artists, Wennie Huang, decided to write her own grant to be able to travel to the FSU MoFA from New York City to interact with classrooms and give an opening night performance (in conjunction with the display of her artwork). She received an additional stipend of a few hundred dollars from FSU MoFA grant money.

Annual budgets available to art teachers varied considerably from school to school. In Leon County annual art budgets were school based instead of district based. With a range of fifty cents to four dollars per student, some schools endured bare bones budgets and others enjoyed generous budgets. Some schools also received additional funds from parent–teacher organizations (PTOs). Several art teachers with very low budgets applied yearly for grants in the community to supplement their monetary allocations. At least one school ran its art program almost entirely from an annual community grant.

Buck Lake Elementary, a school with an ample art budget, PTO support, and funding from multiple grants modeled much of the constructivist co-curatorial process through Visions of the North Florida Environment, the first and extensive project and exhibition in the series of five discussed in this book. With The Story, the third project in the series, one of the art teachers from the Visions project suggested a change in the makeup of co-curatorial committees from single school representation to multiple school representation. The inclusion of art teachers from various schools within one project tended to negate the influence of an abundance or lack of art funds at a school in its relationship to the constructivist co-curatorial project at hand. For student response work, teachers submitted artwork in any size, media, technique, or style. Work could be done by a student alone or by a collective or collaboration of students. Co-curatorial committees viewed highly economical media, like pencil, paper, and crayons as valuable as more expensive media like paint and canvas. One of the most memorable and profound student display artwork submissions over the course of these five projects used basic media in a collective fashion. Students at Riley Elementary contributed to a poetry book in which each collaged page spotlighted a poem written and illustrated by a student. All illustrations featured pencil and crayon. Since the inequity of art funding at schools made busing students to the museum for tours a financial challenge for some teachers on the co-curatorial committees, grant funds were used for those schools to help pay for charter buses for the project and exhibition titled The Story. Grant funds were also used to pay for school district buses for the Generations project and for the Waging Peace! project. Other schools charged each student a small field trip fee to cover the school bus transportation costs which combined bus driver hourly wages and mileage charges.

Selecting the Artists and Artworks

Over the course of 18 years, works by internationally and/or nationally acclaimed artists like Faith Ringgold, Samella Lewis, Maya Lin, Judy Chicago, Linda Stein, and Trevor Bell as well as works by artists with greater regional fame like Dean Mitchell, Clyde Butcher, Romero Britto, and James Gibson were selected by co-curatorial committees. The works of these artists signaled the tone for the five projects and exhibitions, projecting a high level of quality, meaning, artistic scope, and cultural diversity. Local and lesser-known regional artists were also represented. Although Linda Stein, Dean Mitchell, and Clyde Butcher visited the FSU MoFA to interact with students, the co-curatorial committee enjoyed a large pool of available talent for in-person student interaction from lesser-known artists.

During the co-curatorial process members of the committee selected artwork for inclusion in the exhibitions utilizing one of two methods. With the first method, which was used for most of the projects, teachers and/or the curator of education submitted digital imagery of artwork for consideration. These artworks reflected members' previous research of artists and their judgments about the viability of these artists' works for the project and exhibition and suitability for their own pedagogy. The committee could also determine a "call for entries," the second method which was used for the last project, *Waging Peace!* In either case, as previously indicated, the co-curatorial team spent monthly meetings during an entire year looking at the images and choosing the artworks. When a member of the committee submitted potential imagery for consideration, that committee member provided contextual, historical, and critical background about the work and the artist, often with projections about use of the work in the classroom. When a "call for entries" was employed, the call was sent by museum staff to free outlets that advertise exhibition calls, such as local cultural or arts organizations' across the country, art publications in print, and digital publications like websites. The curator of education, with intern assistance, responded to incoming replies from "calls for entries," collected entry forms and digital artwork images, and organized information for the co-curatorial team members' consideration.

When selecting works the committee members were cognizant of the needs/levels of understanding of students of different age groups. Artwork selection was a co-curatorial consensus process. Artworks were selected through a discussion of the quality and appropriateness of the work for the exhibition, viability for use in the classroom, and potential interaction of the artists with students and teachers. Works, however, did not need to meet all of these conditions to be included but those that did made for a richer, wider-reaching overall project. The two most important considerations were as follows: 1) How did the artwork fit into the theme of the show? Did it support the meaning/impact desired? 2) Was the artwork appropriate for use with kindergarten through 12th grade students?

After consensus was reached concerning the selected artwork, artists were contacted by the curator of education and/or museum interns, sometimes with help from a committee member who experienced a personal connection with an artist. For *The Story* project many committee members made personal contact with artists prior to official paperwork communication from museum representatives. For example, before official contact with the artist Sydney Scherr, a committee member for *The Story* project, Linda Johnson, directly invited her participation and went on to arrange additional interactions with the artist. Sydney Scherr worked in metal, enamel, and wood. Linda Johnson, a middle school art instructor, also was trained to work in metal and belonged to the Florida Society of Goldsmiths, Northwest Chapter (FSGNW) based in Tallahassee. The FSGNW sponsored Sydney Scherr's travel to Tallahassee to give a workshop to its membership. The artist agreed to also meet in the classroom with Linda Johnson's students during that trip and agreed to participate in the project's exhibition. The response artwork from this student–artist interaction appeared in the parallel student display at the FSU MoFA titled *Stories K-12*.

During one of the monthly co-curatorial meetings for the *Generations* project, all co-curatorial members sent personal letters, based on a model letter composed by the curator of education, to individual "adopted" artists explaining the project and inviting each of them to participate. In most cases the work of each artist "adopted" by a committee member had originally been submitted to the committee by that member for consideration of inclusion of the work in the exhibition.

Official Paperwork

For all artists and artwork, the curator of education and interns completed the official exhibition paperwork which encompassed loan forms, insurance coverage lists, shipping arrangement notifications, and catalogue information request forms.

All of these except the submission of insurance coverage lists were addressed by the same official communication. An official communication to each artist started with a cover letter which provided:

- an overview of the exhibition
- a museum invitation to participate
- a brief description of pertinent information addressed in attached documents and forms
- the deadline for return of forms with signatures.

Attachments with the cover letter included a loan form providing basic information and requesting basic information to be returned to the FSU MoFA. The loan form stated dates of the exhibition and the deadline date for arrival of work on site. In addition, the form gave requirements/parameters for digital images to be sent to the museum. Requested information included:

- lender's (usually the artist's) name, address, and contact information
- full identification of the artwork to be loaned to the museum (artist, title, medium, size, date, insurance value)
- authorizations for reproductions of the artwork for publicity, publications, and educational purposes
- social security numbers or Federal Employer Identification numbers in case of unforeseen potential payments or reimbursements.

Loan forms also included shipping arrangement information like the following:

- requirements for preparation of work for shipping (ready to hang; no use of glass unless work was hand delivered)
- means of shipping
- requirements of return shipping
- packing information (work to be returned in same packing)
- insurance information (insurance companies will not cover work damaged due to packing issues originated by artists; claims must be justified by documented market value of the work)
- special exhibition requirements (provision of detailed directions for some installations or arrangements for personal responsibility of installment; personal responsibilities for works with electronic functions)

- important dates (due date for delivery of work, pickup date for return of work to artist by shippers, date for deinstallation and pickup of hand-delivered work).

Attachments additionally included a document covering catalogue information and text. This document outlined information and items needed to be sent by the artist for inclusion in the exhibition catalogue. Return items consisted of:

- a digital image of the artwork (meeting digital size requirements for publication and printing)
- sometimes a portrait image of the artist (again with digital size requirements)
- sometimes a résumé or vita
- a written short biography and/or an artist's statement
- forms to be filled-in by the artist to outline his or her employment or career position, contact information, and a list of five awards/exhibitions.

After the return of signed documents and forms, an insurance value list for all works in the exhibition was compiled, with dates needed for coverage, and submitted to the FSU MoFA director who maintained insurance contracts for the museum. In addition, at the return of documents and forms from artists, work began on the writing/editing of catalogue text and organization of imagery for the project's publication.

Planning Artist Interactions, Teacher Workshops, Other Events

Once the artworks were selected, planning for the rest of the project began. One of the considerations in the selection of artwork was the potential for artist interactions with students. Using notes and ideas jotted down during the selection process, artist/student interactions were first brainstormed, then refined, and finally implemented. Questions sparked co-curatorial committee discussion. Which artworks held the most potential for student meaning making and discovery of/introduction to materials and techniques? Which artists might be willing or available on a practical basis to work with students? What would the interactions with the students look like? Would the interactions incorporate hands-on artmaking, artist demonstrations of technique, discussion, or talks/lectures about the artists' own artmaking concepts or about their own histories as artists? The curator of education, sometimes with intern help, contacted artists for whom teachers indicated high interest and then checked availability of those artists and their willingness to interact with students. Availability included practicalities. Budgets usually offered some remuneration to artists and generally little travel expenses. A short list of artists willing and available to interact was generated. This shortlist included not only the artists' willingness but also the potential types of interactions with students, any practicality issues revolving around money or travel, and a possible scheduling window for each artist. Then teachers on the co-curatorial team were given the opportunity to request dates for scheduling interactions with artists. Artist–student interactions varied considerably from project to project, school to school. Sometimes students traveled to artists' studios; more often artists visited schools. Some teachers booked only one interaction with one artist while some booked several and occasionally an artist returned to a classroom for multiple visits.

Next the co-curatorial team considered which artists afforded the potential for teacher workshops. Again, questions guided discussion and decision-making. In what ways would workshops with artists under consideration expand teachers' knowledge and support teachers' in-service credit toward recertification? During the *Waging Peace!* project the Linda Stein workshop, which was supported financially by the Tallahassee Holocaust Education Resource Council (HERC), "did double duty" by supporting recertification credits in art and by supporting the district's Holocaust Education in-service goal. Other workshops focused on art processes. For example, in concert with the project *In Print: The Language of Art*, a workshop featured exhibition printmakers and their techniques. The related workshops of the five projects covered in this book played a valuable role in continuing art teacher education especially during times when district in-service dollars for the arts were in short supply.

The co-curatorial committees also offered workshops with speakers other than artists. These included teachers, authors, museum educators, and the like. They also occasionally partnered with other organizations and held workshops at other community locations. A two-day teacher workshop during the *Visions of the North Florida Environment* project was held the first day at the FSU MoFA and the second day at the Mary Brogan Museum of Art & Science. The printmaking workshop was held in the printmaking lab at Florida State University under the direction of printmaker, Kabuya Bowens, an FSU professor and artist in the *In Print* exhibition. The workshop featuring Ela Weissberger during the *Generations* project was held at the Mission San Luis historical site.

Project events comprised the third area considered by the co-curatorial team after artwork/artist selection. During some projects like *Generations*, events overlapped with artist interactions, as in the case of the Aletha and Robert Butler plein air Saturday event at Mission San Luis. The daughter and father team demonstrated their technique and then worked with/talked with students, parents, and teachers as students experienced painting plein air themselves. Sometimes events overlapped with the development of teacher workshops. For *The Story* project the *Preface* event, which consisted of four parts, occurred a year before the exhibition and focused on the underlying narrative concept of various types and pieces of art. In the first part which antedated the other three *Preface* components, images of narrative pieces from the MoFA permanent collection were made available to classrooms to act as impetus for student response work. In the second part, student response work was hung side by side in a small show with the professional permanent collection artwork. In the third component of the *Preface*, the FSU MoFA hosted a reception for this show for students, their families, and their teachers which was followed by the final unit of the event on the same night. A teachers' only buffet dinner was served while an award-winning author of children's literature discussed the integration of visual arts and writing. Teachers received recertification credit for attending. At other times alternate types of events did not merge or overlap. During the *Waging Peace!* Project, a member of the co-curatorial committee developed a traveling and interactive installation that proceeded to four schools, a rolling event unto itself.

Planning for student displays became the fourth area of consideration by co-curatorial committee members as lack of enough space for the concurrent student shows became an issue. Space within the FSU MoFA proved problematic due to the size of the student displays. Schools that were not involved in project implementation or the operations of co-curatorial committees but used the catalogues, teachers' packets, and images of artworks from the show as inspiration for their students' response work were included in satellite student displays. The co-curatorial committees tapped and reserved extra exhibition space with community locations for this "overflow" of student work. Announcements detailing requirements for participation and locations of alternate venues were sent to interested art teachers. The local community responded supportively. During different years community venues included Tallahassee Community College Art Gallery, Tallahassee City Hall exhibition space, the Gallery for Innovation and the Arts at the R. A. Gray Building (a state-run space), and the LeRoy Collins Leon County Public Library. Each alternative venue planned its own separate opening night festivities.

Transportation

Busing students either to an artist's studio or to the museum for tours or other events was a challenge financially but also logistically due to in-school schedules for daily student arrivals, departures, and lunch. Once timetables for exhibitions, artist interactions, and events were established by co-curatorial committees, planning the moving of students from place to place began. It was necessary to determine the sum of money available from grants for busing students, which schools needed money and the requisite amounts, and to whom payments were to be made and when. Art teachers on each co-curatorial committee worked with the curator of education to first establish which schools needed assistance. Schools who submitted requests for funding for busing determined monetary amounts by calculating hourly wages for bus drivers added to mileage costs. Thus, a final amount requested depended on a school's distance from an event. The cost of busing per school ranged between $50 to several hundred dollars. Some schools wanted only one bus trip and some wanted buses for a multiplicity of classes and trips. Teachers also provided identity and contact information for persons at schools who could answer monetary questions and who received the payments for busing. Payments usually came in the form of reimbursements. Schools that could do so provided their own funding for buses. Addressing busing windows for some artists' interactions (like the field trip taken with an artist to a state park) and exhibition tours were often begun months in advance. Teachers on co-curatorial committees were advised to speak to their pertinent administrative personnel at the beginnings of school years because start dates for these shows took place in May due to university department calendars. The last two weeks of May, the end of the school year, brought district mandated busing blackout dates. For one project, *The Story*, charter buses were hired to circumvent the issue.

Teachers' Packets and Catalogues

Usually, a teachers' packet was written during a group session the year before a project exhibition opened and at the advent of summer immediately after the last day of teacher planning. Artists and artwork curated into the exhibitions served as the basis of content for plans and writers of plans selected artists and artworks according to their interests. Teachers' packets provided coverage for a sizable selection of artwork and artists but did not cover the total of any exhibition. Responsibility for developing lesson plan formats and writing was shared primarily among the members of the respective co-curatorial committees. Teachers took the lead and museum interns contributed by assisting with group procedural or operational tasks and writing additional plans at times. Each lesson plan reflected a teacher's pedagogical emphases and style, but each plan adhered to a presentation format to give the packet a sense of cohesiveness. For the *Waging Peace!* teachers' packet, each lesson plan started with a title for the plan followed by a brief biography of the artist, one or several state standards, grade level, time needed for the lesson, a session activity description, objectives, materials, activity procedures, and means of evaluation. Often these writing sessions were turned into opportunities to earn in-service credit which helped to motivate teachers to participate and meet their recertification requirements.

Editing and preparing the layout of teachers' packets was undertaken by the curator of education with help from museum interns. Working in teams, interns were charged with the visual design of individual lesson plans as well as the design of the overall packet. This included decisions about aspects like typography, choice of imagery, cover designs, introductory pages, and arrangements of space on pages. Initially FSU MoFA interns copied and compiled packets on paper and disc for school mail distribution to teachers throughout the district. Later packets were distributed to teachers using only digital methods which included posting on the FSU MoFA website. The earmarked date for packet completion was at least a semester before the exhibition and typically late summer before teachers returned for preplanning of the school year in which the project exhibition was mounted. Every art teacher in the district received a teachers' packet, either in hard copy in the early years or digitally in the later years. If requested, packets were also distributed to teachers outside the art field and outside the district. Teachers then used the packets in conjunction with exhibition catalogues for suggesting, planning, and implementing lessons in the classroom.

Catalogue production followed a somewhat different process. After artists returned digital imagery and catalogue information forms to the museum, work began on composing catalogue drafts. Compiling information and material for publications as well as editing and finalizing drafts to submit to the publication designer was the responsibility of the curator of education. Once submitted and the catalogues were laid out, the curator of education teamed with the designer to decide refinements and proofread all text. For the first two projects, *Visions of the North Florida Environment* and *In Print: The Language of Art*, posters were produced which acted as mini-catalogues. For the last three projects (*The Story*, *Generations*, and *Waging Peace!*), full catalogues were published.

For three projects, *Visions of the North Florida Environment*, *In Print: The Language of Art*, and *The Story*, teachers on the co-curatorial committees chose participating artists for which to write first drafts of biographies for publications. For *The Story* each biography followed the trajectory of a narrative, but briefly within 150 words. Each biography included a character or characters, a setting, a plot, a conflict, and a resolution. All addressed the same theme—the story of the artist's journey to his or her then current realization as an artist. For the *Generations* publication, teachers contributed to the development of the paths of legacy concepts and the related legacy icons used in the catalogue. For the *Generations* and *Waging Peace!* catalogues, artists' biographies were not used. Instead, artists provided "artist's statements" which related to the theme of each exhibition. In all three catalogues, a full page was allotted to each artist which included his or her imagery with the textual information provided.

The museum contracted with local professional printers for a completion of the catalogue process. As with teachers' packets, the targeted deadline for completion was at least a semester before the project's exhibition or in late summer before teachers' preplanning days. Catalogues were distributed by the curator of education with intern assistance: 10 copies to each artist in the exhibition; 30 copies to each co-curatorial committee member which allowed teachers to use catalogues with classes; one copy to each additional art teacher in the district; and to others upon request. The museum made catalogues available to the public free of charge as they visited the exhibitions. As mentioned, teachers used the catalogues in conjunction with teacher packets for planning and implementing lessons.

Preparation of the Exhibition Cards, Invitations/Flyers

Approximately one semester before each show opened, the curator of education worked with the appropriate museum staff to advertise the project's exhibition. Exhibition postcards and any other printed advertising materials were created by the publications designer. Exhibition postcards were distributed by the museum to artists and the museum's mail list about one to two weeks prior to the exhibition opening. Exhibition information was posted by the museum's communications officer to the museum's website, sent to a museum email list, and announced via various social media outlets. Press releases announcing and describing each exhibition were sent to traditional outlets like the arts section of the local newspaper and local arts council calendar.

Exhibition postcards and other pertinent exhibition announcements were then distributed to teachers digitally and/or by hard copy. Art teachers assisted in announcing the exhibitions by copying and sending flyers home with students, creating posters and/or flyers to display at schools, emailing messages to parents, broadcasting exhibition information on schools' morning news programs, and conveying special invitations to the families of students whose work appeared in the student display section of the exhibition.

Artwork Arrives at the Museum

Approximately one month before the project exhibition's start date, artworks began to arrive. This "one month in advance" timeline was due to the small work force at the FSU MoFA and proper "registrarial" protocols were necessary. Interns assisted with every step. The curator of education supervised the registrarial process. Works were unpacked, preserving packing methods and materials for return. Works were labeled, condition reported, and checked for hanging or installation issues. The curator of education then worked with the preparator. Together, they determined the layout of the exhibition works including signage and didactic wall texts for the exhibition of professional work and the student display. Signage and didactics were ordered or produced in house. Professional work was hung, with exceptions, according to the usual museum standards of spacing and 56–60″ eye-level viewing of the center of pieces or groups of pieces. Student displays were often hung salon style in class groups, sometimes from "floor to ceiling," using a variety of methods including push pins. The preparator hung the shows, again with intern assistance.

Co-curatorial committee art teachers spent varying lengths of time working with their students to produce art for the student displays. Length of time ranged from a few weeks to a year depending on the art teacher and number of lessons taught from the exhibition artworks. Art teachers chose student artwork from these lessons. Artworks were labeled and then mounted, often on construction paper. Digital and hard copy summations of student names and titles were forwarded to the museum, and artworks were delivered about two weeks prior to the start date of the exhibition. Teachers not on the committee delivered their students' artworks to the alternative venues, such as the Tallahassee Community College Gallery or City Hall. The number of student artworks per school varied by exhibition based on space and the number of schools represented on the co-curatorial team. This number, however, was not restrictive due to the salon style method of exhibition for the student displays mounted at the FSU MoFA. Inclusivity was the priority, not exclusivity.

The first two projects, particularly the student display parts of the projects, followed somewhat different procedures. For the *Visions of the North Florida Environment* project, the co-curatorial committee members, all from Buck Lake Elementary, hung the student display at the LeRoy Collins Leon County Public Library themselves. For the *In Print: The Language of Art* project, the student display was hung at the Gallery for Innovation and the Arts, a public gallery space in a state building which housed the Museum of Florida History. The *In Print* student display showcased student works from 12 schools which combined the work done by students of teachers on the co-curatorial team and teachers not on the co-curatorial team. The show was hung by the museum's preparator.

Opening Night

Project exhibitions typically ran from a date in May to a date in July, a time selection influenced by the university calendar. The co-curatorial committee viewed each exhibition as the climactic action/occurrence for the overall project with classrooms visiting the exhibition for tours during the last month of the school year. Teacher workshops often followed during the first part of June and were succeeded by time available for summer camp tours. Opening receptions, filled with activity and energy, often occurred after the actual start date of the exhibition. Receptions, which included refreshments, took place during the early evening hours generally on a weeknight or Friday night. The co-curatorial committee conveyed the "specialness" of opening receptions to students who attended with their friends and families. Make and take tables featuring minds-on and hands-on activities were placed in the museum galleries, each table in front of an artwork on which it was based. Materials used were supplied by the FSU MoFA and included at one time or another colored pencils, crayons, markers, stencils, printmaking stamps and ink, collage materials from magazines and xeroxes, stickers, natural materials like leaves, yarn, glue, scissors, pipe cleaners, air-dry clay, visual and language arts worksheets, paper, and a host of other assorted "clean use" mixed media. Typical visual and language arts worksheets directed students to create their own imagery, or add to imagery presented, and often to answer critical thinking questions. For example, a worksheet could present the student with a figure from a painting in which the background played an out-sized role in conveying the message or the meaning of the work. The worksheet would then direct the student to provide an alternative context for the figure by creating a different background using the materials laid out on the make and take table. Finally, the worksheet would direct the student to rename the work of art in light of his/her newly created background. In addition, the worksheet might ask the student to give one reason for the new title. Activities at make and take tables were designed to help students observe exhibition artwork more closely and construct meaning. Students moved from table to table, many spending the entire opening reception immersed in these activities.

Nearly all make and take activities were originated and fabricated by interns under the supervision of the curator of education who checked each step of the process as the intern proceeded. To plan and prepare for a make and take table, each intern wrote a lesson plan, titled the make and take activity, gathered the necessary materials, organized the process into extremely simplified step by step directions, made samples to display, and created and copied any worksheets to be used. The time needed for each activity was not to exceed 15 minutes. Each intern also fabricated xeroxable signage for his/her table which included the title of the activity, directions posted for students and parents, and sometimes simple definitions or other information the intern deemed valuable. During the *Waging Peace!* reception, the make and take table titled "Design an Ecosystem Drawing" included a didactic providing an age-appropriate definition of the word "ecosystem" and the word "landscape." Each intern implemented his/her own make and take activity by setting up the table, working directly with students and parents during the reception, providing direction and explanation, and answering questions. In the event an intern experienced scheduling conflicts, the intern found and trained a substitute before the opening night reception.

Receptions included student productions in such areas as dance, theater, readings, poetry recitation, choir, musical instrument performance, and more. This broadened the participation of each school and brought a wider audience to the project exhibition. For instance, during *The Story* reception high school students greeted visitors in "pop art" costumes inspired by the Romero Britto work included in the exhibition. Although arrangements began months in advance, final performance schedules were developed by the curator of education during the semester of each opening reception. School performance participation was recruited on a voluntary basis by art teachers on co-curation committees through contacts with other teachers at their schools.

A number of artists attended opening receptions to interact with students and parents informally or formally. Artists sometimes signed posters or catalogues at receptions. For the *Generations* reception, Carrie Ann Baade sold prints of her exhibition work and donated the money to a school for art supplies. For *The Story* reception, the artist Wennie Huang gave a performance symbolizing her Taiwanese heritage using her exhibition installation.

Student Tours

The curator of education and interns under her supervision conducted minds-on and hands-on tours of the exhibitions for students. Often touring students were divided into smaller groups who moved in simultaneous rotating sessions from tour leader to tour leader for distinct approximately half hour sessions with changing but complementary emphases. Some sessions emphasized a primarily hands-on approach with interactive discussion leading to "clean materials" art-making. Other sessions emphasized a primarily minds-on approach. During the *Generations* exhibition students in a minds-on session critically and verbally engaged with two works by two artists from the first and second generations of the Florida Highwaymen Movement which hung in the exhibition side by side. During tours at the elementary level, the leader introduced the two works and two artists as well as the group of artists to which they belonged. Discussion questions to the touring group centered on the learning that moves from an older generation to a younger generation, often from teachers to students like themselves.

The tour then quickly switched to "playing" the "Seven Second Game." During a quiet and timed seven second period, students were charged with seeing and recalling every detail possible in the Highwaymen works while the tour leader stood behind the group. Students then turned away from the artwork to verbally relate to the tour leader their recalled details. After this verbal response ended, students once again viewed the works to check the recalled details. At this point, the tour leader evolved the discussion into a compare and contrast exercise. Two questions were asked: Which details seem to show something the younger generation artist learned from the older generation artist? Which details seem to show the younger generation artist wanted to do some things differently than the older generation artist? Final questions to the group related the exercise to their own lives: What do you learn in art class from your teacher? What would you like to teach someone else about art? What would you like to teach someone else about these artworks?

Students on occasion visited student displays at community locations in conjunction with their FSU MoFA tours. After touring the FSU MoFA during the *Visions of the North Florida Environment* project, school groups visited the student display at the Leroy Collins Leon County Public Library to view their own artworks inspired by the pieces of the professional exhibition. During the *Waging Peace!* project several school groups first toured the FSU MoFA and then visited the exhibition titled *Waging Peace at the Plant*, a satellite exhibition which featured some student artwork. The number of classes, grade level, and timing of visits were scheduled during the last co-curatorial meetings of these projects. Students of co-curatorial committee members received first choice for tours.

Implementing Teacher In-Service Workshops

School system credit toward recertification was arranged by the curator of education months prior to workshops, often with assistance from individual co-curatorial committee members. Requirements and paperwork to ensure credit varied depending on the type of workshop and the amount of potential credit offered. Some types of workshops required paperwork to be completed by the FSU MoFA and submitted to the appropriate school board office, and some types of workshops simply required attending teachers to fill in and submit their own paperwork. In all cases, liaison contact with the appropriate officials at the school board office was imperative. Occasionally the arrangement of some details required more than emails and phone calls, and in-person contact was necessary.

Workshops were often offered a day or so after the end of the teacher school year, frequently during the first days of June before teachers scattered for the summer. Workshops scheduled at this time took place over a two-day time span with morning and afternoon sessions. Many sessions featured local artists whose works were curated into the exhibitions. Many were hands-on artmaking classes. One session for the *Generations* project included a trip to the bronze sculpture studio of a father and son team. The flyer advertising "Working with Generations Artists" encouraged teachers to attend with the following message: "This institute is just for you! Have fun! Be an art student again."

Not all workshops, however, followed the artmaking format. *The Story* work-shops offered no artmaking sessions. The program handout described the session for artist Adrian Fogelin as follows: "The award-winning author talks about her books and the story writing process she employs. She will briefly focus on *The Sorta Sisters* for which she also created the illustrations (two are on display in *The Story*). She shares some strategies she uses to get students started in creative writing." Another session, a collaboration, was explained: "Eluster [Richardson], one of the artists whose work is on display in *The Story*, and Betty [James], a life-long educator from Gadsden County, collaborated on a children's book about another artist in the exhibition, Dean Mitchell. Betty authored *Against All Odds: The Dean Mitchell Story* and Eluster illustrated it. They talk about their joint production." Several sessions featured panels of art teachers from the co-curatorial committee who talked about their pedagogical use of the work from the exhibi-tion in their classrooms. And a curator of education from the Ringling Museum traveled to the FSU MoFA to "lead a tour of the *Story* exhibition with special emphasis on the educational attributes and utilization of the works on display."

Many of these sessions took place in the galleries of the FSU MoFA. Artmaking sessions were often held in university art classrooms. Because the sculpture lab at Florida State University housed a furnace, installation artist and glass-blower Caroline Madden demonstrated glass-blowing and provided teachers the chance to try the process in conjunction with the workshops offered with *Visions of the North Florida Environment*. Several workshops were held during the school year and were open to other teachers other than art teachers. Although primar-ily attended by art teachers in the district, workshops such as the *Generations* Workshop featuring Ela Weissberger and the *Waging Peace!* Workshop featuring Linda Stein were attended by other teachers. These two workshops also provided examples of all-day programs for which teachers would be absent from school. For these workshops specific co-curatorial members worked with school board personnel to make funds available to pay for substitutes. All workshops were free and the FSU MoFA provided attendees with a complimentary lunch. Workshops were primarily supported with grant monies and donations which also subsidized the whole of these projects as previously described.

Striking the Show

At the close of each of these projects, the curator of education supervised the return process of artwork with the help of interns. When the exhibition was dismantled, all work was condition reported and repacked in the same materials in which it was sent to the FSU MoFA. Shipping was generally arranged via Federal Express or UPS dependent upon the artist's preference during incoming shipping, and arrangements were made for personal pickup of work that had been hand delivered. Artists were contacted to verify the return of work. Teachers collected student display work and pieces were returned to students usually at the beginning of the next school year.

Afterword

At the end of projects, co-curatorial committees felt a sense of accomplishment. After finalization of each of the five projects, a selection of members of each co-curatorial team informally reviewed the project to determine a means of sharing that accomplishment. Members of co-curatorial committees gave several presentations at the National Art Education Association Conferences and the Florida Art Education Association Conferences. One presentation was made to the Florida Association of Museums Conference as well as the Art & Design Education for Social Justice Symposium hosted by Florida State University. Presenters at the National Art Education Association Conference on *Visions of the North Florida Environment* included the environmental photographer Todd Bertolaet, one of the artists curated into the exhibition. Using slides of his own artwork paired with student artwork for the *Visions* student display, he demonstrated the positive influence of the experience, that is the way his body of work began to change during and after the project. An essay on *The Story* was published by a pair of committee members for the journal, *The International Journal of the Inclusive Museum*. An essay on the *Waging Peace!* project was published by a trio of co-committee members and a graduate intern for *The Journal of Art for Life*. Co-curatorial committee members gladly cooperated with research through interviews for an article which gave a qualitative assessment of the last project (*Waging Peace!*) for the publication *The International Journal of Arts Education.*

Table 1: Constructivist Co-Curation—Who Does What?

Museum Educator	Art Educator Committee	Community
• Initiate process (of the five projects at the FSU MoFA, the museum educator initiated the constructivist co-curation process three times)	• Initiate process (art educators initiated the constructivist co-curation process twice) • Initiate show idea (art educators initiated all five project/show ideas/themes)	
• Take show idea to museum director to determine scope, placement, schedule, and possible grant funding		
• Call meetings • Recruit members for curation team primarily from schools, but secondarily from the community • Maintain organization, communication, and timeline	• Attend meetings • Participate with committee • Suggest additions to committee primarily from schools, but secondarily from the community	• Attend meetings • Participate with committee

• Determine budget, exhibition dates, and possible funding sources for the project with museum director	• Determine possible needs for transportation funds, otherwise school art budget is specific to each school	• Provide ad hoc funds for such things as workshops, guest speakers or other assorted details, use of space, or contributions in-kind
• Suggest artists and artworks	• Suggest artists and artworks	
• At times, develop and send a "Call to Artists"	• Help define content and scope of the "Call to Artists"	
• Select artwork • Decide on possible interactions with artists and potential workshops for teachers	• Select artwork • Decide on possible interactions with artists and potential workshops for teachers • Preliminary planning for transportation to the museum	• Suggest in-kind or direct contributions for display space, artists' interactions, or potential workshops
• Write catalog entries, lesson plans, and teacher packet with assistance from museum interns	• Write catalog entries, lesson plans, and teacher packet	
• Edit, prepare, and print catalog and teacher packet with museum intern assistance		
• Distribute catalogs and teacher packets with intern assistance • Prepare exhibition cards, invitations, flyers	• Use catalogs and teacher packets to plan instruction • Implement lesson plans for student creation of artwork based on professional artists' work selected for exhibition	

(Continued)

• Schedule artist inter-actions with schools • Facilitate artists visits/interactions	• Schedule artist inter-actions and visits via museum staff • Implement artist inter-actions with students	
• Assemble professional artists' work selected for exhibition	• Continue class lesson plans for continuation of production of art-works inspired by professional artists' work selected for exhibition	
• Work with preparator to hang professional artists' artwork • Work with preparator to hang students' artwork	• Mount and label student artwork • Deliver student artwork to museum	• Hang student work when community facility is used as an annex
• Distribute invitations and flyers to schools and community	• Copy invitations and flyers • Send invitations and flyers home with students	
• Create and prepare, with museum interns, hands-on activities and materials for exhibition opening • Begin planning live student performances inclusive of music, dance, theater, recita-tions, etc. for exhibition opening	• Occasionally create and prepare hands-on activities for exhibition opening • Make inquiries at schools to arrange for student perfor-mances for exhibi-tion opening	

• Address transportation/ busing issues to determine which schools need assistance to pay for buses for school visits to the museum • Schedule school group visits/tours	• Submit transportation assistance requests/ information if needed • Schedule school group visits/tours	
• Give exhibition tours for school groups with help of museum interns	• Bus classes to museum for exhibition tours	
• Plan and facilitate teacher in-service,	• Plan, facilitate, and attend teacher in-service	• Facilitate process, space, and/or funding for teacher in-service
• Strike exhibition and return artist work	• Pick up student work from museum and return to students	
• Write articles and/or prepare presentations for state and national conferences	• Write articles and/or prepare presentations for state and national conferences	

Table 2: Sample Meeting Agenda:

Generations Project: Rolling Monthly Agenda Beginning February 28, 2012

Curatorial idea: Generations

This concept deals with legacy, work that shows the passing of information and skill in the fine arts and fine crafts to the next generation through the following ways:

- from artist parent to artist child which includes artists of a family dynasty
- from artist teacher to artist student

(Continued)

- from artist to society, but in a way that passes on some aspect of cultural heritage (e.g., through the work of the Native American ceramist Maria Martinez).
- from art movement first generation to art movement second generation

Points for discussion:

1. Meetings: last Tuesday of each month

2. February: see #9 below—a. final selection; b. select artists to adopt; c. get contact information; d. provide info for files at MoFA; e. brainstorm ideas for using this imagery with students/curriculum/ lesson plans; f. share ideas

3. March—a. write to artists to secure works (utilizing provided format); b. suggestion: meet the afternoon of Monday Mar 26 (1:00–4:00 pm; perhaps during lunch; will serve lunch)—teacher planning day, to write letters during this session (Julie McBride will check with Curriculum Coordinator to sponsor our meeting & make a countywide announcement to provide officialness for this meeting that some teachers may need); c. continue to explore ways to utilize artists in the classroom (how can the artist interact with students in school and from afar with multiple schools and sessions); d. share ideas

4. April—review acceptances for show to finalize checklist of artists & artwork; b. plan for *In Our Steps* exhibition and workshop

5. May Preview—*In Our Steps* (in the Walmsley Gallery)—a. work must adhere to one or more of the four concepts of legacy; b. just students in curatorial teachers' classrooms this year will be included; c. single works to be framed; d. if space, will allow one composite work; e. no size restrictions for teachers' work; f. hand in work on Tuesday, April 24, also a meeting date (includes work by teacher and single works by one or two students dependent on space; if space, will allow one composite student work; potentially involve

parent/grandparent collaboration); g. exhibition dates: Monday May 7–Friday June 1; h. reception—Friday May 11, want to keep a primarily community audience (adults and children) for this event and want to extend this event to 3.5 hours for purposes of teacher recertification credit; i. schedule for event

> 4:30–5:00 p.m.: setup (teacher involvement in activities for kids to do)
> 5:00–6:30 p.m.: kids/parents/hearty hors d'oeuvres; activities
> 6:30–7:30 p.m.: keynote: Faith Ringgold
> 7:30–8:00 p.m.: questions and book-signing
> - Follow-up required for TEC credit—provide plan for utilizing this information in the classroom

6. June—a. catalogue and accompanying lesson plan book (catalogue deadline—catalogue must be written and printed during the summer of 2012 to be distributed in the Fall semester for use in the classroom; grant monies also make this timetable necessary); b. workshop procedure (follow the same procedure as with *The Story*—lesson plans and bios, etc. will be written at an all-day workshop the day following the last day of school—Tuesday, June 5. Curatorial member volunteered her school as a site for workshop due to central location; computers available; continental breakfast and lunch); c. suggestions for catalogue pages (incorporate some sense of legacy/flowchart/family tree; Shannon Takacs's submission of legacy icons; bio to include basic, background information as well as artistic influence—artist's legacy; main entry in catalogue will be an artist's statement by artist that deals with the issue of legacy; image of artist important—use photo that demonstrates legacy; sections by point of theme/legacy)

7. Review of partner institution involvement

   - Mission San Luis—updated activities/events (scheduled already: parent/child day highlighting various processes used in a number of pieces in the exhibition, hands-on); additional idea—Xavier Cortada (separate exhibition focusing on this artist; from Miami

(Continued)

and available to come to Tallahassee; Spanish heritage and mixing of cultures; Mission already owns some of his work; information was sent after meeting in October)

- Master Craftsman Studio—satellite exhibition of Charles Hook work and parent/child workshop (iron pour)
- Tallahassee Museum—exploring possibilities?
- TCC—will again host student work by those who will join the project in the last semester

8. Maya Lin—sponsored by art instructor from Raa Middle School?

9. Begin final selection of work—a. pare down list of works; b. select artists to adopt (before next meeting get contact information; provide info for files at MoFA); c. brainstorm ideas for using this imagery with students/curriculum/lesson plans

Notes from January 31, 2012

1. Potential group writing of letters to artists at March meeting: suggestion to do it during the day on the teacher planning day—March 26. If not Tuesday, March 27 at regular time: 4:30 pm
2. Preview events discussed: Faith Ringgold will be our speaker—see above
3. Catalogue format discussed—see above
4. Instructor from Raa Middle School asked about Maya Lin—perhaps she will sponsor Maya Lin
5. PowerPoint of pieces selected from September, October, November, January to be made

Process Document: *Waging Peace!* Call to Artists

From the Florida State University Museum of Fine Arts (FSU MoFA)

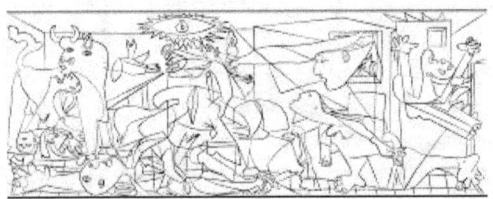

In the spirit of Picasso's *Guernica*
Waging Peace!: Call to Artists

Printable Entry Form on the FSU MoFA website (please note: this form works best when opened with Safari or Internet Explorer)

Contact Information

If you have any questions please send a message to: Viki D. Thompson Wylder, vwylder@fsu.edu or call (850) 645-4681.

Exhibition Theme

In the spirit of Picasso's *Guernica*, the members of the selection committee for the *Waging Peace!* exhibition, are seeking artworks that are a comment upon:

- a response to, solution towards, or consequences of peace or its absence.
- active progress towards or questioning of the nature and possibility of peace, overcoming conflict, promoting, striving towards, seeking, investigating the journey of, and achieving peace.
- potentially multiple levels of the possibilities mentioned, i.e.: personal, spiritual, regional, cultural, geographical, worldwide, etc.

All the above are acceptable sub-categories of the concept of the *Waging Peace!* exhibition, but **please note:** ideas should examine the topic of peace beyond pastoral scenes, tranquility, heaven, or clichéd symbols and the like.

Rules of Entry

POSTMARK DEADLINE for entries is, January 31, 2017.

Artists are eligible to submit works without regard to sex, race, creed or national origin. Artists must be 18 years of age or older. Artists must reside in the United States. All media is eligible for consideration. Mixed media, larger pieces and installations or collaborations are encouraged. There is a no entry fee. A maximum of two (2) works per person may be submitted. Digital images must be in jpeg format. Maximum image file size is 8MB. Slides WILL NOT be accepted.

For two-dimensional pieces provide one (1) image per work. For three-dimensional and installation pieces artists may provide two (2) images per work—a front and rear view or an overall view and a detail. Whether submitting images by email or CD, name each image file with the initial of your first name followed by an underscore, your last name and a number for the file. For example, if your name is Jane Doe, you would name the first work: J_Doe1 and the second, J_Doe2 (if you have a detail view simply put detail after the number: J_Doe1detail). Video based media submissions are eligible for consideration but must be in Quicktime or Windows Media Player format, and should be no longer than a two-minute trailer. No SASE is necessary-CD's will not be returned.

Although the Museum does not impose size restraints, artists whose work weighs more that 150 pounds crated and/or exceeds standard Fed Ex and UPS length and girth measurements, requiring the use of freight shipping, will be responsible for BOTH incoming AND return shipping (see Shipping of Accepted Entries for further details).* Work must be original and prepared for exhibition (i.e. ready for hanging or other appropriate installation), and must be reasonably adaptable to gallery installation. No framed work, other than hand-delivered, may be shipped with glass; artists must use Plexiglas in framing.

Method of Selection

The competition is juried by a committee of educators. Committee members select works based on their own merit and relevance to the theme of *Waging Peace!* Selections are made from the digital images submitted, so it is imperative that quality images be provided to insure fair judging. The Selection Committee will meet in February and March 2017 to make selections and artists will be notified of acceptance or non-acceptance no later than April 15, 2017. **The exhibition is currently scheduled for May 11 to July 8, 2018.** Accepted works must be in the Museum between April 11 and April 18, 2018 unless other arrangements have been made. All dates are subject to slight changes. Committee members and the FSU Museum reserve the right to reject, upon arrival, any work of unacceptable craftsmanship and quality not discernible in the image.

Insurance and Limitations

All work will be insured from the point of arrival through the duration of the exhibition and in most cases will also be insured through return transit (see Shipping of Accepted Entries for exceptions). Claims for full loss must be justified by prior sales amounts equivalent to the value of the claim.

Claims for partial loss will be based on materials and the artist's labor expenses to repair the work. Please be advised that most damage to works occur in transit. You, the artist, are responsible for securing incoming transit insurance if you so desire. If damage is noted upon unpacking you will be notified via email, which will include photo documentation of the damage. It will be your responsibility to file a claim for any damage incurred during the incoming shipping. Should you note any damage upon return of your work—if you qualified for insured, return transit—you must document the damage with photographs and immediately notify the Museum.

Artists sometimes choose to present works on paper (drawings, photographic images, prints) without frames and this presentation method will be subject to review at the Museum; the Museum may be unable to hang works presented without frames, due to insurance requirements, but will proceed on a case by case basis. In the instance of damage to a photographic work or print, the artist's damage claim will be limited to the cost of reprinting the image(s) or repairing damage incurred to the frame or other mounting support. Invoice, receipt, estimate or other documentation must be provided to support the re- printing and/or remounting expense. The damaged print or photograph then becomes property of the FSU Museum of Fine Arts.

Shipping of Accepted Entries

Artists must provide for incoming shipping and insurance to the Museum. Artists whose work weighs more than 150 pounds crated, and/or whose work exceeds standard Fed Ex or UPS length and girth measurements, requiring the use of freight shipping, will be responsible for BOTH incoming AND return shipping costs and arrangements, including transit insurance. A prepaid return shipping label must be provided by the artist in the above instances, along with any return shipping commercial invoices. In most cases, except those as outlined above, the Museum will provide insurance, return shipping via common carrier (UPS or Fed Ex will be used in most instances). Artists who wish to have their works returned through a fine arts shipping company or artists whose works need to ship via a freight company, will have to do so at their own expense (both incoming and return). Works will be returned packed in the same materials and manner in which they were received, therefore crates, boxes and other shipping containers must be strong enough for the return trip. Artists who choose to hand-deliver their work to the Museum must also pick up their work. The Museum will not reimburse travel. Delivery and pick up hours are Monday-Friday, 8-4. We are NOT able to accommodate weekend deliveries.

Special Exhibition Requirements

Any special exhibition requirements MUST BE submitted in writing accompanying the entry. If an installation work wins entry, the Museum of Fine Arts sets the following conditions: The artist must provide specific installation instructions or be willing to deliver and install the work him/herself. If the artist chooses to deliver and install, he/she is then responsible for the de-installation and pick-up of the work the week following the close of the exhibition at his or her own travel expense. The installation, if equipped with electronic functions, must be set up by the artist to be viewer activated or be able to run continually for 7 hours daily. Such lengths of time present problems of wear and tear on an artist's machinery and should be considered before submitting an entry with electrical or mechanical components. All equipment must be provided by the artist, unless otherwise arranged with the Museum.

Catalogue/Sales

A color catalogue is produced, and all artists who enter will receive a copy. Accepted artists will each receive a set of at least 10 complimentary catalogues. The Museum DOES NOT take a commission on works sold as a result of the exhibition. Interested buyers will be referred directly to the artist.

Instructions to Enter

Complete the printable entry form and e-mail to vwylder@fsu.edu with images (put *Waging Peace!* Entry in the subject line), or mail with your CD (if not emailing images) to: FSU Museum of Fine Arts, *Waging Peace!*, 530 West Call Street, Rm 250 Fine Arts Bldg., Tallahassee FL 32306-1140. The entry must be postmarked on or before the deadline of January 31, 2017. If forms are not received via e-mail or mail by this deadline, the entries will not be processed. If *Waging Peace!* Entry is not in the subject line, the entry will not be processed.

Links

Printable Entry Form (please note: this form works best when opened with Safari or Internet Explorer)

Contact Information

If you have any questions please send a message to: Viki D. Thompson Wylder, vwylder@fsu.edu or call (850) 645-4681.

Courtesy: Florida State University Museum of Fine Arts.

Process Document: Sample Cover Letter, Artist Loan and Catalogue Forms, *Generations* exhibition.

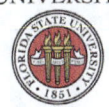

FLORIDA STATE UNIVERSITY | *The* COLLEGE *OF* VISUAL ARTS, THEATRE *&* DANCE
Museum of Fine Arts

COLLEGE *OF* VISUAL ARTS
THEATRE *&* DANCE
Sally McRorie, Dean

ADVISORY COMMITTEE

Jack Freiberg
Assoc. Dean, CVAT&D
David Gussak
Chair, Art Education
Carolyn Henne
Assoc. Dean, CVAT&D
Lynn Hogan
Assoc. Dean, CVAT&D
Cameron Jackson
Director, School of Theatre
Adam Jolles
Chair, Art History
Allys Palladino-Craig
Director, Museum of Fine Arts
Patty Phillips & Russell Sandifer
Co-Chairs, School of Dance
Francis Salancy
Asst. Dean for Dev., CVAT&D
Eric Wiedegreen
Chair, Interior Design

MUSEUM *OF* FINE ARTS

Allys Palladino-Craig
Director, MoFA
Editor-in-Chief, MoFA Press
apalladinocraig@fsu.edu

Wayne T. Vonada
Senior Preparator
wvonada@fsu.edu

Viki D. Thompson Wylder
Curator of Education
vwylder@fsu.edu

Teri R. Abstein
Museum Studies &
Communications Officer
tabstein@fsu.edu

Jean D. Young
Registrar of Collections &
Fiscal Officer
jdyoung@fsu.edu

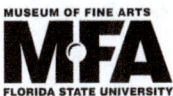

MUSEUM OF FINE ARTS
MoFA
FLORIDA STATE UNIVERSITY

May 1, 2012

Artists/Lenders
Generations

Dear Artist:

As your original contact has undoubtedly indicated, you will here find enclosed information needed for the inclusion of your works in the exhibition titled *Generations*. The exhibition will include artists of international, national, and regional reputation.

Please note that, with some exceptions, the Museum of Fine Arts will provide for shipping (see attached information on shipping). In addition, the Museum was able to acquire grant funds for a catalogue (see attached information on catalogue).

This title of the exhibition is indicative of the theme selected for this show – all works in the exhibition will indicate legacy in some way – from one family member to another, from a teacher to a student, from a specific culture to the culture-at-large. The exhibition, and program to accompany it, is unique in its conception, planning, and process. A committee of Tallahassee/Leon County K-12 visual arts and language arts teachers from 16 schools (and three other cultural organizations, Mission San Luis, the Council on Culture and Arts, and the Tallahassee Community College Gallery) are joining the Museum to curate the exhibition and plan the educational program and activities surrounding the exhibition. This includes an educational packet, with lesson plans written by teachers on this committee, to be sent to all visual arts teachers (and others) in this school district. A goal is to insert the images from this exhibition into the academic curriculum of schools within Leon County. The works in this exhibition will be used as a stimulus for student projects and art production (K-12). A parallel exhibition of K-12 work will be developed. Other activities include teacher workshops and a program of interaction between students and artists. We hope that a large population of students, teachers, and parents from this district will visit this exhibition. We are working with administrators to seek their advocacy and assistance. The Leon County School System – public and private – has in excess of 2500 teachers and 27,000 students. As stated, the Museum will print a catalogue.

We feel the works selected for this exhibition will make a contribution in terms of aesthetics as well as meaning. The committee sees art as a powerful communicator, as a powerful inspiration for children and adults. This exhibition is one means to encourage a deep and lasting engagement with the arts for people of all ages.

If you have any questions/comments, do not hesitate to contact us. **Please review all materials. Please fill in any missing items or correct any mistaken information you find.** We are looking forward to the return of loan forms, catalogue information, and digital images.

We are delighted to be working with you. The exhibition will be memorable!

Sincerely,

Viki D. Thompson Wylder

Viki D. Thompson Wylder, PhD & Committee
Curators, *Generations*

Committee Members & Participating Schools & Organizations:	
Maria Augustyniak – Trinity Catholic	Marcia Meale – Conley
Sara Chang – Pineview	Julie McBride – Gilchrist
Teresa Coates – Raa	Evelyn Pender – Sullivan
Qadira Davidson – Bond	Donald Sheppard – Montford
Jeff Distefano – Rickards IB	Lindsay Douglas – Mission San Luis
Fran Kautz – Buck Lake	Shannon Takacs – Lincoln
Linda Johnson – Deerlake	Amanda Karioth Thompson – COCA
Katharyn Jones – Pineview	Laura Thompson – TCC Gallery
Eileen Lerner – FSUS	Walter Thorner – Riley

530 West Call Street, 250 Fine Arts Building, Florida State University, P.O. Box 3061140, Tallahassee, FL 32306-1140
Telephone: 850.644.6836 • Fax 850.644.7229 • www.MoFA.fsu.edu

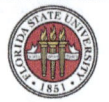

FLORIDA STATE
UNIVERSITY | *The* COLLEGE *OF* VISUAL ARTS, THEATRE *&* DANCE
Museum of Fine Arts

COLLEGE *OF* VISUAL ARTS
THEATRE *&* DANCE
Sally McRorie, Dean

ADVISORY COMMITTEE

Jack Freiberg
Assoc. Dean, CVAT&D
David Gussak
Chair, Art Education
Carolyn Henne
Assoc. Dean, CVAT&D
Lynn Hogan
Assoc. Dean, CVAT&D
Cameron Jackson
Director, School of Theatre
Adam Jolles
Chair, Art History
Allys Palladino-Craig
Director, Museum of Fine Arts
Patty Phillips & Russell Sandifer
Co-Chairs, School of Dance
Francis Salancy
Asst. Dean for Dev., CVAT&D
Eric Wiedegreen
Chair, Interior Design

MUSEUM *OF* FINE ARTS

Allys Palladino-Craig
Director, MoFA
Editor-in-Chief, MoFA Press
apalladinocraig@fsu.edu

Wayne T. Vonada
Senior Preparator
wvonada@fsu.edu

Viki D. Thompson Wylder
Curator of Education
vwylder@fsu.edu

Teri R. Abstein
Museum Studies &
Communications Officer
tabstein@fsu.edu

Jean D. Young
Registrar of Collections &
Fiscal Officer
jdyoung@fsu.edu

MUSEUM OF FINE ARTS

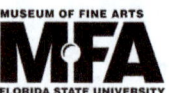

FLORIDA STATE UNIVERSITY

Generations

LOAN AGREEMENT FORM
Please return Loan Agreement Form to the Museum between May 14 and May 18, 2012.

This agreement addresses the temporary loan of work(s) between the Florida State University Museum of Fine Arts (hereinafter referred to as the "Museum") and Lender (specified below).
LENDER:
ADDRESS:
CONTACT PERSON:
PHONE/FAX: **E-MAIL:**
LOAN to ARRIVE BETWEEN:
DATES of FSU EXHIBITION: May 10 - July 12, 2013

For each work please indicate/confirm the following information: title, date, medium, dimensions (important for labels) and value. For shipping, see attached instructions. Please return one copy of this Form to the Museum for insurance/exhibition purposes.
WORK(S) COVERED BY THIS AGREEMENT   **INS. VALUE:**

I agree to loan Florida State University Museum of Fine Arts the work(s) listed above on the condition that said property is insured by Florida State University Museum of Fine Arts as specified in the attached shipping instructions.

PHOTOGRAPHIC REPRODUCTION
Do you authorize the Object(s) to be reproduced by and for the Museum (check all that apply): the Museum will utilize reproductions for all these purposes. This exhibition will publish an accompanying catalogue.

☐   Press and Publicity
☐   Publications
☐   Educational Purposes
Please provide one of the following on disc or via e-mail with the loan form:
☐   digital images: high resolution
☐   digital images: minimum of 300 dpi at 4" x 5" or large format; usually 5 - 25 MB each
      (over 18 MB, must send disk; under may e-mail)

Credit Line (if applicable)

_____   _____
Lender's Signature   Date

_____
Print Name
For potential payments or reimbursements a SSN # or FEID# is required (please fill in even if you do not foresee a payment or reimbursement): _____

Viki D. Thompson Wylder   *May 2, 2012*
Museum Representative's Signature   Date

Viki D. Thompson Wylder   850-644-1299
Print Name   Phone #

vwylder@fsu.edu   850-644-7229
E-mail   Fax #

530 West Call Street, 250 Fine Arts Building, Florida State University, P.O. Box 3061140, Tallahassee, FL 32306-1140
Telephone: 850.644.6836 • Fax 850.644.7229 • www.MoFA.fsu.edu

Florida State University Museum of Fine Arts.

Shipping Instructions

Incoming Shipping

The Museum encourages work to be hand-delivered or shipped via Federal Express. The University holds an account with Fed Ex. Other arrangements will be decided on a case by case basis. Work will be insured in transit to the Museum via accepted carrier.

Artworks must arrive at the Museum between April 2 and April 5, 2013. Unless other arrangements have been made all works selected for the exhibition must be in the Museum by April 5, 2013. Work(s) must arrive prepared for exhibition, that is ready to hang or prepared for other appropriate installation. No work, other than hand-delivered, may be shipped with glass; unless artists hand-deliver work(s), artists are required to use plexiglas for framing.

Return Shipping

The Museum will provide insured, return shipping via accepted carrier with the exceptions listed in #1 and #2 below. Artists must notify the Museum of any address or telephone changes in the event of a move. If you wish your work to be returned to a different location from your mailing address please indicate this clearly to avoid any confusion. We cannot ship to Post Office Boxes, so please provide a shipping address if your mailing address is a Post Office Box.

1. Exception Circumstances Using a Carrier

Artists who choose to ship their work through a fine arts shipper and artists who are outside the US or Canada will be required to arrange and pay for both incoming and return shipping and transit insurance. Works must be return-shipped within 25 working days of the exhibition closing date (by August 16, 2013). The Museum must be informed of the exact date of pick-up. Crates which exceed 65" in any direction or weigh over 150 lbs. will be the artist's responsibility for return shipping. This constitutes an oversized shipment and is usually more costly and difficult to handle.

2. Hand-Delivery

If an artist hand-delivers his/her work, the artist must also arrange to pick up the work within the 25 working days following the exhibition closing date (by August 16, 2013; for installations, see "Special Exhibition Requirements" below). The Museum does not reimburse travel expenses incurred for self-delivery.

Packing and Insurance

Artists are asked to take extreme care with the packing of their artwork as works are returned packed in the same materials and manner in which they are received. Insurance guidelines require that the Museum of Fine Arts be released from any liabilities incurred against the object(s) resulting from the artist's packing materials and manner. In case of accident, the insurance carrier will require that a full loss claim be justified by the documented market value of the work. This will require prior sales amount records equivalent to the value of the claim.

Special Exhibition Requirements

Special exhibition requirements must be in writing and accompany the work. Installation artists are required to do the following:

1. The artist must provide specific installation instructions or deliver and install the work him/herself. If the artist delivers and installs, he/she will de-install and pick up the work within 5 working days following the close of the exhibition (by July 19, 2013).

2. The installation, if equipped with electronic functions, must be set up by the artist to be viewer-activated or must be able to run continuously. All equipment must be provided by the artist unless otherwise arranged with the Museum.

Shipping Dates to Remember

Between April 2 and April 5, 2013: delivery of work to Museum of Fine Arts.
By August 16, 2013: pick up by shippers for return to Lenders.
By July 19, 2013: hand-delivered installation work de-installed and picked up.

Catalogue, etc.

A catalogue will accompany the *Generations* exhibition. The catalogue will afford each artist at least one artwork image and one image of the artist with the information as outlined below. The catalogue will be composed to appeal to varying audiences and levels of expertise.

Please send/fill in the following. Return them with the loan form. If sending via postal service, please print legibly.

1. **Artist's Biography**: Please send a resume/vita and a biography. These will be used by curators/teachers for a variety of purposes including tour information and classroom study.

2. **Artist's Statement**: Please write 175 words or less but write the statement in keeping with the concept of the exhibition and one of the three aspects of legacy. Your statement will talk about the relationship of your work to the concept of legacy.

Legacy in this exhibition is viewed as the passing of information and skill in the fine arts and fine crafts to the next generation through the following ways:
- from artist parent to artist child (or from one member of the family to another)
- from artist teacher to artist student
- from artist to society, but in a way that passes on some aspect of cultural heritage from a specific culture to the culture-at-large (for example, through the work of Native American ceramists such as Maria Martinez).

You may send this statement either by e-mail or fill in this form by hand:

Name, exactly as you would like to have it published:

_____

Artist's statement: addressing the issue of legacy; 175 words or less:

_____

_____

_____

_____

_____

_____

_____

_____

Artist's initials just as you would like to have them appear at the end of your statement: _____

3. **Artist's position and contact information**: this is for your benefit so that interested collectors/museums/curators/buyers may get in touch with you.

Fill in the blanks:

The artist is a/an (position or job title): _____

at (place of employment): _____

and maintains a studio in (city): _____ (state): _____

(studio address): _____

website: _____

gallery (affiliations you might like to have mentioned in the format "The artist is represented by ...."

_____

(e-mail): _____

4. **Awards/Exhibitions**: list the most recent first. Awards may include honors, fellowships, residencies, grants, scholarships, and so on.

	Year	Award and/or Exhibition Title	Awarding Institution	City	State
1.					
2.					
3.					
4.					
5.					

Forms – Dates to Remember: Return all between May 14 and May 18, 2012 which include

- Loan Form
- Artist's Statement
- Artist's Position and Contact Information
- Awards/Exhibitions
- Digital Images: Each Artwork & One Image of the Artist

Send all via e-mail or by United States Postal Service.

Courtesy: Florida State University Museum of Fine Arts.

Generations Interaction with an Artist
Artist's Trip to Tallahassee
Second Generation Highwayman

Date:
First choice: Saturday, April 27
Second choice: Saturday, April 20

Estimated # of Schools & Students:
Five schools: Conley Elementary, Buck Lake Elementary, Pineview Elementary, Bond
Elementary, Florida State University School
Students: approximately 65 to 70 students with at least one parent per family.

Location & Amenities:
Mission San Luis
Tent available and chairs

Materials to be used by students:
Oil pastels on paper using boards for support

Honorarium and Cost:
Honorarium of $575 plus the cost of one night's food and accommodation in Tallahassee

Cost???   Hotel: $150
                 Transportation: $100
                 Food: Dinner, breakfast, lunch – $80

Total: $905

Process Document: *Waging Peace!* Announcement Card

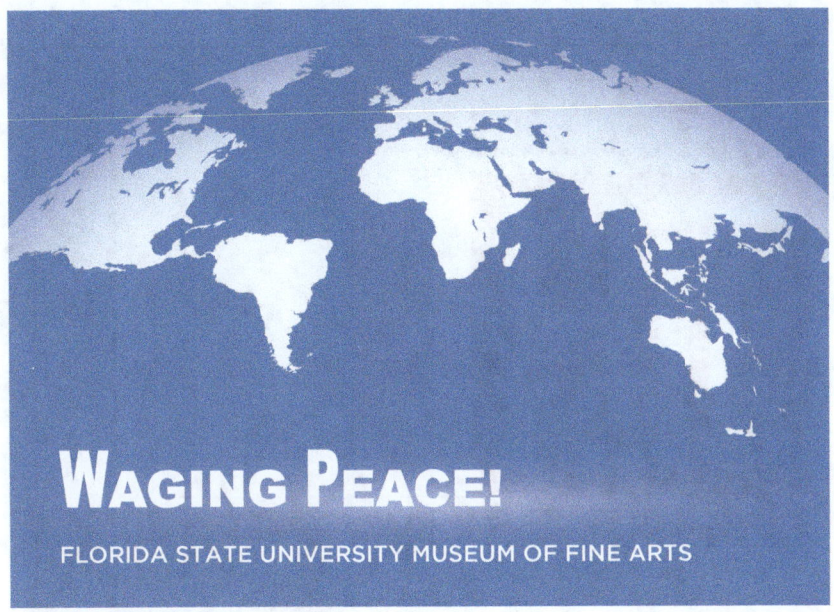

WAGING PEACE!

FLORIDA STATE UNIVERSITY MUSEUM OF FINE ARTS

Museum of Fine Arts

Opening Reception
May 17, 2018 ● 6-8pm

Exhibition—May 14-July 7, 2018. Co-curated by the Council of Educators and the Museum of Fine Arts. *Waging Peace* is a project supporting special educational programming for the K-12.

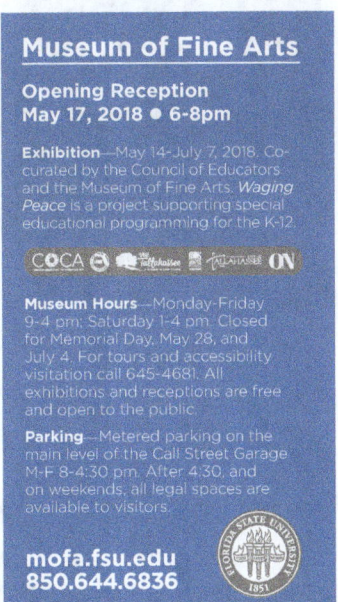

Museum Hours—Monday-Friday 9-4 pm; Saturday 1-4 pm. Closed for Memorial Day, May 28, and July 4. For tours and accessibility visitation call 645-4681. All exhibitions and receptions are free and open to the public.

Parking—Metered parking on the main level of the Call Street Garage M-F 8-4:30 pm. After 4:30, and on weekends, all legal spaces are available to visitors.

mofa.fsu.edu
850.644.6836

FSU Museum of Fine Arts

530 West Call Street
250 Fine Arts Building
College of Fine Arts
Tallahassee FL 32306-1140

Return Service Requested

Non-Profit Org.
U.S. POSTAGE
PAID
Tallahassee, FL
Permit # 55

Courtesy: Florida State University Museum of Fine Arts.

Process Document: publicity in the local newspaper for the *Generations* exhibition and student display.

LOCAL NEWS » TALLAHASSEE DEMOCRAT » WEDNESDAY, MAY 22, 2013

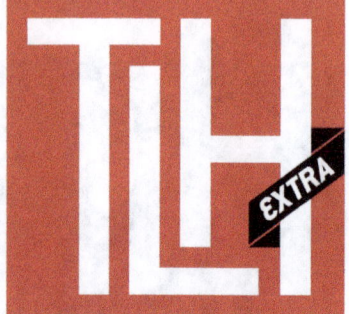

LIMELIGHT EXTRA

Get a jump on your weekend entertainment plans every Wednesday, and pick up the Limelight section on Friday

**By Randi Atwood
and Mark Hinson**
Democrat features editor and senior writer

Art

THIS IS THE FIRST 'GENERA-TIONS': Students from kindergartens, elementary, middle and high schools around the city will have their latest creations on display when **"The Younger Generations"** group show opens with a reception from 6:30 to 8 p.m. Thursday at the Tallahassee Community College Fine Art Gallery, 444 Appleyard Drive. It is free.

THIS IS THE NEXT 'GENERA-TIONS': See original pieces by such internationally and nationally known artists as Maya Lin, Faith Ringgold, Judy Chicago, Trevor Bell, Carrie Ann Baade, Eluster Richardson, William Harper and many more when the **"Generations"** exhibition officially opens with a reception from 6:30 to 8 p.m. Friday at the Florida State University Museum of Fine Arts, corner of Copeland and Call streets. It is free.

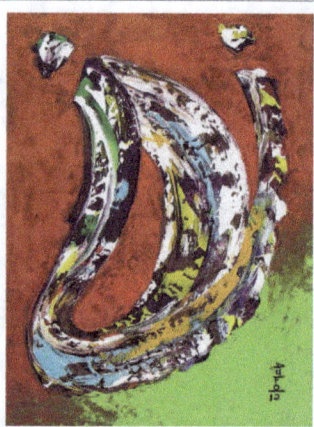

"Memory" by Jean Charles Duffaut is on display at the FSU Museum of Fine Arts as part of the "Generations" exhibit, which has its official opening Friday.

Courtesy: Florida State University Museum of Fine Arts and the *Tallahassee Democrat.*

Process Document: article in the local newspaper for the *Waging Peace!* project.

Tallahassee Democrat - 05/16/2018   Copy Reduced to 81% from original to fit letter page   Page : C01

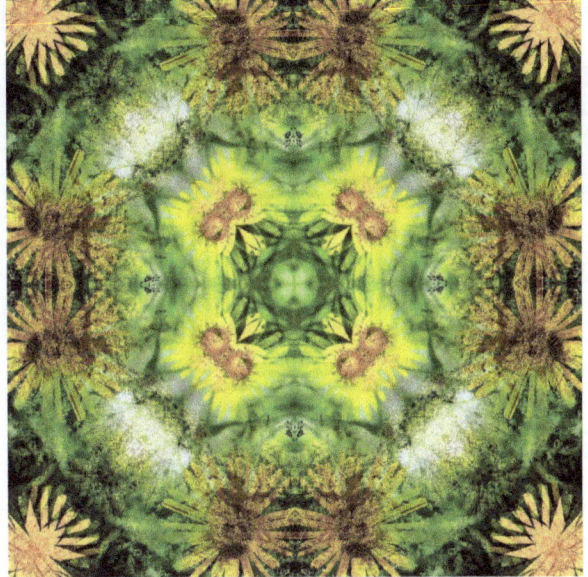

Sara Chang's photographic collage mandala will be on display at FSU's Museum of Fine Arts along with many other peace related artwork by national and local artists, AMANDA THOMPSON

Acting with art

Waging Peace exhibit reaches into the classroom

Amanda Karloth Thompson
Council on Culture & Arts

"How do we proactively practice peace in our lives?" Local artist and educator Sara Chang often contemplates this question. Her photographic collage mandalas symbolize wholeness and balance. She finds the process of creating them is meditative and allows her to achieve a state of inner peace.

Chang is one of 40 artists whose work has been selected by a team of local educators to be shown in the Waging Peace exhibition at the Florida State University Museum of Fine Arts (MoFA). The concept of peace is infused throughout her work as both an artist and the reading coach at Pineview Elementary School.

"Every day I try to practice what the Dalai Lama teaches us: connect to all sentient beings and practice loving

See EXHIBIT, Page 2C

Waging Peace exhibit

FSU MoFA's exhibit is on display from May 14 – July 8. The opening reception is on Thursday, May 17 from 6-8 p.m.

The Anderson Brickler Gallery's exhibit is on display from May 19 – June 9. The opening reception is on Saturday May 19 from 2-5 p.m.

COCA's exhibit at the City Hall Art Gallery is on display from May 9 – July 9. The opening reception is on Thursday, May 24 from 6-7:30 p.m.

The Plant's exhibition is on display through May.

To learn more, visit www.Tallahasseeseearts.org for details.

Tallahassee Democrat - 05/16/2018   Copy Reduced to 69% from original to fit letter page   Page : C02

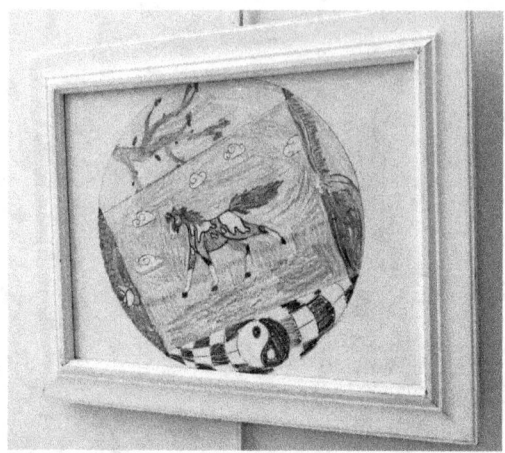

Tranquil Symbols by Saskia Kapoor-Sisask of Montford Middle School is on display at the City Hall Gallery.
AMANDA THOMPSON

Exhibit

Continued from Page 1C

kindness and compassion," she shared. Her advice to others searching for personal balance is to "be patient and stay in the moment to experience awareness. Be proactive, not reactive." She contends that one of the best ways to achieve this is through art making. It's "a creative process, not destructive," she said.

This is one of the driving principles behind the Waging Peace exhibit, the sixth show at MoFA to be co-curated by educators in the community. Leading the charge is Dr. Viki Thompson Wylder, Education Curator at the museum. To her, the operative word is "waging."

"I don't want anyone to think of peace as passive," she said. "Peace is an active process. You have to be involved, think, act, do. We have a whole host of global problems and each one of us needs to make a contribution."

That includes children. "We need to start talking to kids when they're little or we won't have people who feel they can do something and speak up."

In an effort to carry that forward, the curatorial team also created an educational guide to compliment the artworks selected for the MoFA exhibition. "That's important," explains Wylder, "because it starts the process of integrating the exhibit into the classroom."

For the past several months, these lessons plans were implemented across the community and many of the artworks created by K-12 grade students will be exhibited at MoFA and in extension exhibits at several other venues as well.

One of the members of the curatorial team is Donald Sheppard, art teacher at Montford Middle School. He said "anytime students feel like they can participate in a positive way, it's valuable for them. This theme gives them an opportunity to make a statement about their world and even be influential. We're seeing our youth rising up and taking charge. They have something to say and they can do that through their art. An image can move us to action. If not action, at least dialog and contemplation. That's powerful."

Sheppard was especially pleased that the Waging Peace theme allowed for multiple interpretations. Students used a wide variety of materials, techniques and imagery. "Just to see so many different ideas, it has been encouraging. It says to me that there's room at the table for everyone. Diversity has quite a place here."

Inspired by Sara Chang's mandalas, some of Sheppard's art students created their own. Using colored pencils, sixth-grader Saskia Kapoor-Sisask created a personal mandala she titled "Tranquil Symbols" which represented inner peace. A few of Sheppard's students, like eighth grader Jaden Story, chose to focus their attention outward.

Sheppard explained that in Jaden's piece titled "The Lion and the Lamb," she "intentionally placed these symbolic animals together. She's astute with value and contrast and she included those principles of art to make a statement about commonalities versus things that make us different."

Many students used techniques like collage or mosaic and art elements like contrast and balance that reinforce the artwork's message. "What you work with speaks as well," said Sheppard. "When you choose your medium, it becomes an avenue for what you want to say. These students get that."

As much as the selection of materials helps push the message of peace forward, the Waging Peace initiative has modeled the concept of collaboration and inclusivity from the beginning. A truly cooperative effort, there are numerous community partners involved in the Waging Peace project including MoFA, the Council on Culture & Arts (COCA), The Plant, the Anderson Brickler Gallery, The Holocaust Education Resource Council, and many area schools.

Sheppard, Wylder, Chang and many others have worked together to build a positive visual representation of what peace can look like in our schools, community, nation and world. Though the possibility of enduring peace can seem, at times, far away, Sheppard is hopeful.

"When you're moving something that's heavy, one person might move it an inch but when we all get together, get around it, and use our energies we can pick it up. Waging peace is something we all believe in and we've had the opportunity to gather around and now it's time to pick it up and go."

There are several exhibitions related to the community-wide Waging Peace project. They are all free and open to the general public. To learn more, visit www.TallahasseeArts.org for details.

Amanda Karioth Thompson is the Assistant Director for the Council on Culture & Arts. COCA is the capital area's umbrella agency for arts and culture (www.tallahasseearts.org).

Courtesy: Tallahassee Democrat, Council on Culture and Arts, and Amanda Karioth Thompson.

Impact and Outcomes: The Efficacy of the Constructivist Co-Curation Method

Beginnings

As an elementary art teacher, two moments stood out for me as transformative over the course of the 18 years and 5 projects of this constructivist co-curatorial history. The first was the night I walked into the Florida State University Museum of Fine Arts (FSU MoFA) and met the student docents at the opening reception for the exhibition associated with the original project, *Visions of the North Florida Environment*. The student docents opened my eyes to a broader concept of art education and its possibilities. Each student docent focused on one artist and his or her work. The level of engagement, knowledge, and pride that the students demonstrated in "their" artists' works of art took art education to a new level, from mere attraction to the surface qualities of an artwork to something personal and meaningful. The students' frame of mind changed, from a "required study of art history" outlook to something that went beyond the classroom into the lives of the students, families, and community. They "owned" the art and saw the art as worthy of thought, examination, and discourse. Art history became meaningful and alive as parents, friends, and community members were able to experience the works in a new way through the eyes of the students.

The second moment came a few days before the reception for the final and fifth show in the project series, the *Waging Peace!* exhibition. The co-curatorial committee for *Waging Peace!* decided on a last-minute inclusion of an installation art piece addressing a school shooting. This second moment brought the realization of the ability of the constructivist co-curation method to respond in real time to a tragic current event—the shootings at Parkland High School on Valentine's Day in 2018. The fact that the co-curatorial team could respond and curate an installation artwork into the *Waging Peace!* exhibition a few days before the show's opening illustrates one of the main strengths of the process. The process is flexible and responsive to the input and the needs of the community.

> The five projects with exhibitions, artists' interactions, artworks brought to the classroom, field trips to the museum, and other related activities expanded school art programs within and outside the classroom. These all played an important role in expanding the depth of the art curriculum and making art real to the students. Art became something happening now not just in the past.
>
> —*MM*

As a Curator of Education at a small museum, I needed methods that provided the "biggest bang for the buck" literally and educationally. Constructivist co-curatorial projects banged the biggest of any educational programs offered at the FSU MoFA. Though budgets for the co-curated projects were generally limited to several thousands of dollars, the impact on teachers, students and community was significant. Each co-curatorial project engaged committee art teachers for two to four years. The three co-curatorial projects that included art teachers from multiple schools (*The Story*, *Generations*, and *Waging Peace!*) engaged committee representation from 11 to 15 institutions and in turn engaged the student bodies of their schools affecting a potential collective total of approximately 5,500 students for each project. By the end of each of these three projects, however, the number of teachers who wanted to involve their students nearly doubled during the projects' last semesters. For *Generations*, which opened in 2013, 26 public schools, or over half of the public schools in the local school district, eventually participated. *Generations* ultimately attracted 12 more schools and their art teachers during the last semester. As a result, about 4,700 additional students were affected either through classroom presentations and activities, inclusion of their work in a student display, visitation of the main professional exhibition and/or a student display, attendance at an opening reception, or participation in a museum tour. In the end, the number of students potentially affected in some way by the *Generations* project totaled nearly a third of the student body in the county school system at the time. Many students experienced multiples of these project interactions especially when their teachers worked on the co-curatorial team. Students frequently expressed a sense of knowledgeable intimacy with and "ownership" of these projects and their components, particularly the exhibitions, artworks, and spaces that housed them.

As this discussion of school, teacher, and student participation suggests, the constructivist co-curation method expanded the FSU MoFA audience. As teachers joined project co-curatorial committees their own participation and meaning-making associated with the exhibitions and selected artworks affected their pedagogy, classroom interchange, and their enthusiasm for the museum and its offerings. This, in turn, influenced their students and their students' families. Students from across the county experienced artists' interactions, often in their own classrooms. They visited the museum either through field trips to tour these exhibitions or with their families and friends to receptions and other offerings. During the 18 years in which these projects were enacted, thousands of students with their extended families enjoyed seeing student artwork on display as well as the professional artwork that stimulated the student responses. This family audience tended to bring attendees who were new to the museum and its exhibitions and programs. Participating teachers and their students hailed from schools that spanned the economic spectrum, from lower socioeconomic Title 1 schools to schools populated with students from affluent neighborhoods. The interest in and commitment to the FSU MoFA generated by these projects stood in contrast to the "normal" interest in museum programs and projects that generally brought a more surface or casual regard by individual teachers and their students with an occasional field trip to an exhibition. A difference in participation with the FSU MoFA from the 2006 to 2007 year when no such project was coming to fruition to the 2007–2008 year when *The Story* project culminated in an exhibition is striking. During the 2006–2007 year, the FSU MoFA Education Program conducted approximately 140 tours/events for all types of groups, on- and off-site school and community groups, with approximately 4,300 attendees/participants in total. During the 2007–2008 year, the FSU MoFA Education Program conducted approximately twice the number of tours/events, inclusive of all group types, with approximately 12,500 attendees/participants. Museum to museum comparison/contrast is difficult since each museum is unique. But these numbers seemed noteworthy for the FSU MoFA, a museum with five to five and a half employee positions. In an international research study of private museums published in 2016, nearly 40% employed less than 5 staff and nearly the same percentage indicated an annual visitation of 5,000 or less (Bouchera et al., pp. 34–36).

—VDTW

Inherent Qualities of the Constructivist Co-Curation Method from the Art Educator's and Museum Educator's Viewpoints

The constructivist co-curation method inherently included aspects that supported its success. From the art education perspective, inherent in the constructivist co-curatorial process was the easy incorporation of the changing philosophies and pedagogies of the field—Discipline-Based Art Education, Art as a Visual Language, the Big Idea, and Social Justice Art Education—with the constructivism utilized by the MoFA Education Program. Meaning-making by committee members, particularly teachers, was also inherent in the process. Teachers suggested project themes based on enduring ideas or purposes of art that already held meaning for them. As the process proceeded, as committee members viewed and analyzed artwork for exhibitions, those meanings expanded and deepened. Teachers tapped into those meanings to devise lesson plans, programs, activities, and artists' interactions with their students. This meaning-making also guided the planning and choreography of tours of the exhibitions by MoFA's Education Program. This continual making of meaning spurred a greater commitment to each project as a whole and the use of the artwork curated. It created a drive to match theory and pedagogical method to the meanings understood while remaining compliant with state standards. Teachers' investment and effort in the process transferred to their students. In an article written as an assessment of the last project (*Waging Peace!*), teachers who were interviewed for the assessment conveyed the sense of authenticity of their students' work. "Participants observed that student engagement in the project was authentic. They were not simply practicing or using what they learned because they had to; they wanted to—and in positive and civic-minded ways" (Hamrock et al., 2019, pp. 9–10).

Ultimately the most important aspect of the constructivist co-curation method was the inherent franchising of the disenfranchised. Simply by working with the public schools, a more varied demographic perspective was initiated for the museum. From the opening decade of the last century to the early decades of the 21st century, public schools as an aggregate have been increasingly charged with reaching all populations as defined by K-12 age range, race, ethnicity, and economics. With committees of teachers taking the lead in defining themes for exhibitions and opening participation to additional schools in the final semesters of most projects, the five projects detailed in this book became educationally relevant to the needs and interests of a wide array of students and their families. Difficult concepts like "peace" were examined on multiple age appropriated levels. Opening nights brought new audiences who actively participated in hands-on activities at stations positioned in front of original artworks, some of international reputation. Traditional and nontraditional families, each uniquely structured, engaged in art together. Students stood in front of works like the sculptural piece by Bradley Arthur titled *WMDs* to explain to their families or friends that the work was about bullying. The museum opening nights were not quiet nor neat. Generally, people did not dress up but came in the clothes they were wearing during the day. Opening nights were "alive" and filled with people from every walk of life.

From the museum's viewpoint the constructivist co-curation method secured a mesh of school system requirements with FSU MoFA procedures that ensured projects and exhibitions mounted were used by a wide audience of teachers and their divergent school populations inclusive of immediate and extended families of students. Using their own contextual and experiential knowledge of the audiences targeted, teachers and others on the committees continually judged choices in proposed artwork, programs, and activities. These assessments proved comprehensive due to the background of co-curatorial members. Committees reached across a spectrum of teachers to include primarily K-12 art teachers but also teachers from the general elementary classroom, from English for Speakers of Other Languages programs, and from a homeschool cooperative. Liaisons from other museum and gallery programs as well as community organizations were also included on the committees. This range of committee participants demonstrated the ability of the constructivist co-curation method to easily incorporate representatives from fields of teaching other than art as well as representatives from institutions other than schools. Teachers' years of experience and academic preparation varied, but a number of teachers held higher degrees at the master's and doctorate levels. The committee for the *Waging Peace!* project included three art teachers, two at the elementary level and one at the middle school level, with doctorates in art education and many years of teaching experience. These three teachers also represented schools with diverse populations economically and racially/ethnically. School typology extended from a school with a socioeconomically challenged population, a Title 1 school, to a school with a socioeconomically advantaged population. When taken together, these three teachers also represented an overall school population in which approximately 56% of the students were within minority classifications, exceeding the overall 42.6% minority percentage of the student population in the public school district in which the museum resided. The inherent process of informal front-end needs and formative assessments by this cross section of teachers provided direct insight into the requirements of individual schools and the school system as a whole by including population diversity, schedules, rules, standards, and overall scope and sequence. Importantly this method provided a close-up view of the necessities of teachers who must work with these interlocking aspects. Thus, this method was helpful to the FSU MoFA, a small museum with limited staff or ability to finance or find the time for formal needs surveys or formal program evaluations.

Over the course of the 18 years in which these projects came to fruition, co-curatorial members suggested the involvement of multiple community organizations. Generally, when a community organization was invited to participate in a project, that organization was represented by a member on the committee, but not always. When the student display for *Visions of the North Florida Environment* was mounted at the LeRoy Collins Leon County Public Library, no representative of the library sat on the committee. This contrasted with a representative of the Tallahassee Community College Gallery who participated on co-curatorial committees and hosted two "overflow" student displays. Some organizations offered other services in which mutual needs of the project and the organization were met. The Holocaust Education Resource Council (HERC) supported two projects with funding for speakers for teacher workshops. These workshops met specific objectives of the projects while also meeting the community educational goals of HERC. In addition, they contributed to the Holocaust awareness objectives set by the public school system for teachers. Other participatory community organizations included museums such as: the Mary Brogan Museum of Art & Science; Mission San Luis, which celebrated the Native American and Spanish heritage of the area; galleries like the Anderson Brickler Gallery that focused on African American art; and arts organizations like the Tallahassee Council on Culture and Art and the do-it-yourself art space named The Plant. Community organizations like The Plant emphasized art as a connective tissue among the FSU MoFA, K-12 schools, and the community at large. Participation in the art workshops and exhibition The Plant offered for the *Waging Peace!* project attracted artists, teachers, K-12 students, university students, and the general public. Jennifer Hamrock, who represented The Plant on the co-curatorial committee observed, "It is a space that brings together groups of people that don't normally interact [including the] homeless...My hope was for people to come together and make art together, leaving behind pretentious or definite rules about what art should be, and to connect while creating" (Wylder, personal communication, 2020).

In addition to fostering the participation of community organizations, the constructivist co-curation method inherently encouraged the contributions of university interns who assisted with all steps in the process. Involvement was never superfluous. They attended co-curatorial meetings and, though often quiet, were invited to contribute to discussions. Under supervision they wrote lesson plans, designed the graphics of teachers' packets, created and implemented make and take activities, contacted artists for official paperwork reasons, unpacked and repacked artwork, conducted condition report inspections, attended layout sessions for exhibitions, and installed labels and didactics. Occasionally an intern's involvement over several semesters warranted membership on a co-curatorial committee, such as the intern who contributed extensively to *The Story* project even determining the catalogue entry for the Gee's Bend artist Mary Lee Bendolph. In addition, a graduate intern joined the team who published the postproject assessment article on the fifth project of the series, *Waging Peace!*. Through this process interns were given the benefit of a productive inside look at multiple facets of the actual life of the museum. As one intern put it, "You won't be a pencil pusher" (V. D. T. Wylder, personal communication via note from FSU MoFA intern, Danielle Steele, Spring, 2014). Together, the participation of community organizations and university interns amplified the contextual real-world space for the development and implementation of these projects including their concepts, exhibitions, and program offerings.

Holistic Value of the Constructivist Co-Curation Method: Teachers, Students, the Museum

The value of the constructivist co-curation method is holistic, affecting teachers, students, the museum, and its relationship to its audience. The constructivist co-curatorial process provided value at three levels for teachers: professional growth, flexibility, and enhanced student learning experiences. From primarily stand-alone positions, that is, each art teacher was often the only art teacher at a school, teachers received the opportunity to join an active and effective community. The constructivist co-curatorial process provided art teachers with a group that engaged earnestly and cooperatively in the work of art education. As the teams for each project developed, multiple perspectives were offered.

Informal and collegial conversations with peers expanded concepts and served as a form of in-service as teachers struggled with novel constructs or ideas and changing art education theories and pedagogy. Within the realm of formal professional development, the museum provided quality workshops at no charge which were based on the exhibitions or utilized participating art community members, which in turn helped teachers gain points toward recertification. From a teaching perspective, no longer feeling like a sole practitioner, instead working with and learning from and with peers informally and formally, was one of the main values of this process.

The flexibility of the constructivist co-curatorial process, whether referring to committee size or project content, was extremely valuable from the art teacher perspective. The functioning of the committee was not dependent on everyone attending every meeting making membership on the committee possible while juggling real life schedules. There were times when a committee member participated by speaker phone. Teachers could be on the committee from the start or join the project later as noncommittee members with limited school participation during the semester before the exhibition. The process seamlessly adapted to changing art education theories, state standards, scope and sequences, and district mandates. The process unified exhibitions with art curriculum and provided additional primary and secondary resources. The teacher packets provided background information, lesson plans, and images and the catalogs were often used as booklets for students to browse, read, or use in class to inspire their own work. The museum staff often brought artworks or arranged for artists to visit classrooms. They dealt with the arrangements freeing teachers to concentrate on student learning.

For students the value lay in the constructivist co-curatorial process' ability to enhance student learning through multiple experiences: they met artists, they interacted with original works of art, they had opportunities to engage in artist talks, they visited the museum, and they showed off their own works of art in a professional setting. The projects developed by this process demonstrated to K-12 students a valuation of students' concepts, critical thinking, and effort particularly as seen in the artwork in the student displays mounted for each project. The students whose schools participated in these co-curatorial exhibitions extended their knowledge of artists but also of media and processes. Participating in these projects made art real and accessible. Students developed a sense of pride in their work. The curated exhibitions provided students a first-hand view of primary resources from a range of high-quality professional art that was chosen

Inspired by a *Generations* artist, Buck Lake Elementary students
constructed meaning by creating Assemblage Sculpture.

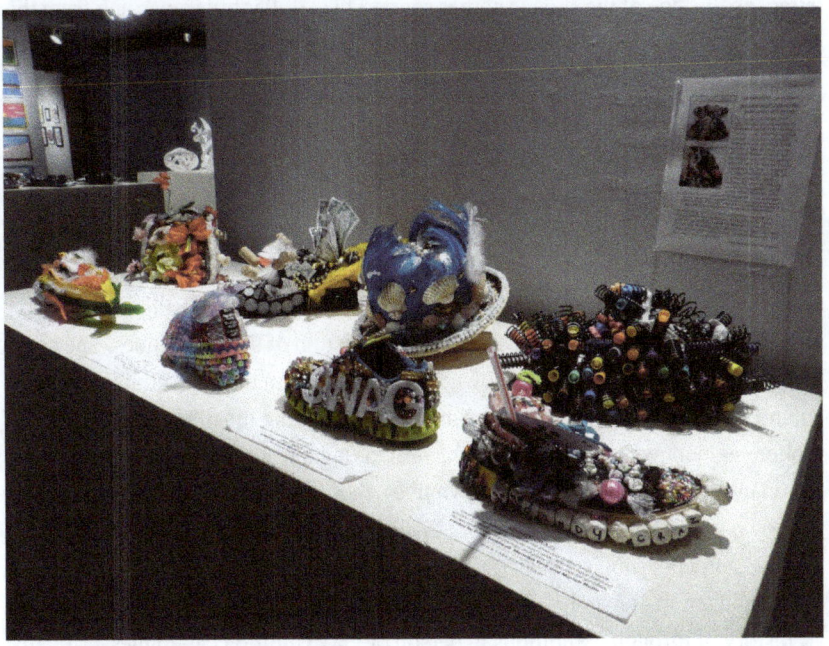

Courtesy: Florida State University Museum of Fine Arts.

with them in mind. Museum visits provided opportunities to engage in opening
night celebrations, hands–on art activities, and interactive tours that made the
museum space the students', not some intimidating building where they did not
belong. The constructivist co-curatorial process expanded the school art program
beyond the classroom. These projects engaged not only the students but brought
in the broader community, particularly through students' families and friends, to
celebrate art in personal and meaningful ways.

Student display artworks often attested to a pedagogical emphasis on creative
solutions to the problems of conveying visual meaning. During the *Generations*
project, Buck Lake Elementary students working in groups under the direction
of art instructor Sonia McDowell produced assemblages of "swag" shoes with
money and goods glued to them. Each "swag" shoe assemblage was created by
a distinct student group who discussed choices, planned, and collaboratively

transformed a shoe. Shoes were thickly covered in beads, trinkets, and toys that would attract students. One assemblage even mounted the word "swag" in white letters on the side of the shoe. Another sported fake dollar bills emerging from the shoe's interior. Interestingly, these assemblages revealed that shoes themselves had become part of the concept of swag—the goods that attract students. The wearability of the shoes was no longer important; their only value remained in their attractiveness as "swag." These works conveyed the human, humorous, and often foolish attraction to contemporary cultural trifles devoid of real-life value and they also commented on the reduction of the actual value of practical objects, in this case shoes, to a surface value. One goal of the making of the shoe assemblages was an understanding of the artwork by the *Generations* exhibition artist Nancy Youdelman who inspired the production of the swag shoes. She combined disparate materials in her own work to create meaning. Another goal was an understanding of ways to notice and understand the meaning of imagery. By looking at Nancy Youdelman's work, verbalizing her messages, and connecting her imagery and messages to their own lives, these students were able to construct their own works and convey their own distinct meanings to an exhibition audience.

As this process shows, these projects offered K-12 students a start to finish view of the production of making art within contemporary culture—studying artworks in art history or through exhibitions in person or via exhibition catalogues, critically analyzing artworks, transferring and merging information gathered from these artworks with personal views and messages, generating new artwork with fresh or related meanings, using skills and materials available, and with pride offering their original artwork to audiences. This process also offered students aspects of artmaking and viewing that pertain to an educated life in general. Art provides a means to engage in visual critical analysis and visual communication, important skills in the visual emphasis of the world in which we all live. Art shows the value of accepting connections outside the norm to convey meanings or reveal issues and thus to solve problems. Art relates to life and provides the ability to respond or comment on issues. This constructivist co-curatorial process nurtured the ability of museum and school art educators through deepened engagement with prolonged projects and their exhibitions to show K-12 students the value of art within society and particularly the value of the art world.

The constructivist co-curation method changed the relationship of the FSU MoFA with a large part of its audience and a swath of its community. This method is facilitative and not authoritarian. For the targeted audience and community members it made the FSU MoFA a welcoming place of knowledge, imagination, curiosity, relatability, and meaning-making rather than an elitist bastion of authorities and patrons. The FSU MoFA instead became a place of equity where teachers, their students, and community members felt ownership of the space and felt they held a stake in the FSU MoFA and its success.

The constructivist co-curation method was essentially a nonhierarchical one in which the museum, schools, and community members acted as partners. This equitable stance encouraged large numbers of teachers, hence their students, to participate. For several projects over half of the art teachers in the school district involved their classes. The constructivist co-curatorial process allowed a small museum education program to extend its reach to a broader audience while deepening meaningful interaction with that audience. The process proved replicable; it was repeated five times. As the constructivist co-curatorial process gave teachers, students, and community members a bigger stake in the life of the FSU MoFA, the process likewise gave the FSU MoFA Education Program a bigger stake as well. For those who worked in the Education Program, curator and interns both, the constructivist co-curation method produced a deep sense of satisfaction, the feeling of "making a difference," and an appreciation of "being of service."

Future Outcomes

The inherent attributes and holistic qualities of the constructivist co-curation method as outlined here show the process is beneficial for any school or museum education program. The method incorporates a nonhierarchical decision-making process that promotes multiple perspectives which in turn nurtures a joy in the recognition of the deep meaning conveyed by works of visual art. The process nurtures understanding and appreciation of school culture by the museum and of museum culture by the school. The process is valuable to both in their goals of meeting the needs of their overlapping constituencies. The process is flexible and replicable. The constructivist co-curation method has the potentiality to proceed from a pioneering method utilized by a single museum education program and local school district to becoming standard operating procedure for many museum education programs and school districts. In so doing, the constructivist co-curation method also provides the potentiality to expand the sense of community place and participation at multiple levels in museum life in general and ardently nurture the next generation's keen understanding of the value and purpose of art, the museum, and the art world.

REFERENCES

Introduction

Blatt-Gross, C. (2017). Creating community from the inside out: A concentric perspective on collective artmaking. *Arts Education Policy Review, 118*(1), 51–59. https://doi.org/10.1080/10632913.2016.1244781

Buffington, M. L. (2014). Power play: Rethinking roles in the art classroom. *Art Education, 67*(4), 6–12. https://doi.org/10.1080/00043125.2014.11519277

Clark, G., Day, M., & Greer, W. (1987). Discipline-based art education: Becoming students of art. *Journal of Aesthetic Education, 21*(2), 129–193. https://doi.org/10.2307/3332748

Darts, D. (2006). Art education for a change: Contemporary issues and the visual arts. *Art Education, 59*(5), 6–12. https://doi.org/10.1080/00043125.2005.11651605

Dewhurst, M. (2010). An inevitable question: Exploring the defining features of social justice art education. *Art Education, 63*(5), 6–13. http://www.jstor.org/stable/20799831

Dobbs, S. M. (1992). *The DBAE handbook: An overview of discipline-based art education.* The J. Paul Getty Trust. https://files.eric.ed.gov/fulltext/ED349253.pdf

Feldman, E. B. (1970). *Becoming human through art: Aesthetic experience in the school.* Prentice-Hall.

Garber, E. (2004). Social justice and art education. *Visual Arts Research, 30*(2), 4–22. http://www.jstor.org/stable/20715349

Hein, G. (1998). *Learning in the museum.* Routledge.

Stewart, M. G., & Walker, S. R. (2005). *Rethinking curriculum in art*. Davis.

Chapter 2: Constructivism–A Broad Theoretical Basis for the Museum and School-Based Art Education "Constructivist Co-curation" Method

Czajkowski, J. W., & Salort-Pons, S. (2017). Building a workplace that supports educator-curator collaboration. In P. Villeneuve & A. Rowson Love (Eds.), *Visitor-centered exhibitions and edu-curation in art museums* (pp. 239–249). Rowman & Littlefield.

Ebitz, D. (2008). Sufficient foundation: Theory in the practice of art museum education. *Visual Arts Research, 34*(2), 14–24. http://www.jstor.org/stable/20715471

Hein, G. (1998). *Learning in the museum*. Routledge.

Koke, J., & Ryan, K. (2017). Mechanisms for integrating community voices into exhibition development. In P. Villeneuve & A. Rowson Love (Eds.), *Visitor-centered exhibitions and edu-curation in art museums* (pp. 47–56). Rowman & Littlefield.

Pegno, M., & Farrar, C. (2017). Multivocal, collaborative practices in community-based art museum exhibitions. In P. Villeneuve & A. Rowson Love (Eds.), *Visitor-centered exhibitions and edu-curation in art museums* (pp. 169–181). Rowman & Littlefield.

Villeneuve, P., & Rowson Love, A. (Eds.). (2017). *Visitor-centered exhibitions and edu-curation in art museums*. Rowman & Littlefield.

Chapter 4: Project #1–The Influence of Discipline Based Art Education

991bigjohn. (2009, May 30). *Vincent Van Gogh—Starry Starry Night with Don Mclean*. YouTube. https://www.youtube.com/watch?v=DD1ih3Q9otE

Anderson, T.L. (1997, September). *A model for art criticism: Talking with kids about Art*. School Arts, 97 (1), 21-26.

Anderson, T. & Milbrandt, M. K. (2005). *Art for life: Authentic instruction in art* (pp. 102--106). McGraw-Hill.

Clark, G., Day, M., & Greer, W. (1987). Discipline-based art education: Becoming students of art. *Journal of Aesthetic Education, 21*(2), 129–193. https://doi.org/10.2307/3332748

Dobbs, S. M. (1992). *The DBAE handbook: An overview of discipline-based art education*. The J. Paul Getty Trust. https://files.eric.ed.gov/fulltext /ED349253.pdf

Epstein, D. (2003, Summer). *Transforming education through the arts challenge: Final project report* [Abstract]. Grantmakers in the Arts. https:// www.giarts.org/article/transforming-education-through-arts-challenge

Feldman, E. B. (1970). *Becoming human through art: Aesthetic experience in the school*. Prentice-Hall.

Florida Department of Education. (2020, March 23). *A chronology of events: 1990–2000*. https://www.fldoe.org/accountability/assessments/k-12-student -assessment/archive/history-fl-statewide-assessment/hsap9000.stml

Florida State University Museum of Fine Arts. (2002). Introduction in *Visions of the North Florida environment* [Poster], (verso).

Thompson Wylder, V.D, Kautz, F., McDowell, S., Sullivan, B., Braswell, C., Janasiewicz, L., Reeves, L., Frinks, D., & Haff, D. (2003). *Visions of the North Florida environment: Comprehensive art education at work* [Unpublished manuscript]. Florida State University Museum of Fine Arts.

Chapter 5: Project #2—The Influence of Traditional Formalist Theory and Practice

Childers, C., Cohen, L., Little, K., & Thompson Wylder, V. D (2003). *In print: The language of art* [Teachers' packet]. Florida State University Museum of Fine Arts.

Childers, C., Cohen, L., & Little, K. (2003). *In print: The language of art* [Exhibition poster]. Poster Verso. Florida State University Museum of Fine Arts.

Feldman, E. B. (1970). *Becoming human through art: Aesthetic experience in the school*. Prentice-Hall.

Feldman, E. B. (1992). Formalism and its discontents. *Studies in Art Education*, *33*(2), 122–126. https://doi.org/10.2307/1320360

Florida State University Museum of Fine Arts. (2003). Introduction in *In print: The language of art* [Poster], (verso).

Chapter 6: Project #3–The Influence of the "Big Idea" Approach

Little, K. (2008, January 25). Fogelin guest artist [PowerPoint slides]. In [Slides showing interaction of *The story* artists with Lawton Chiles High School art students] (pp. 10–17). Personal PowerPoint.

Mrs. Greenberg's 4th Grade. (2008). *Poetry inspired by nature* [Unpublished manuscript]. Riley Elementary, Tallahassee, FL.

National Board for Professional Teaching Standards. (2000). *Early childhood and middle childhood/Art standards.* https://www.nbpts.org/wp-content/uploads/2021/09/EMC-ART.pdf

National Board for Professional Teaching Standards. (2001). *Early adolescence through young adulthood/Art standards.* https://www.nbpts.org/wp-content/uploads/2021/09/EAYA-ART.pdf

Stewart, M. G., & Walker, S. R. (2005). *Rethinking curriculum in art.* Davis.

Thompson Wylder, V. D. (2005). *Curatorial statement* [Unpublished notes]. Florida State University Museum of Fine Arts.

Thompson Wylder, V. D. (2007). Acknowledgments: Telling the story. In *The story* (pp. 4–6). Florida State University Museum of Fine Arts.

Chapter 7: Project #4-Revisiting the "Big Idea" Approach

Fletcher, M. (2012). Mark J. Fletcher. In *Generations* (p. 17). Florida State University Museum of Fine Arts.

Florida Department of Education. (2014; updated 2022). NGSSS—Visual art. In *Next generation sunshine state standards—The arts, 2014*. https://www.flrules.org/gateway/readRefFile.asp?refId=3100&filename=1.%20Proposed%20NGSSS%20for%20Arts.pdf

Stewart, M. G., & Walker, S. R. (2005). *Rethinking curriculum in art.* Davis.

Thompson Wylder, V. D. (2012). Acknowledgements, Generations: An enduring idea. In *Generations* (p. 3). Florida State University Museum of Fine Arts.

Youdelman, N. (2012). Nancy Youdelman. In *Generations* (p. 43). Florida State University Museum of Fine Arts.

Chapter 8: Project #5-The Influence of Social Justice Art Education

Anderson, T. (2009). *2010 kids' guernica*. Florida State University Museum of Fine Arts.

Arthur, B. (2018). Bradley Arthur. In A. Palladino-Craig (Ed.), *Waging peace!* (p. 11). Florida State University Museum of Fine Arts.

Blatt-Gross, C. (2017). Creating community from the inside out: A concentric perspective on collective artmaking. *Arts Education Policy Review*, *118*(1), 51–59. https://doi.org/10.1080/10632913.2016.1244781

Buffington, M. L. (2014). Power play: Rethinking roles in the art class-room. *Art Education*, *67*(4), 6–12. https://doi.org/10.1080/00043125.2014.11519277

Chau, D. (2018). Du Chau. In A. Palladino-Craig (Ed.), *Waging peace!* (p. 14). Florida State University Museum of Fine Arts.

Darts, D. (2006). Art education for a change: Contemporary issues and the visual arts. *Art Education*, *59*(5), 6–12. https://doi.org/10.1080/00043125.2005.11651605

Dewhurst, M. (2010). An inevitable question: Exploring the defining features of social justice art education. *Art Education*, *63*(5), 6–13. http://www.jstor.org/stable/20799831

Garber, E. (2004). Social justice and art education. *Visual Arts Research*, *30*(2), 4–22. http://www.jstor.org/stable/20715349

Girard, L., & Stuart-Tilley, M. (2018). Waging peace by bridging communities. In Y. Zhu (Ed.), *Waging peace!* [Teachers' Packet] (pp. 80–83). Florida State University Museum of Fine Arts.

Hamrock, J. (2018). The Plant on Gaines Street. In A. Palladino-Craig (Ed.), *Waging peace!* (p. 62). Florida State University Museum of Fine Arts.

Hamrock, J., Fendler, R., & Freeman, A. (2019). "Waging peace"!: An art museum as a resource for partnerships. *The International Journal of Arts Education*, *14*(3), 1–14. https://doi.org/10.18848/2326-9944/CGP/v14i03/1-14

Jones, K. (2018). Waging peace tent. In Y. Zhu (Ed.), *Waging peace!* [Teachers' Packet] (pp. 29–34). Florida State University Museum of Fine Arts.

Marc, S. (2018). Stephen Marc. In A. Palladino-Craig (Ed.), *Waging peace!* (p. 26). Florida State University Museum of Fine Arts.

Schwadron, H., & Bruker, M. (Choreographer, Research Director). (2015). *Klasse* [Dance Film]. http://www.hannahschwadrondance.com/klasse

Shechter, J. L. (2018). Judy Lipman Shechter. In A. Palladino-Craig (Ed.) *Waging peace!* (p. 37). Florida State University Museum of Fine Arts.

Stein, L. (2018). Linda Stein. In A. Palladino-Craig (Ed.) *Waging peace!* (p. 40). Florida State University Museum of Fine Arts.

Takacs, S. (2018). Collectively Peaced Gown [Label didactic for artwork of that title]. *Waging peace!* Florida State University Museum of Fine Arts.

The Kearney Center. (2015). *Who we are: Mission statement.* https://kearneycenter.org/our-mission/

The Plant. (2018a). *Building a community together: A collaborative 3-d art project.* https://theplantartscenter.wordpress.com/waging-peace-at-the-plant/

The Plant. (2018b). *Draw or doodle: What would a peaceful world look like to you?* https://theplantartscenter.wordpress.com/waging-peace-at-the-plant/past-waging-peace-at-the-plant-workshops/

Thompson Wylder, V. D. (2018). The logistics of *waging peace.* In A. Palladino-Craig (Ed.) *Waging peace!* (p. 6). Florida State University Museum of Fine Arts.

Zhu, Y., & Mendoza, N. (2018). All people have a place on earth. In Y. Zhu (Ed.), *Waging peace!* [Teachers' Packet] (pp. 50–53). Florida State University Museum of Fine Arts.

Chapter 10: Conclusion–Impact and Outcomes: The Efficacy of the Constructivist Co-Curation Method

Bouchara, C., Bossier, M., Howald, C., Liu, S., Noe, C., Woo, K., Xu, C., Sun, Y., & Ren, W. (2016). *Private art museum report.* Larry's List & AMMA. https://www.larryslist.com/report/Private%20Art%20Museum%20Report.pdf

Hamrock, J., Fendler, R., & Freeman, A. (2019). "Waging peace!": An art museum as a resource for partnerships. *The International Journal of Arts Education, 14*(3), 1–14. https://doi.org/10.18848/2326-9944/CGP/v14i03/1-14

www.ingramcontent.com/pod-product-compliance
Lightning Source LLC
Chambersburg PA
CBHW070215190526
45161CB00002B/88